Advance Praise for *Sometimes Brilliant*

"One of the best books I've ever read, period. An extraordinary adventure, scientific odyssey, and spiritual journey of the highest orders. Beautifully written and deeply inspiring; a klieg light in the darkness. Brilliant in every way!"

> —Dean Ornish, M.D., founder and president of Preventive Medicine Research Institute, clinical professor of medicine at UC San Francisco, and author of *The Spectrum* and *Dr. Dean Ornish's Program for Reversing Heart Disease*

"*Sometimes Brilliant* is simply remarkable. Filled with inspiration and humor, Larry Brilliant's memoir chronicles his spiritual and professional journey that includes fighting for social justice in America and helping to eradicate smallpox in India. *Sometimes Brilliant* is a candid assessment of a tumultuous time and an insider's account of what can be achieved through the sheer force of a shared vision."

> —Sheryl Sandberg, COO of Facebook and author of *Lean In*

"Larry Brilliant has been an incredible inspiration to me as a spiritual adviser, teacher, and friend. He has dedicated his life to helping others and making the world a better place—from eradicating smallpox to addressing global inequality. Larry also helped ignite my personal passion for advancing children's healthcare, and for that I'm grateful. His life story is nothing short of remarkable and this book will serve as an enduring inspiration for many generations to come."

> —Marc Benioff, chairman and CEO of Salesforce

"Larry Brilliant's story would be worth reading just for the fascinating cast of characters he introduces and the turbulent times he describes so vividly. But the book also offers us a more valuable gift: a rare bridge between science and spirituality, and a reminder that real progress in improving the lives of other human beings is within our grasp."

—Steven Johnson, author of *The Ghost Map* and *How We Got to Now*

"Truly magnificent. *Sometimes Brilliant* mixes a gripping story, a primer on compassionate service, and a guide to purpose-driven social action into a can't-stop-reading narrative. Larry Brilliant tells an entrancing tale, one we need more than ever: as us-and-them hate gains the spotlight, he restores faith in the power of unity toward a greater good. *Sometimes Brilliant* is in turns wise, funny, and inspiring—and always terrific."

—Daniel Goleman, author of *Emotional Intelligence* and *A Force for Good*

"Maharaji has now written another book and this is it."

—Ram Dass

"Steal this book! Steal this book! No, wait, that was Abby Hoffman from the 1960s. Now I say: Buy this book! Buy this book! It's a really uber-awesome slab of tree flesh. This book is a true-life adventure of a life well lived to make the world a better place."

—Wavy Gravy, Clown Prince and Master of Ceremonies at Woodstock

"My friend Larry Brilliant has had an exceptional career and an outsized impact on global health, but he took a path less traveled that included work in the civil rights movement, seeing the world by bus, and embarking on a great spiritual journey. In *Sometimes Brilliant,* Larry gives us an honest, forthright, and entertaining depiction of his unique experiences and how they helped him play a vital role in the eradication of one of our planet's most ancient plagues."

—Al Gore, 45th vice president of the United States

"This book reads like an adventure novel, by one of the most innovative figures in global health telling the fascinating tale of smallpox eradication—one of the great triumphs in public health."

—Peter Piot, director of the London School of Hygiene and Tropical Medicine

"A brilliant storyteller reveals a life of endless curiosity. Having worked with and known the author for forty-three years I can verify that some of these stories may actually be true! I highly recommend this book."

—Bill Foege, M.D., MPH, recipient of the Presidential Medal of Freedom, former director of CDC, and author of *House on Fire*

"This is the story of a life that you couldn't make up if you tried. Inspiring, terrifying, touching, and transcendent, with a cast of characters from the widest possible spectrum of humanity. Dr. Brilliant takes us on the last leg of a relay race against a horrible death that mankind has waited ten thousand years to complete—while also engaging us on his inner journey of discovery, despair, and ultimately triumph. You can hear the knock on the door of a billion house calls in his prose, his love, and a lifelong journey that celebrates the human experience. An astounding book to treasure and devour. Dr. Brilliant is a superstar and I am honored to be a small part of the effort to let everyone else in on the secret."

—Jay Walker, founder of Priceline.com

"What do you get when you cross Steve Jobs's India with Wavy Gravy and the Grateful Dead, Google with the PayPal founders? What a welcome relief to see this story of someone with soul and a great healing spirit coming out of Silicon Valley, to actually— literally—help in saving the world. This is the wonderful book we will all give to our children, as they look for mentors and career inspiration—after staying up reading it ourselves."

—Mark Anderson, CEO of Strategic News Service

"In an age of global crisis, *Sometimes Brilliant* is a beacon of hope. An improbable and engaging account of how the world came together to eradicate one of the most deadly diseases in our history. A must-read for those dedicated to create necessary and lasting change."

—Judith Rodin, president of the Rockefeller Foundation

"Larry Brilliant is an extraordinary man who has lived an extraordinary life. *Sometimes Brilliant* is a mesmerizing read—at once one man's unexpected journey through life, a window inside some of the most unique social and spiritual movements of the 1960s and 1970s, and the story of how people from a dozen nations came together to eradicate one of the world's most terrible diseases. I can't recommend this book highly enough."

—Jim Wallis, author of *America's Original Sin*, president of
Sojourners, and editor-in-chief of *Sojourners* magazine

"I couldn't have made up a story half as interesting or thought provoking as what I just read in these pages. Hard to put down and easy to feel inspired, *Sometimes Brilliant* should really be titled *Simply Brilliant*. This terrific book brings to light the power of the karmic yoga path. Do yourself a favor and read it."

—Chade-Meng Tan, author of *Search Inside Yourself* and
Joy on Demand

"Larry Brilliant has touched many lives in person all over the world. The famous, the not-so-famous, the establishment, and the counterculture all figure in this remarkable memoir. *Sometimes Brilliant* will touch still more lives with its humanity. An extraordinary life extraordinarily well lived."

—Stephan Chambers, the Marshall Institute for Philanthropy
and Social Entrepreneurship, London School of Economics

"Fabulous! A wildly inspiring, wondrous, improbable, heartbreaking, and triumphant tale. Makes you want to do beautiful courageous things."

—Jack Kornfield, founder of Spirit Rock Meditation Center
and author of *A Path with Heart*

"*Sometimes Brilliant* is an epic, life-transforming story, about the triumph of Love against all odds. Larry's mystic, long and winding hippie trail emerges from the era of sex, drugs, and rock and roll and leads toward saving the world's poor from deadly diseases. Our globe urgently needs Doctor America's vision. *Sometimes Brilliant* is an eye-opening tale of a true superhero, friend of humanity, and servant of God. In *Sometimes Brilliant,* readers will see an America which is hopeful, fearless, and champion of the underdog. *Sometimes Brilliant* should be required reading for students at all universities across the globe and for world leaders who want to find creative solutions to overcome the myriad threats of the twenty-first century."

—Salman Ahmad, founder of the rock band Junoon, professor
of Islamic music at Queens College, Polio Goodwill
Ambassador, and author of *Rock & Roll Jihad*

"On its surface, *Sometimes Brilliant* is a gripping, illuminating, and entertaining inside look at one of the greatest medical triumphs of our time—wiping smallpox from the face of the planet. But at a deeper level, it is a compelling argument for pursuing a life that productively combines both serendipity and intentionality, rather than one to the exclusion of the other."

—Roger L. Martin, Institute Director of the Martin Prosperity
Institute at the Rotman School of Management

"Dr. Larry is more than sometimes brilliant. He has written an epic tale about the massive program to eradicate smallpox from the face of the globe, as predicted by our guru, Neem Karoli Baba. He combines the deep tenets of living a spiritual life with an activist's heart-full desire to relieve suffering—the perfect illustration of what is meant by fulfilling your life purpose through karma yoga. And his brilliant light shines on."

—Parvati Markus, author of *Love Everyone*

"*Sometimes Brilliant* is heartfelt and deeply inspiring, from Larry's stories of the 1960s, to his spiritual quest and relationship with Maharaji, and in the amazing story of the eradication of smallpox. I read with a sense of wonder and suspense, and continue to reflect on how what seems impossible can become possible when we work together for the greater good."

"Now I know why Larry Brilliant has the wonderful capacity to form bonds not of political or social convenience, not for transactional gain, not of temporary duration, but lasting bonds of love and purpose. In this book he beautifully describes the experiences, the moments, the insights that nurtured this capacity. Read it and cry. Read it and laugh. Read it and be in awe."

"I am excited about *Sometimes Brilliant* and the opportunity for those who may have been in a hole and missed the dynamic ministry of Dr. Brilliant to become acquainted with this brilliant man through his written story. Oh, by the way, when I met him at San Quentin, he was there as a volunteer to offer an evening of ministry to the inmates—that's Brilliant!"

Sometimes Brilliant

(Sometimes Not So)

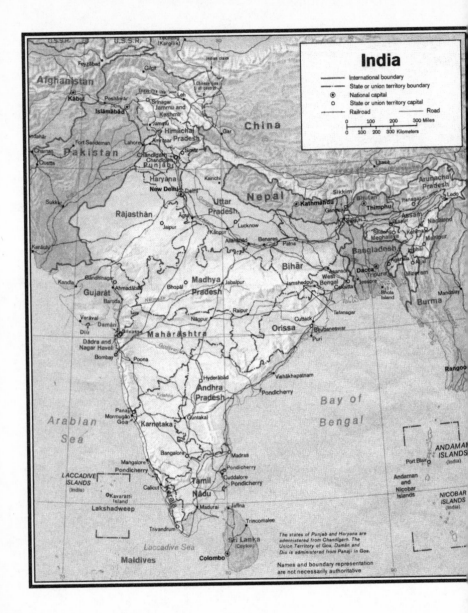

Sometimes Brilliant

The Impossible Adventure of a
Spiritual Seeker and Visionary
Physician Who Helped Conquer
the Worst Disease in History

Larry Brilliant

 HarperOne
An Imprint of HarperCollins*Publishers*

HarperOne

FIRST EDITION

Designed by SBI Book Arts, LLC

Library of Congress Cataloging-in-Publication Data has been applied for.

ISBN 978–0–06–204923–0

16 17 18 19 20   RRD   10 9 8 7 6 5 4 3 2 1

To Neem Karoli Baba, who touched my heart, opened me to feel love for everyone, and showed me the way to live a life of service. And to my wife, Girija Brilliant, who loved me so much she dragged me kicking and screaming to India. We have had three wonderful children together, and this is one more chance for me to tell Joseph Seva Brilliant and Iris Sarada Brilliant how proud I am of them and how much I love them, and for us all to remember our beloved Jonathan Eugene Skanda Brilliant, who died from cancer much too young. He would have done a very close read of this book, teased me about the pompous parts, and then laughed loudly and lovingly at just the right places.

Contents

Author's Note — ix

1   *In Medias Res,* The Middle of Things — I

2   Nickelodeons — 11

3   Woodstock on Wheels — 31

4   Magic Bus Trip — 49

5   Renunciation — 77

6   Initiation — 93

7   You Are No Doctor — 115

8   Prophecy — 129

9   Apprenticeship — 155

10   Karma Yoga — 187

11   Escape from Central Prison — 201

12   After-Death Experience — 215

13   Tales of the Jungle — 241

14   City of the Tatas — 267

15   Smiling Buddha — 295

16   The Goddess of Smallpox Fights Back — 321

17   The Final Inch — 337

18   The Case for Optimism — 365

Epilogue — 375

Acknowledgments — 397

Further Reading — 413

Credits — 415

Author's Note

At the heart of this book are two interwoven miracles.

The first miracle occurred in the middle of the Cold War, when doctors from more than two dozen countries including Russia and America set aside their enmity and fought alongside each other to defeat a common foe that had killed billions of children over millennia—smallpox.

The second miracle was that a young hippie doctor living in a Himalayan ashram was sent by his teacher, an old Indian guru, to work for the United Nations and be part of the campaign to eradicate this disease. The guru predicted, "Smallpox will be quickly eradicated. This is God's gift to mankind because of the hard work of dedicated health workers."

Less than three years later, all naturally occurring *Variola major,* killer smallpox, was gone.

Forty years ago, I was that hippie doctor. It is long past time for me to tell you about these miracles as I experienced them.

My memory is not clear enough to recall events as vividly as I would like but I have tried my best to capture the spirit of what really happened while trying to balance the effects of the passage of so much time. I have placed quotation marks around conversations I participated in directly or heard from trustworthy sources, but I don't pretend to remember word for word conversations from forty years ago; details have surely been modified by the passage of time. Conversations with my teacher Neem Karoli Baba, the guru who opened my heart, were often in Hindi and were translated mostly by Ravi Khanna, Dada Mukerjee, or by my wife, Girija, or me as our Hindi improved. We recorded many of these conversations each day in our spiritual diaries. And we wrote down every word of his improbable prediction the day he made it. Lest we get it wrong, we sent it out to dozens of our friends soon after.

The reporting on the smallpox campaign is accurate: it's sourced, researched, and drawn from my own experiences in the field, the actual World Health Organization (WHO) files, the numerous reports I wrote for WHO, both my own and my wife's contemporaneous diaries, and the academic book I wrote on the subject when I was a professor at the University of Michigan, shortly after smallpox's eradication (*The Management of Smallpox Eradication in India*), as well as confirmation from the incredible men and women alongside whom I worked, shoulder-to-shoulder. Thankfully, many are still around to hold my feet to the factual fire. You will find additional sources on the history of smallpox and its eradication at the end of the book in the "Further Reading" section, on page 413. I hope you will read some of them to get a broader view of the miracle of the campaign.

In this book I have retained the Indian geographical names as we used them on our reports and epidemiological maps in the 1970s. Cities and jurisdictions are referred to by the names they were called at the time. Bombay instead of Mumbai, for example, and Calcutta instead of Kalighat, Chotanagpur instead of Jharkhand, Kumaon instead of Uttarakhand. This archaic nomenclature is not intended to disrespect India's rapid modernization but to reflect the journey taken at that time.

The people I write about are real people, but some of the names have been changed in order to prevent unnecessary embarrassment to individuals whose identification might cause pain to their families. In some cases, their actions were questionable.

For any mistakes I might have made regarding names and dates, and wherever I have failed to adequately thank those who were due more credit, I apologize in advance. Forgive me, too, for failing to include the names of the thousands of public health heroes—doctors, vaccinators, search workers, and volunteers—who worked on the program. I so wish I could memorialize every man, woman, and child sickened or killed by smallpox. To do them real justice would require a library, an archive, a monument.

As I retell some of these stories today, they sometimes strain even my own credulity, but as my father often said, before launching into one of his own intriguing tales, "It is a great story, and it has the extra, additional, incremental benefit of being true."

Sometimes
Brilliant

CHAPTER 1

In Medias Res,
The Middle of Things

Perseverance furthers.

—I Ching

A pril 10, 1974, was hot. India hot.

Our jeep wove through the overgrown jungle, bounced over the undulating washboard road, and halted in front of the Tatanagar railway station. Slanted rays of the afternoon sun reflected off the station's fading whitewashed walls, a stoic reminder of the British ambition to link every corner of colonial India by rail.

The Indian-made jeep, marked with the official blue and white seal of the United Nations, quickly attracted a crowd. Outstretched arms grabbed at us through the open windows. Thin limbs and tired bodies pressed closer, rocking the vehicle. Zafar Hussein, the paramedical assistant assigned to me by the Government of India, gently asked the crowd to move back in Hindi and then in a language I did not understand. When space cleared he carefully and respectfully opened his door. I followed.

My foot had barely touched the ground when I heard a wail: "Doctor Sahib! Doctor Sahib! Saita, saita!" Doctor! Doctor! Help, help! A gaunt young mother in a bright red sari carrying a little boy jumped up from a squat, broke through the crowd, and stumbled straight for me. Twigs from the neem tree, a traditional—though futile—treatment for smallpox, fell from her lap. "Doctor! UN doctor! Please. I beg you. Help me. My baby is very sick."

Her boy was four or five years old. The woman held him out to me, motioning for me to take him. When I hesitated, she pushed the child into my arms, like an offering in a temple, her eyes pleading, never leaving mine.

The boy's black hair was matted with sweat and mud, his eyes lined with kohl, the black substance Indians often use on children to protect their sight from the harsh sun. But his eyes were fixed wide open and opaque; his arms and legs dangled limp from his body. His face was streaked with blood. I held him and looked closer. He was emaciated, covered with pocks. Smallpox's telltale buckshot pattern—deep red pustules a quarter-inch round everywhere—looked like angry little volcanoes ready to erupt. The lesions on his hands and feet had coalesced into an almost continuous graph; I could barely identify individual pocks. The boy had no healthy skin left on his arms and legs, no space to fit even a fingertip between his sores.

Zafar and I looked at each other. We knew. We sighed.

The boy was not sick. He was dead, gone moments before our arrival, one more casualty of *Variola major,* one of nearly two hundred thousand sickened or killed during the Indian smallpox epidemic of 1974. Most were children. His death must have been agonizing—the disease had transformed his lifeless hands into bloody pieces of meat and had taken his sight before it had taken his life.

I looked down at the boy's still body, which seemed so slight, so light, so soft. It was hardly there, as if his soul had fled the torment of the disease, risen up from what the Indians called his atman, or personal soul, to merge with Brahma, the great soul, the eternal soul that we all share, the oneness of God. I had arrived too late, but even had we arrived while he was still alive, there would have been nothing any doctor could have done. There is no cure for smallpox. That was why the epidemic had to be stopped from spreading, why it had to be prevented before it could kill other little boys and girls. That was why we had only a single goal: eradication.

For many rural or traditional Indians in the 1970s, smallpox was not a disease in the way we understand such illnesses—an infection caused by a virus or bacteria. An Indian child in some villages might be thought to be visited by a goddess, the pock marks a sign left behind by Shitala Ma—the "cooling mother," both protector and destroyer. Her annual visit, commonly occurring each spring, was both a blessing and a curse. She was personified as a fierce and wild-looking goddess, a bit like Kali the Destroyer, astride a wild donkey, carrying a winnowing fan and whip or scourge. It was the tip of her whip that caused the painful welts of smallpox. Shitala Ma determined life and death according to some mystifying calculus.

But I knew that a virus, not a goddess, had killed this boy; he was killed by the same ancient disease that had felled billions of men and women, boys and girls, a plague that for ten thousand years or more had slain peasants and princes, damsels and doctors, kings and queens, emperors and dictators.

A disease that, before Edward Jenner's discovery of vaccine in 1796, commonly infected nearly everyone it attacked, and killed one of three who contracted it. No amount of wealth or power could offer protection until Jenner's discovery. In the twentieth century, as many as half a billion people died from smallpox, more than died in all the wars and genocides of those turbulent times combined.

Smallpox was a disease so common and so ubiquitous that it is easy now to understand why it was seen as something more than just a disease, something otherworldly, not a plague of the material plane. This was true not just in India, but in countries as distinct as Japan and Nigeria and many other parts of the world where other smallpox gods or goddesses ruled.

When I looked at the dead boy in my arms, I knew he was part of a long, unbroken chain of transmission that had killed untold numbers of humans every year for thousands of years. I knew he was part of one of the longest-running epidemics of all time. What I did not yet know, as I held his tiny body, was whether this boy's death would be the final link in this chain, a tragic exclamation point punctuating the end of the terrible hold smallpox had had on human history. And I did not yet know whether the prediction of my guru Neem Karoli Baba would come true: that God would lift this one form of suffering from the shoulders of humanity and pull the disease of smallpox out from the roots.

As I look back now, four decades later, I am troubled that I never discovered the boy's name, or that of his mother. Why hadn't I asked? Why have all those faces—the thousands of boys and girls with smallpox whom I saw or held or walked past—merged into a single memory, a montage of their young lives?

They are no longer individuals now, but statistics and numbers and points on a graph or curve. It was not because they were brown and I was white, they were Indian and I was American. Or because I had become a numb and distracted public health doctor, no longer a clinician living by the Hippocratic Oath. There were simply too many dead and dying; the numbers overwhelmed my ability to remember each of their faces and names.

I do not and cannot speak for all of us—the smallpox warriors, as we have since been called. We were eager young Americans, Russians, Brits, and Swedes, and especially heroic Indians and Bangladeshis, called by the fierce urgency demanded by our deadly enemy, smallpox.

The boy was one of two thousand smallpox victims in Tatanagar, a rich industrial city in the northeastern Indian state of Bihar. Famous for its steel exports, this year the city's major export was disease—and it was exporting smallpox faster and farther than any other city in the modern era. Smallpox was everywhere, attacking everyone; neither religion nor caste, gender nor age acted as a barrier to keep smallpox from infecting anyone who was not vaccinated.

I had arrived in Tatanagar earlier that morning from the neighboring state of Madhya Pradesh, where my team and I had been working for much of the year to conquer smallpox. We had nearly ended smallpox in much of India while doctors from two dozen countries working side by side with Indian colleagues furiously fought against the disease. But out of nowhere, a cascade of seemingly random outbreaks rained down on Madhya Pradesh and other states, erasing most of what we had achieved. Perhaps we had overestimated how close we were to our target, zero cases of smallpox. Overnight, areas of India that had been declared free of disease woke up to a shower of new smallpox cases. In Madhya Pradesh, my team—Russian epidemiologist Lev Khodakevich, Zafar Hussein, and I—raced to investigate a dozen newly infected villages. We made our maps and timelines, interviewed survivors and their families, traced their routes, but only solved the mystery when we realized that each outbreak had begun with a passenger on a train from Tatanagar. Out-of-work villagers had gone in search of jobs in the steel and coal industry. The first case in every outbreak in Madhya Pradesh had been a young man who had come in contact with someone who was sick with smallpox while they were looking for work, or at work, in Tatanagar. Soon they too would come down with fever and pain, making them feel sicker than ever before in their young lives. With the eruption of pustules on their hands and face came a single thought: *Shitala Ma has come for me. I want to go home to die.* Their journey home by train or bus spread smallpox throughout India, to cities in the Himalayas in the north and villages in the south, and even to neighboring countries.

The sudden appearance of my jeep with the WHO United Nations Smallpox Eradication Program seal on the doors must have seemed an answer to the prayers of those suffering at the train station in Tatanagar, especially the dead boy's mother. But sadly, my arrival was grim evidence that smallpox was far from eradicated; it was spreading around the country, cough by cough, scab by scab, touch by touch.

The mother's plaintive cries brought me back to the moment. My stomach tightened, my legs felt weak in a familiar way, and the dead boy in my arms seemed to grow heavier. Her brightly colored sari now seemed to mock us. "Rama Nama Satya Hai! Harika Nama Satya Hai!"—God's name is truth; only God's name is true—I whispered under my breath, like Hindus do when they pass a funeral in the street or at the burning ghats. The moment was filled with a mother's unbearable pain, Zafar's kindness, and my helplessness. I could offer no consolation to the victims, no optimistic rallying cry to the smallpox workers. No words are adequate in the face of a child's death, especially from a disease that could have been vanquished lifetimes ago.

Zafar took the boy from my arms, sat down with the mother, and offered condolences in her dialect. When he uttered the Hindi expression, "Your son is no more," her screams pierced the quiet. She had already known that he was dead; mothers always do. Yet when our jeep arrived, she hoped God would show mercy on her child, as mothers always do.

I looked at the hundreds gathered on the lawn of the train station, where in better times Indian travelers would have congregated with their families, their possessions wrapped in bright fabrics, perhaps eating lunch out of a metal *tiffin,* or teasing children excited about their first ride on a train. As I made my way through the crowd to the platform, beggars reached for small coins—the usual toll for passing. I put a fifty-paisa coin in an elderly man's hand, checking for smallpox vaccination marks or telltale scabs or scars of an old infection; his companions were unvaccinated.

At the front of the station, where there should have been a line of passengers waiting to purchase tickets, a dozen or so bodies had been carefully stacked like cords of wood, neatly wrapped in shrouds made of their own dhotis or saris. The unclaimed corpses awaited family members to come and perform the final rituals; failing that, they awaited the *shudras,* or untouchables, to gather and cremate them.

Looking up toward the ticket office I watched a living skeleton of a man buy a ticket. As he turned away, clutching his ticket, I saw the pustules, smallpox lesions, on the fingers of the hand holding the ticket. *Oh shit. He will carry this disease with him on his way home, infecting passengers for hundreds of miles.*

The vision of a hand covered with active smallpox grasping a train ticket did something to me that seeing piles of dead bodies had not. *This city must be quarantined. No one must be allowed to leave Tatanagar without a vaccination.*

I felt in over my head as I watched Zafar talk with the wailing mother. I was just a young kid from Detroit, still in my twenties, on my first real job out of medical school. My wife and I had come to India two years earlier as hippies and spiritual seekers with Wavy Gravy on the Hog Farm commune buses with forty of our communal friends. Like many young people of our generation we drove along the Silk Route, now the Hippie Trail, from London through Turkey and Afghanistan over the Khyber Pass to Pakistan and then to Nepal. After trekking in the Himalayas, my wife and I lived for a year in the ashram of our guru Neem Karoli Baba. We called him Maharaji.

Nestled in the Himalayan foothills, in the spot on the map where India, Nepal, Tibet, and China come together, Maharaji's ashram was part of the Kumaon Hills, a land filled with thousand-year-old temples and ashrams, yogis and *babas,* saints and mystics—genuine fakirs, as well as a few fakers. The Kainchi ashram gets its name from the Hindi word for "scissors," a clever physical description of the meandering Kainchi River and spiritually apt: the river cuts off the everyday world from a decidedly mystical realm. Even casual visitors who had no spiritual connection to Kainchi remarked that it felt otherworldly and as rock solid as the stone out-croppings of the Himalayan foothills from which it seemed to emerge. But beyond the complex of temple buildings there was something special in the air, a sparkling effervescence that tingled up your spine when you came around the bend to see the panorama of the temple dedicated to Hanuman, the monkey god, or when you walked across the brightly colored bridge that separated the heavily trafficked road from the peace and quiet of the monastery.

I could have stayed forever with Maharaji, my wife, and our new friends—the "Das brothers" as we called those who had followed Ram Dass on this Himalayan pilgrimage: Ravi Das (now Judge Michael Jeffery), Kabir Das, Balaram Das, Dwarkanath Das, Krishna Das, and Jugganath Das (Dan Goleman) and Gita, Sita, Mira, and Sunanda—all Westerners with new Indian names, many of whom had arrived before me on their spiritual search. From our base in the ashram, Maharaji sent us on pilgrimages throughout India to meet holy men and women, to learn yoga and meditation. But one day, Maharaji pulled me aside and, giggling, told me, "You have other things to do, Doctor America." That was what he called me then. I wanted a spiritual name like one of the Das brothers, but he called me Doctor America. "You will go to villages giving vaccinations." I thought he was telling me I was a failure as a meditator and seeker. And I had almost forgotten I was ever a doctor. Maharaji insisted. "With the help of dedicated health workers," he said, "God will eradicate a terrible disease, smallpox. And Doctor America will become a United Nations doctor."

When I became a UN doctor I was twenty years younger than most of my colleagues. The huge number of dead and dying, the vast amount of suffering in Tatanagar from an epidemic raging out of control, was overwhelming. I was adrift and far away from the help of colleagues in Delhi. There were no mobile phones, no faxes, and telegraph service was poor. It could take hours or days to arrange one call to headquarters. And in that instant when I passed that nearly weightless dead child to Zafar, I felt the full weight of failure. My body shook. I wasn't the best person to be at Tatanagar, and I certainly should not have been the only UN doctor here in this Dante's Inferno, but I was here and *now* was the only moment that mattered. I felt on my own with nothing but faith to guide me. Faith in what? God? Faith that what Maharaji had told me would come true? Faith in the science of epidemiology? Arriving in Tatanagar and seeing the piles of dead bodies—men, women, and children, the latest victims of *Variola major,* the newest offerings to Shitala Ma—made me realize how much I had underestimated the enormity of the work that my inscrutable guru had sent me out to do.

CHAPTER 2

Nickelodeons

Coming empty-handed, going
empty-handed—that is human.

—Zen Master Seung Sahn

I don't know what made me leave my dorm room cave on that
gloomy November day in 1962 in Ann Arbor to listen to a man
I knew little about, Martin Luther King Jr. Dr. King was not yet
that famous, he had not yet given his "I Have a Dream" speech on
the Washington Mall, he had not yet won the Nobel Peace Prize,
but the *Michigan Daily* ran a small announcement that he was
speaking at Hill Auditorium the next day and I decided to go.

I had been lying in bed, for days or maybe weeks. The pain
was in my head—the most important person in my life, my father, was dying and I was just a kid with no idea what I would
do without him. Outside, the world teetered. Nuclear madness
in Cuba. Federal troops on patrol after violent reactions to the
first black student admitted to Ole Miss. Bob Dylan singin' "A
Hard Rain's A-Gonna Fall." I hardly noticed.

I locked myself in my room, gorged on candy and comics—
Superman, Captain Marvel, Spider-Man—any story of a wonky

weakling who could transform into an all-powerful hero. I was seventeen, in my second year of college in Ann Arbor. I was the awkward, nerdy son of the smoothest, strongest man I'd ever known.

When my dad answered the phone, "Mmm . . . yelloh," it sounded like "mellow," which he was. Mellow, tall, handsome, with wavy black hair now turning to white—he had been forty-two when I was born, fifteen years older than my mother, who said he looked like Clark Gable. He was thin and athletic, a former boxing champ we were told, with a pencil mustache and a gambler's easy way. He had gotten good at numbers, not the kind you learn in school, but *running numbers,* selling illegal punch cards on the streets. He had dropped out of school and by age twelve was working for bookies and mobsters, collecting the money, returning with cash to pay off any winnings.

He had arrived from a place he called Belarussia—White Russia—five years earlier, when he was seven, with his bricklayer father Luis and seamstress mother Bessie, both Orthodox Jews from the shtetels. He became a fighter because he had to, he told me; life for Russian Jewish immigrants was tough on the streets of Detroit. He was skinny and needed to defend himself.

I remember seeing a photo of him in boxing shorts and gloves, pounding a punching bag. He was probably the same age then as I, when hiding in my dorm room—seventeen. The photo hung framed in his office at Brilliant Music Company.

Dad loved the racetrack, and took my younger brother, Barry, and me there and to opening day for the Tigers, Bobby Lane and the Lions, and especially Red Wing hockey games—his favorite bets. He would tip an usher to get us seats near the penalty box so he could get me a broken stick from my idol, Gordie Howe. Cops and mobsters alike would greet my dad like their oldest friend. They would tease him about some boxing match he had won or lost. Sometimes they noted his Masonic ring; other times he would point out a member of the Purple Gang, Detroit's version of the Jewish Mafia that he had grown up with.

I knew he had been a tough kid, but by the time I was born those days were mostly behind him. Brilliant Music, his company, was on the margins of the legitimate business world. Dad leased nickelodeons, jukeboxes like Rock-Olas and Wurlitzers, to restaurants, bars, and bowling alleys. In the bars and restaurants, customers fed the machines with coins, and Dad's men came weekly to collect them, left some percentage behind, and brought the rest to the office. It was an all-cash business, the kind the mob loved. No papers, no problems. My dad had the largest jukebox "route" in the Midwest, and the Mafia made it clear that it wanted to take it away from him.

I was woken one night by terrifying cries from my parents' bedroom. Mom was sobbing. Dad had just left the house, carrying his revolver, to answer a "man-to-man" challenge from a mobster she said was named Buffalino, who told my dad on the phone that if he did not meet him on Hastings Street, "the boys" would kill me and Barry. It was 2 A.M. Buffalino never showed, but the next day Barry and I were taken away from our home. This remains one of my most vivid childhood memories. Mom took Barry to stay with Catherine Miller, our black housekeeper, in the projects. Catherine—Barry and I called her "Cackie"—a big, warm, loving black woman, housekeeper and surrogate mom, was with us for more than ten years. She was perhaps more my mother than my own mom.

Dad took me out to Willow Run airport and put me on a two-engine propeller flight alone to Cleveland, where my grandparents lived. Before the plane took off, my dad told me he was sending me away "so the gang won't kidnap you." I didn't know what the Mafia was then, but I remember the "unaccompanied minor" stickers and little brass wings that a stewardess pinned on my shirt, marking me as a first-time flyer. Grandma Ida was my favorite, so for me the trip to Cleveland was more a vacation than an escape from harm.

That threat on our lives caused my dad to make a decision. One night in high school my mom and Barry and I sat around our first television set and watched my dad, in Washington, DC, testifying in front of the Senate's McClellan Committee investigation into the Mafia's extortion practices in the jukebox industry. The Detroit newspaper ran a photo of my dad on its front page. Journalists called him "courageous." Bobby Kennedy phoned and even came to our house once, and thanked *my* dad.

The mob retaliated. They shot and killed my dad's store manager, a tough looking but kind man named Hugo who I remember because of the way he kept me occupied: he would bring bags of nickels for me to look through. I organized them all by date and kept the rare ones.

Within weeks of my dad's return from Washington, a teamster truck mysteriously jumped over two streets, a median strip, and an embankment to barrel down the wrong side of the road and slam through the front glass window of Brilliant Music Company. The crash ignited a fire that gutted my dad's business.

"Well, I knew that they were going to do something," my dad explained to me. "They went after the store, not us. So you kids are safe now."

After the office burned down, Dad closed the company. The Mafia had its revenge; Dad was nearly bankrupt. After that he tried to reinvent himself in other small businesses: aluminum fabrication, the then–cutting edge technology of vacuum tube testing, and a new company called Draw-Matic Engineering, which manufactured electrically operated curtains and window dressings.

As strong as he was, he became a broken man. I came home from Ann Arbor for a weekend and found him in our den reading one of those detective books that arrived every month in the mail. Dad was sitting in his green reclining chair. He smiled when he saw me and asked me to sit on the ottoman to talk. He told me his stomach cancer that we thought had been cured by an operation had become a new cancer, or maybe it was a different cancer—it didn't matter—but he had something called a sarcoma. The doctors told him he would be dead within a year.

I was the eldest son, the firstborn on both sides of our immigrant families. I was no longer a child, but I had never seen death personally. I did not have any experience. Dad and I walked to the front door, where we stood crying and talking. In his weakened state, he stumbled backward into the coat closet. Embarrassed, he quickly got up and said, "I'm not afraid of dying, son. I'm just worried what will happen to you and your brother."

The next day I woke up to cries of agony. I found my father on the floor of the bathroom, writhing in pain. He had an impacted stool and asked me to remove it. "Do the best you can with what you've got," my father always said. So I did my best. But I had no inner resources to keep from falling into depression as he got sicker and started to slip away. I returned to Ann Arbor and burrowed into my dorm room and waited and cried and hid until I saw the notice about Dr. King.

The small group of students who showed up to hear Dr. King speak didn't fill even half of Hill Auditorium. The university president was embarrassed. But King wasn't. He looked out at the sparse audience and laughed and said, "This way there will be more of me to go around. Those of you that want to, come on up here." Many of us accepted Dr. King's invitation and moved to the front of the auditorium, some even climbing the steps to the parquet floor of the stage and sitting in a semicircle around him. I wanted to get close, to feel that there was still some warmth in the world when mine was going cold.

King spoke like no one I had ever heard. There was a world of suffering outside my own that I didn't know about. There were Americans who couldn't eat at a dime-store lunch counter, who couldn't walk through town without fearing for their lives. They couldn't vote, they couldn't use most public bathrooms, and they couldn't sit in the front of a bus. They couldn't get an education like mine, lucked into it as I did by winning a math competition. King transmitted something, an intense feeling of righting such wrongs, of bending the arc of history toward justice using the weapons of love and peaceful civil disobedience. He painted a vivid word picture of a better future, one in which we were all in it together in a land of peace and harmony.

We sat transfixed. Time stopped. Those few hours seem like years of inspiration. None of us was ever the same.

I became infected with the virus of activism, the virus of optimism, the virus of championing human rights. Without being conscious of it, I signed up with an alphabet soup of organizations: NAACP (National Association for the Advancement of

Colored People), CORE (Congress of Racial Equality), SNCC (Student Nonviolent Coordinating Committee), and SDS (Students for a Democratic Society). For a moment I forgot about my dad's sarcoma and my own suffering. I took up the cause of civil rights and the fight against an unjust war in Vietnam. A few hours in the presence of this amazing man and my social isolation and emotional depression had found its antidote—the march for justice and the movement against violence. His power and wisdom were unlike anything I had experienced with professors or rabbis.

Most of my friends joined marches in Alabama and Mississippi over the next two summers. I stayed with my dad but made it to a march in Washington, DC, for freedom, social change, and civil rights. I alternated between being in school, visiting my family in Detroit, and attending sit-ins and teach-ins. I learned nonviolent civil disobedience from African American churchgoers, followers of Dr. King. Four or five of us at a time would pretend we were in Mississippi or Alabama and order a soda at the lunch counter at the Detroit Woolworth's or Sanders Confectionery. One of the church members would pretend to be a bad guy and smack us on the back, like a Zen master does to wake up a young initiate, without warning. We learned to not react, absorbing blows without hitting back, trying to forgive the assailant or even to love our enemy as the great ones from Jesus to Gandhi had taught. Sometimes it worked, sometimes not so much, but we kept practicing.

A lot of hearts were broken on Valentine's Day 1965, the day my father died—having lived longer than the original year doctors had predicted. His cancer had been treated with the crude and heavy chemo of the day, and he had gotten pneumonia.

After three years of fighting, he lost his strength, his hair, his humor, and his will to live. The doctors summoned me from Ann Arbor, as he mercifully, in their estimation, slipped into a coma. He had a breathing tube and was on life support. They were certain he would never reawaken and asked me to sign the permission forms to stop the drugs that were keeping his heart beating and let him die in peace.

My mother was emotionally unable to make that decision. My brother, Barry, three years younger, was too young by law to have a say. My mother had told the doctors I was in medical school, which was not true, but I had worked a summer at that same hospital as an orderly emptying bedpans for strangers. I sat with my dad. A few weeks earlier he had said, "Larry, I won't be able to leave you boys much money, but I will leave you something worth much more: a good name, a respected name." Looking at the face of the man I loved so much I could see he was no longer there. The doctors were right. He was gone. Though he could not hear me, I talked to him anyway and told him how much I loved him and what a great father he had been. I cried and signed the documents.

Five days later, during shiva, the Jewish week of mourning, my mom's dad, Abraham Sherman, sat me and Barry down to tell us he would now be our father. Grandpa was a kind man, also raised in the shtetels of Russia, and was now leading the Jewish family rituals. He had gotten low chairs for us to sit on and covered all the mirrors in the house with sheets so that the mourners could not groom themselves or display any vanity. No one was permitted to take food out of a house during the mourning period, but they sure could bring food in: the rabbis and members of Temple Israel came to the house with what seemed like hundreds of casseroles. Dad's Masonic and Shriner brothers were there every day, making sure my dad would be buried in his Masonic apron.

Desperate for a break from the organized grieving, I asked Grandpa Abe to come upstairs to my room so I could show him a rare coin I'd found in the pile of change from Dad's jukeboxes. He was breathing heavily by the time he reached the landing. It was a buffalo nickel from a 1917 die that had an "8" struck over the "7" such that both numbers showed. Most coins have a mint mark showing the city in which they were struck, and this one was struck in Denver during the Spanish influenza and World War I. That nickel always made me wonder who held it, touched it, and what kind of life they led—poor or rich, soldier or civilian, sick or well. It was rare and valuable.

When an ambulance came for Grandpa Abe in the middle of the night, I was sure it was because I had asked him to climb those stairs to see the nickel. He was dead by the time they got him to the hospital. My mother had lost her husband and her father in less than a week; she watched helplessly as her world crumbled. Grandpa had died because of my selfishness and my stupid nickel.

For years, I carried around guilt about killing my grandfather, making him climb those steps to see my goddamn nickel. The only person I ever confessed that guilt to was Elaine, my first love. She was so classy; she was fifteen and I was sixteen when we met at an AZA high school dance in Detroit in 1960. AZA, "Aleph Zadik Aleph," was a fraternity for Jewish teenagers. Our theme song was "Izzie, Ike, Jake, and Sam. We are the boys that eat no ham." Elaine had gorgeous brown hair and a big inviting smile. She lived half a dozen blocks away, and we both went to Mumford High School. On one of our first dates, I stopped the car in the middle of the Ambassador Bridge connecting the United States and Canada; we got out and kissed a long sweet teenage kiss on the international border, to the sounds of honking and hooting from the traffic backing up behind us. Living in Detroit so far from the coasts, I couldn't think of any other way to manufacture something as sophisticated and romantic as that kiss on the bridge on the border. Elaine and I weren't seeing each other by the time of Dad's funeral, but when she walked in the front door during shiva, I fell in love with her all over again. She could understand my loss; her own father had died when she was only a child.

My dad left my mom with a house and a car but no life insurance or income. I would be okay at college; my tuition and expenses were paid by the math scholarship I had won. Following my dad's example, I developed a side business of coin-operated vending machines that I placed in girls' dorms, maybe hoping for other kinds of investment returns. Barry was still in high school, so my mom, broken as she was by events, went back to work selling jewelry. Barry and my uncle took over dad's last company, Draw-Matic Engineering.

As activism took hold of me, I became more of a philosophy nerd, deeply immersed in what philosophers wrote about suffering. The English utilitarian philosophers Jeremy Bentham and John Stuart Mill wrote about leading a life in pursuit of the summum bonum, the greatest good. Mill concluded that the greatest good could be computed mathematically by determining the greatest happiness and multiplying it by the greatest number who were made happy by a given act. He called it the greatest happiness for the greatest number. I saw two ways of doing this myself: either by becoming a defense attorney and saving people like Julius and Ethel Rosenberg from the electric chair, or saving lives by becoming a doctor. My father's cancer might have propelled me toward medicine, but I felt better suited intellectually to being a lawyer. I took the law school admission tests, or LSATs, and did well. I applied to law schools in the East: Harvard, Columbia, and Yale.

"No, absolutely not," my mom said when I told her I wanted to go to Boston for an interview. "You are not going away and leaving me here alone when I've just lost my father and my husband." I could not imagine any kind of moral code that ignored my newly widowed mother's pleas. After burying my father and grandfather, it was nearly summer, too late to apply to any of the Michigan law schools. And though I had finished nearly all my coursework for my senior year, I never completed the last class, a thesis on ethics, and so I never did get an undergraduate degree.

A few months after my dad died, in August 1965, I rode my motorcycle to a dentist's office in downtown Detroit to have my wisdom teeth removed. I hadn't thought much about riding back home after a round of nitrous oxide, so I waited a bit to let my head clear. An hour later, I started home but was still a little woozy, so I pulled over to get myself together—into the parking lot of Wayne State Medical School. Looking up at the building, it occurred to me: *Maybe medical school might actually be a good option after all.* Propelled by nitrous and youthful exuberance, I parked my bike and went in.

As luck would have it, the admissions director was in the office that summer day. He was a pathologist way ahead of his time, working on using the body's immune system to ward off cancer. He was very kind when I told him about my dad, Grandpa, and my desire to do good in the world. The dean did not seem bothered by my lack of an undergraduate degree, maybe because I was such an improbable candidate.

It was too late to sit for the Medical College Admission Tests, or MCATs, "But," the dean was quick to add, "we have some old versions of the test here. If you are willing to take them right now in the office, it would give us an idea if you should ever think of a medical career under any circumstances now or later." I sat in an empty lab room filled with faucets and sinks, glass jars and the pungent smell of formaldehyde. A student helper timed the test, collected my answer sheet, and told me to wait while administrators scored it. "Well, I guess there really is a first time for everything," the dean said, looking over my test, tapping his fingers on my motorcycle helmet, which I had left on his desk. "We've had a last-minute cancellation, so I guess it's not impossible to have a last-minute admission." I was accepted to Wayne Medical School and could stay in Detroit. And I would sell that damn nickel to pay for it.

Medical school was easier than I expected. I was blessed with a good memory, and memorization was what the classes mostly required. After a while, however, I found I was much more interested in the politics in the streets than the bodies in the morgue; the "Movement"—civil rights, human rights, equal rights—seemed more urgent. I still did well in my classes, but I could not ignore the seismic changes in the world happening around me.

I threw myself into organizing, working with many socially conscious groups. I founded the Detroit chapter of a radical group called the Student Health Organization, a kind of marriage between SDS and the Medical Committee for Human Rights (MCHR). I became the editor of their magazine, *The*

Body Politic. I was so engrossed in these activities that my friends at medical school nicknamed me "the Phantom." I attended board meetings of the American Civil Liberties Union (ACLU). I set up a free clinic in the Detroit housing projects and raised money—and got food—from rich Detroiters, lots of them Republicans and churchgoers, as well as from Movement lawyers and restaurants. Lines of doctors volunteered their time. It is true that the movements for civil rights and against the Vietnam war split the country in half, but unlike today, when the split is between classes and ideologies, in the 1960s this divide was more generational. Parents and their children were divided by the war. But there were always plenty of kindhearted, high-minded people eager to work on projects for the poor, regardless of political affiliation.

I ran a lunchtime discussion group at Wayne State that we called LICE—Lunchtime in Cultural Euphoria—to which I brought an array of speakers to standing-room-only crowds: the singer Odetta; the political comedian Dick Gregory; the union organizer Cesar Chavez, who slept on my couch because we couldn't afford a hotel room for him; the actor Theodore Bikel; and Dr. Benjamin Spock, the author of the book that raised my generation, *Baby and Child Care.* Ben Spock had become a hero for me—a famous doctor who put his life and reputation on the line to protest the war and was willing to go to jail for his beliefs. I called and asked to interview him for a student magazine, the *New Physician.* I wanted to catch him when he came to deliver a talk at Michigan State. When he said he had no time before leaving for Chicago, I asked whether I could drive him from Lansing and talk on the way. During that four-hour drive, we began a long friendship that only ended thirty years later when

I attended his New Orleans–style funeral in La Jolla, California. After that first meeting, though, I never made a move without checking in with him. He was my role model for what a great doctor, committed to peace and social justice, should be.

The 1960s were a time when we knew that individuals could make a difference. Through our whispers and shouts, our sitting and marching, risking our jobs and education, the fights with our parents, it was all worth it. We had skin in the game. Our brothers, uncles, cousins, and neighbors were caught in a foreign war not of their own choosing, drafted into killing or being killed, or succumbing to drugs and madness. I took every opportunity to do my part, wishing it had not taken so many deaths to get us to act. For me, protesting was punctuated by medical school, rather than the other way around.

When the Chicago chapter of MCHR put out a request for doctors and medical students in 1966 to join a march there, I put on my white coat, grabbed my stethoscope, and drove the three or four hours down to the Windy City. Doctors and medical students—all with white coats and dangling stethoscopes—joined Martin Luther King and thousands of other protesters in a peaceful march through the pro-war and police-lined streets of Chicago. Several hundred of us were arrested. It seems in retrospect, we were too many to be thrown into the Cook County jail. We were corralled into a large park, a few were handcuffed, some of us were fingerprinted, but none were booked. Dr. King just kept on preaching, teaching all of the protestors about nonviolence while we were detained in the park. It seemed surreal and more like church than jail. Every once in a while a chorus of protestors from outside the barriers around the pretend jail would sing "We Shall Overcome," and Dr. King joined in as well.

I spent the summer of 1966 as a volunteer clearing out discarded junk piles in the South Bronx and Spanish Harlem and turning them into "vest pocket" playgrounds. In the summer of 1967 I became a federal employee of the new Office of Equal Health Opportunity, looking for civil rights violations in hospitals in Alabama and Mississippi. One of the other medical student teams was shot at after they did a stealth night inspection of a hospital with multiple violations in Mississippi. After that, our employer, the federal government, shipped me off to San Francisco to inspect hospitals for discrimination.

San Francisco! It was 1967 and ground zero for the Summer of Love, the Age of Aquarius, a nonviolent revolution of good over evil. There was something in the air—in addition to the smell of patchouli and pot smoke. It was impossible to believe that goodness and mercy would not inherit the earth, at any second. Allen Ginsberg had been on Hippie Hill in Golden Gate Park chanting *Om*. There were concerts, parties, and so many girls. Ken Kesey's Merry Pranksters were driving a bus of riotous colors through Haight-Ashbury. You could order home delivery of erotically shaped "Montana Banana" sundaes from a restaurant in the Haight called "Magnolia Thunderpussy." The temptations of sex, drugs, and rock and roll were too much for a young kid who had hardly been out of Detroit, Michigan. I took Oscar Wilde's advice: "The only way to get rid of temptation is to yield to it." I inhaled. Everything, deeply.

The intoxication continued that fall when I hopped the bus caravan to Washington, DC, to join more than one hundred thousand people marching on the Pentagon. Feeling part of a movement so enormous, and feeling so grateful to be in one of the few countries that allowed such a march, was overwhelming. I was not far from where the iconic "Flower Power" photo was snapped of a protestor putting a flower in the barrel of a soldier's rifle.*

The next summer, 1968, exposed me to a darker turn being taken in Europe. I was spending the first semester of my senior year of medical school doing an externship in pediatrics and global health at Guy's Hospital in London with poet and pediatrician Martin Bax. I ended up at a conference in Oxford sponsored by the Medical Association for Prevention of War. My professor of psychiatry from Wayne State, Paul Lowinger, was also there. Paul had been invited to join playwright Arthur Miller, who was in Paris protesting the stalled peace talks there. When he suggested I join him, I couldn't resist.

We stayed at the Hôtel du Quai-Voltaire on the Left Bank, a home away from home for American activists. On the first night, I took my first psilocybin. Over the next few hours, the already magical streets of Paris became painted over by a soft purple hue. A door opened in my mind to something bigger; a vague, undeniable sense that we humans were more than we seemed to be, and that we were a bigger part of and more important to the shape of history than we knew. The war in Vietnam, the city where the peace talks were taking place, the idea of peace, God's most precious gift, all merged in my psychedelic trip, fluid, neither real nor dream.

*If anyone had told me that forty-five years later I would be telling this story to an audience of military brass during a talk I gave at the Pentagon, I would have said they were crazy.

Arthur Miller invited Paul to join him the next night at a celebration of the anniversary of the signing of the French accords with Vietnam at some embassy. I tagged along, still seeing a bit of purple from the psilocybin. After cocktails, the group moved into a large auditorium to hear speakers and watch films. At first the films were all about peace—the peace treaty that France and Vietnam had negotiated, and the desire for peace with the United States. The audience was a potpourri of Third World activists, African nationals, and European diplomats. Someone came through the audience and handed each of the Americans a gift-wrapped box. Inside was a four-inch metal sculpture of a Vietnamese peasant plowing a field with a plow that was shaped like a U.S. fighter jet; the wings of the plane were the plow's handles, and the nose of the plane was the blade. Underneath the plow was a slogan in English, something like: "We will beat their war planes into plowshares." It was a welcome gift, until I found out that the sculpture was crafted out of the metal fuselage of a U.S. plane that had been shot down in Vietnam. An American pilot might have been killed to make this little gift. The film that followed showed Vietnamese artillery shooting down a U.S. plane. The crowd burst into applause as our plane burst into flames and the pilot parachuted to an uncertain fate.

It was hot and stuffy; the walls of the theater closed in on me. The cheering was deafening. I stumbled through the crowd, running out in the middle of the movie. I felt like I was going to vomit. There was no good side to be on during that war, but I could not ever be on the side that cheered for death.

I walked back to the hotel though the streets of Paris, not knowing what to do with the sculpture made from an American plane. Forty years later I am not quite sure why I still have it other than to honor the verses from Isaiah, "They shall beat their swords to plowshares, and their spears into pruning hooks: nations shall not lift up sword against nation, neither shall they learn war anymore."

I did not serve in the army during the Vietnam war; I had been exempted from the draft because of a bony tumor on my knee and because I was enrolled in medical school. I hated the war, but I was not sophisticated enough to realize that those who were drafted did not have the advantages of choice that I had. Like so many in my generation, I made the disastrous mistake of conflating the soldiers who did not have a bony tumor or were not in medical school, who were drafted and had no other choice, with killers. So many of those draftees, those warriors, came back from the war disheartened and confused, only to be abused by people like me and my generation. We were right to fight against our country going to war, and we were right to fight Richard Nixon and Lyndon Johnson or any president who pushed America into a dubious war. But we were so wrong to victimize the kids who were drafted to fight in a war they had no power to start or stop. We should have thanked them. Perhaps keeping the sculpture has been a small reminder of a sin I have tried to make up for over the years.

My childhood pal and med school roommate Jerry Eichner joined me in Paris. We bought a shiny new VW microbus, which we drove to Stockholm to visit John Takman, a doctor who was part of the Medical Association for Prevention of War. He was helping to organize Bertrand Russell's war tribunal, which was in the process of investigating American actions in Vietnam as war crimes. All of northern Europe was unanimous in its opinion of America's actions. We wanted to hear firsthand how they had come to these conclusions. The American government ignored the proceedings, terrified instead of dominoes falling, of the Soviet sphere of influence overtaking theirs.

From there we went to Helsinki and entered the Soviet Union through the Finnish border. The U.S. Embassy advised us not to drive into Russia, as there was war brewing with Czechoslovakia. We ignored their warnings.

An "Intourist guide," a Communist Party minder, traveled with us to Leningrad (St. Petersburg) and Moscow—and then southwest toward where I thought was the village where my father was born. We did a pilgrimage to communist hero memorials, but didn't find the heroes. I wanted to know about three people, Marx, Lenin, and Trotsky, and how their philosophies were addressing social inequalities in Russia. Instead of answering the question, every Russian we met wanted to know if we had three things that they could buy from us and resell: copies of *Playboy,* Beatles albums, and, most of all, blue jeans. I remember trading a pair for a huge cardboard box of Russian goodies: two bottles of vodka, many Russian dolls, and, though I couldn't play them, four or five balalaikas. Our trip was cut short when our guide forced us into Bulgaria and off the road the Soviet military was using to mobilize its forces into Czechoslovakia to crush the Prague Spring. Disillusioned with Mother Russia, we made haste to Istanbul and back to London.

My generation set out to change history, prove that right was greater than might, that America was indeed different, that we were outside the normal stream of history, but not like those who boast of "American exceptionalism" as a cudgel for nationalism. We were a new kind of patriot, believing the actual words of the Declaration of Independence, that America was founded

on the principle that all people—with the emphasis on the word
all—have the inalienable rights of life, liberty, and the pursuit of
happiness. We believed deeply that human and civil rights had
found their home in America, and that all—again the emphasis
is on *all*—people are created equal. Although we were frequently
labeled anti-American, we were motivated by the deepest patrio-
tism, by the idea that a nation "of, by, and for the people" would
only endure if we corrected the social wrongs of discrimination
and disenfranchisement, especially redressing the pain caused
by slavery. It was not a class struggle; it was a generational belief system. Detroit could easily have divided along class lines.
But my memory of those days was that though people disagreed
about the war and civil rights, everyone still wanted to be part
of the same national vision regardless of where they came from.

Whatever had been in the air in San Francisco, the smell of
freedom was spreading, and something new was pervading the
world.

CHAPTER 3

Woodstock on Wheels

Peculiar travel suggestions are dancing lessons from God.
—Kurt Vonnegut

About a month after I got back to Detroit from Europe for my final year in medical school, I took a date to a performance of the Living Theatre, a touring anarchist troupe that had been producing works of Bertolt Brecht, Jean Cocteau, and Gertrude Stein. I had not seen Elaine in more than three years. But somehow there she was, my Elaine, looking radiant, sitting directly in front of me in the theater, with somebody else, another date. For some reason I am unable to explain, I had carried a large, ripe red pomegranate with me to the show. I know not everyone goes to the theater carrying a pomegranate, but it was what I had at that moment, and when I saw Elaine sitting there with someone else, I was so thrilled to see her I just handed her the pomegranate. Our dates could never have understood the meaning of that pomegranate, but we did because we used to talk about pomegranates lying in the back of my father's station wagon discussing Greek mythology among other things. Within a few days, we gave up any pretense that we were not meant to be together and Elaine moved into my apartment near the medical school, and—by the standards of the time—we began living in sin.

To avoid confronting our mothers, we installed two separate phone lines, one in her name and one in mine. When Elaine's mother called her and asked, "Have you seen Larry lately?" she would look over at me on the couch and say truthfully, "I expect to see him soon." Ditto if my mom called. We kept a bowl of pomegranates in our sinful apartment. Neither of us can remember who our other dates to the Living Theatre were on pomegranate night.

Though I proposed soon after, Elaine was too smart to marry me while I was still in medical school—it had become cliché that the minute a guy got his M.D. he would divorce long-suffering wife number one who had supported him in school and move on to marriage number two. After Elaine had finished her master's degree in psychology at the University of Michigan and I graduated from medical school, we got married and had two ceremonies. One was Jewish—rabbi, chupah, glass breaking, and marriage contract for our parents and their friends. The second wedding was later that night, a hippie reception at a rent-a-mansion, the Gar Wood estate on Grayhaven Island, in the middle of the Detroit River. The island had a bridge that we could gate when the party began, to keep the police away. I arranged for a Good Humor ice cream truck and local band Savage Grace as well as musicians from MC5, a Detroit favorite. Our wedding cake sported a huge candy peace sign. Friends brought two punch bowls, filling one with ordinary Kool-Aid and spiking the other with LSD; they posted a big "Electric Punch" warning sign over the spiked bowl. It was a grand party with only one mishap. Grandma Ida, who was game enough to come to both parties, did not know what "electric punch" was, and so she drank from the wrong bowl. She told me a year later that she had the time of her life at our wedding party. She may have been from the old country, but I think she knew quite well why she had such a good time.

I landed an internship in San Francisco, so we packed our apartment and loaded the VW camper for our honeymoon drive west. We drove slowly across the country, sleeping in national parks and exploring. On the drive, rainbows were ubiquitous—on the back window of every VW Beetle or van like ours, hand-embroidered on Levi's jackets and backpacks, on posters for rock shows, on record albums, painted on bodies at festivals. Well before the rainbow flag represented the gay rights movement, the rainbow represented peace, hippies, yippies, the Summer of Love, or simply love. I was taught in Hebrew school that rainbows were God's message of hope. God had summoned Noah and told him that humanity was wicked. Disappointed in his creation, God was going to destroy the world by flooding it. But he wanted to save a few good people and each animal species to repopulate the world after the waters receded. Noah's job was to build an ark to carry those people and animals to safety.

Noah declined. "How do I know that you won't destroy the world the next time you get angry?" God answered, "Well, I wouldn't destroy the world if all of humanity were good, but they're not." Noah started negotiating: "Okay, what if there was one good man in the world. Would you spare the world for his sake?"

God said, "No."

They haggled night and day, day and night, finally reaching an agreement: If there were thirty-six good humans, God would not destroy the world. In Hebrew, thirty-six is *lamed vov,* and "The Lamed Vov" became the name given to these righteous beings. In Jewish mysticism, these saints, whose identity is always secret, protect the world by leading a righteous life. The rainbow was the symbol for this new covenant. The thirty-six righteous ones was for me a kind of shorthand for the rainbow of faces, the rainbow of faiths, that infused the counterculture movement. I have always felt that the love of the righteous would prevail over the centrifugal forces of greed and corruption, anger and hate, selfishness and violence.

Presbyterian Hospital in Pacific Heights, a very wealthy enclave in the very heart of the San Francisco establishment, was where I began my internship, as all internships begin, on July 1. As I walked eagerly through the hospital, it was impossible to miss the message in the welcome the hospital laid out for me: the cover of a 1969 *Medical World News* magazine had been reproduced and pinned up on bulletin boards all over the building.

"Watch out!" the cover declared. "These radical MDs are going to take over medicine." Five of us long-haired, wild-eyed radical medical students were the subjects of the story and the cover photo for this conservative medical journal. I was squatting right in the center, chest out, eyes wide. Someone had gathered copies of that cover photo and displayed them prominently. On a few, maybe for emphasis, a hypodermic needle was stuck in my nose, pinning to it a warning: "Presbyterian Hospital welcomes its new intern, Dr. Brilliant, here to save the world!"

Welcome to San Francisco, land of rainbows.

Elaine began work as a juvenile probation officer in the East Bay. I worked nonstop at the hospital but found time to volunteer some nights at the Haight-Ashbury Free Clinic helping addicts. I kept close ties with MCHR. I taught an extension course for the University of California called Drugs and the Mystical Experience, and prayed that no one from the hospital would learn I was teaching it. Elaine was accepted into law school and was to start the following September.

San Francisco was awash with social experiments, cults and karasses, T-groups and encounter groups, Hindu teachers and Tibetan lamas with their *satsangs* and *sanghas*. There were yoga classes everywhere, dozens of communes, and on Hippie Hill more exotic characters than at Speakers' Corner in London's Hyde Park.

At the hospital in between civil rights and antiwar marches I took patient care very seriously. It was the first time I had hands-on responsibility for the health, and sometimes for the lives, of patients. In a few instances I got into trouble for having long hair, going to antiwar marches, and for taking time off to attend hippie spiritual lectures by a fellow named Baba Ram Dass who had just returned from a transformative experience in India.

At one antiwar march in Union Square, a photographer took my picture and it wound up on the front page of the paper. That was bad publicity. A few of the older attending physicians wanted to kick me out of my internship, which would have pretty much ended my medical career. I found out later that two of the youngest staff doctors—Marty Brotman and Keith Cohn—had risked their own careers by speaking up for me.

I was pursuing a surgical internship. I was particularly fascinated with the work of one surgeon, Dr. Victor Richards, who had the swiftest and smoothest scalpel in the West. After assisting during one of his operations, an intern in my group said, "It's as if the patient's flesh opened in eager anticipation of his knife." I wanted to be by Dr. Richards's side as often as possible. One morning I was assisting on a patient with intestinal cancer. Dr. Richards had to remove part of the colon and create a bypass—a long and complicated surgery, perhaps ten or twelve hours standing and cutting. Several hours in, while I was holding parts of the intestines back with retractor clamps, my right leg buckled and I collapsed, toppling the anesthesia cart and sending bottles of IV fluids spraying everywhere. Lying on the operating room floor I recall thinking, *The tiles are so much colder than they seem when you stand on them.*

Many interns pass out during their first long surgery. But this was different. Long after I was able to get up from the floor, I continued to experience short bouts of paralysis in both legs; I tired easily, and from time to time, my thinking was muddled. Dr. Richards took me on as his patient. Blood tests revealed a very high level of calcium, which would explain the lethargy, slowed thinking, and perhaps the muscle weakness in my legs. But why had my calcium levels skyrocketed?

Dr. Richards diagnosed a tumor of the parathyroids, the four pea-size endocrine glands buried in the four corners of the thyroid at the base of the neck just above the collarbone. He would not be able to distinguish between a benign tumor, an adenoma, or cancer, an adenocarcinoma, until he opened me up and removed samples of the glands for tissue studies. Either way, it was likely that all four glands, which regulate calcium and potassium in the body, would have to be removed. I had assumed that a surgical residency would be the next step in my training, but it was surgery, not training, that was next for me. Richards suggested I take a year off from seeking a residency and schedule the operation for the fall.

As my internship was coming to an end, the local news became fixated on the events happening on the small island of Alcatraz in San Francisco Bay. The infamous prison there had closed six years earlier, and the federal government had declared the land surplus property. In November 1969 a group of American Indians occupied the island and demanded that it be deemed once again "Indian land" on the basis of the hundred-year-old Treaty of Fort Laramie, which had stipulated that all Indian land that had been taken over by the U.S. government and then declared "surplus" must be returned to the original tribal owners. The occupiers, who called themselves the "Indians of All Tribes," demanded that the island be used as a center for Native American spirituality and study and a museum of Indian culture.

At the peak of the Alcatraz occupation, about four hundred Indian occupiers were on the island—many arrived there by jumping off of boats and swimming. They were joined eventually by John Trudell, a Sioux poet who broadcasted daily on Radio Free Alcatraz, providing information for national news coverage. Because of his activism, it was later rumored that John had the thickest FBI file in history. He continuously spoke out against the hypocrisy of the American promotion of freedom abroad while his people were trapped and dying on reservations. He took a leadership role on Alcatraz.

According to a poll, 80 percent of San Franciscans cheered for the Indians to win their standoff with the U.S. government— San Franciscans were shocked by U.S. government policies that continued to strip Native Americans of land and resources. So were many in the Coast Guard. Members of the tony San Francisco Yacht Club ran through Coast Guard blockades to take provisions to the island while the Coast Guard pretended to stop them. But by the middle of the summer of 1970, the Indians on Alcatraz were in trouble. The sympathetic sailors from the yacht club had gone back to their day jobs, and the occupiers were running out of supplies.

The legendary *San Francisco Chronicle* columnist Herb Caen often wrote in support of the occupation of the island, calling with limited success for doctors to provide medical care on the island. John Trudell's wife, Lou, was pregnant; they wanted their baby to be born on Alcatraz, which would make him the first Native American child to be born on Indian-freed land in two hundred years. Herb Caen wrote, "Is there no doctor who will help her deliver her baby on free Indian land?" There was no water, no electricity, scarce food, and little medicine. Sounded like the perfect assignment to me.

My illness, though pressing, was not a medical emergency. I could hold off surgery for a few weeks, or months, but I wasn't allowed to practice at the hospital until I underwent the procedure. Volunteering to go to Alcatraz was a chance to get back to activism while doing something with my medical degree, so I offered to make the house call. At first, I went to the island in the morning on a Coast Guard helicopter and came back on a boat each night. Two nurses from the Medical Committee for

Human Rights stayed on Alcatraz as Lou got closer to her due date. I moved out there soon after for what would turn out to be a three-week stay.

On July 20, 1970, in the former superintendent's house, on a hill overlooking the bay, Lou Trudell gave birth to a boy that they named Wovoka. We had limited clean sheets and water and some emergency medical supplies. When the baby was crowning, when one more push would bring this historical child into a world of spiritual and political import, something made me realize that the father's hands, an Indian's, not a white guy's hands, should be first to touch this baby. The delivery was smooth; perhaps the biggest medical challenge I had was to persuade John Trudell to wear gloves, as the old prison was filled with hiding places for tetanus bacillus, a common cause of infant death in the developing world. I was not going to lose this baby to that bacterium. John caught his son as Lou made a final push. We cleaned the baby up and John hovered over his wife and child, smiling. I had done my job, assisted by the two MCHR nurses, and there didn't seem to be any complications. Lou took her time to caress and bond with her new baby, and then stood up, looked around at the dozen or so people in the living room, and proclaimed: "Is anyone else hungry? Who wants bacon? I'm going to make breakfast!"

The name Wovoka was an intentional choice, meant to send a mystical message to Native Americans across the country. Eighty years earlier, a Northern Paiute medicine man called Wovoka—which means "cutter"—had created the Ghost Dance religion, which Sitting Bull and Geronimo later joined in force. Wovoka prophesized that after he died he would rotate around the Earth, in a kind of heaven. When he was reborn, he said, it would herald the return of the buffalo, the return of the Indian way, and the end of the white man's way.

"Wovoka lives!" shouted a tall lean Indian who had come back from fighting in Vietnam—ex–special forces, Green Beret. He seemed drunk or stoned—he later said he was high on acid. The former Green Beret scanned the room—Lou, John, Wovoka— and then saw me, a white guy in scrubs, a blemish in the Indian painting, something to be edited out of the story. Alcatraz had been taken. Wovoka had returned as prophesied. I was a problem to be solved. He pulled out a hunting knife so fast I hardly saw it, and then had me in a headlock, waving the knife toward my neck when anyone moved.

"Stop it!" John screamed. "Stop it! He's the doctor! He delivered Wovoka!" But this skinny, intellectual poet was no match for the Green Beret, and the Green Beret knew it. "If I can't kill the white man, I'll cut myself! Wovoka was a cutter. I am a cutter too!" he shouted. People poured into the room. Several Indians jumped the Green Beret and pulled him off me. After struggling free of their hold, he slashed his left forearm, spraying blood everywhere like a kid squirting a garden hose. His friends held him down; I sewed him up. He pulled the stitches out and started bleeding again. I sewed him up again. We did this dance three times. Finally, he grabbed me, blood still spurting out of his arm and onto my face, the knife again at my neck. Everyone was drenched in red.

"Wovoka is born! We don't need any of these fucking white bastards on the island!"

I do not remember very much until I heard a shout. "Give me the knife," said Charley, a slight five-foot-two-inch Indian who

40

moved slowly toward the Green Beret on hand crutches, his legs weak from polio. "Give me the knife. Give me the knife," he repeated quietly. And just like that, the Green Beret gave up his knife. Charley lightly cut his own forearm, casually, like he was slicing pastrami, and held his bloody arm against a cut on my face. "Now there's no white man here. Just our blood," Charley said. "Okay?"

Things calmed down for a while and I began to think I might make it off the island without more drama. But the Green Beret started fiddling with his wounds again, tugging at the sutures saying, "I'm ready to die." Blood sprayed everywhere again. If we didn't get him to a hospital, I feared, he would bleed to death.

One of John's friends sprinted off to the dock to the only working telephone, set up by the Coast Guard for emergencies or, they hoped, for when the Indians were ready to surrender. Soon a Coast Guard cutter pulled up at the wharf and we bundled the Green Beret in sheets and got him onto the boat.

A ship bumping through rough waters is not ideal for putting a ligature on an arterial bleeder. To make matters worse, the Green Beret—still tripping on whatever he had taken—continued to pull out his stitches as fast as I could get them in. What should have been a very short ride from Alcatraz to the San Francisco piers seemed to last forever as the sheets got redder and the Green Beret got paler. An ambulance met us at the dock and sped away to San Francisco General, where he was sedated, sewn up, and held on suicide watch. I never saw him again.

Back on the San Francisco dock, news cameras appeared out of nowhere. Reporters pointed microphones at me, asking, "What do the Indians want?" I had never met an Indian until I showed up on Alcatraz, but I ended up on the front page of the

San Francisco Examiner and all over TV news. A local doctor saw the coverage and contacted a radio DJ, Tom Donahue, who was producing a movie called *Medicine Ball Caravan* with Warner Bros. It was about rock-and-roll bands traveling across America and the hippie fans following them in psychedelic buses, camping in teepees, staging rock-and-roll concerts. The doctor, Bob Baron, had already signed up as both medic and extra for the film and suggested to Donahue that Warner Bros. hire me to be a second doctor for the film caravan. It was supposed to be, as the *Oakland Tribune* called it, Woodstock on Wheels. There would be a final blowout concert in Canterbury, England, with Pink Floyd. Warner Bros. offered to fund the clinic I had set up for the Indians on Alcatraz if I agreed to come along without being paid. Elaine and I agreed, packed up our life in San Francisco, turned over management of *The Body Politic,* handed off our apartment to our new tenant, and ran away with the circus for what we thought would be a summer vacation.

The starting point for the Medicine Ball Caravan was on a pier right near the Ferry Building. There were more than a dozen forty-foot buses, loads of band equipment, movie cameras, and wannabe movie extras gathered on the San Francisco waterfront. My first duty was to vaccinate the film crew and all the musicians against smallpox. At the time there was no smallpox in the United States, and I thought then that the vaccinations were overkill. But Warner Bros. expected the cast and crew to go to England for the final concert, and in order to get back into the States everyone needed one of those yellow immunization cards with proof of a recent vaccination. There was a chance some of the caravan might continue on through Europe to India where there was still a lot of smallpox. I did not know much about smallpox and had never given anyone a smallpox vaccination, but it was easy enough.

The first time I met Wavy Gravy was while he waited his turn for vaccination. He put out his arm for me to vaccinate him and his face lit up with a huge smile, his mouth a rainbow, a row of multicolored false teeth he'd convinced a dentist friend to make for him. He was wearing a duckbill hat with an actual duck's bill and a hand-sewn jumpsuit made of patches of American flags, blue sky, and stars. Next to him stood his stunning wife, née Bonnie Jean Beecher, rumored to be the Minnesota beauty of Bob Dylan's "Girl from the North Country." She had abandoned life as a starlet—after appearances in *Star Trek* and *The Twilight Zone*—to be with the poet Hugh Romney. Then Hugh Romney the poet and stand-up comic morphed into Wavy Gravy the fool, the clown, and Renaissance man—a kind, smart, compassionate, hilarious force of nature. The police had beaten Wavy so badly, and so regularly, at protests and sit-ins, that his back was broken several times; later he would need multiple spinal fusions and full body casts. When Wavy figured out that cops do not like to beat up—or be seen beating up—clowns, Santa Claus, or the Easter Bunny, Wavy adopted a clown or holiday persona as the season allowed.

A year before he had been Chief of Please at Woodstock, where he and the Hog Farm, the counterculture descendants of Ken Kesey and the Merry Pranksters, were in charge of security for hundreds of thousands of revelers. "How are you going to provide security without weapons?" a skeptical reporter wanted to know. Wavy said that they would form a "please force." A reporter laughed and said he was silly.

"Do you feel secure now?" Wavy asked.

"Yes," the reporter replied.

"Well, you see, my plan is working."

When rain and mud from an overnight storm threatened to unleash chaos at the festival, Wavy got on stage and uttered the line that defined him and the event: "What I have in mind is breakfast in bed for four hundred thousand of us." The Hog Farm commune, with lots of help, delivered a cup of granola to each person in every tent so that nobody tried to navigate the mess left behind from the storms. This was Wavy's magic. Love and generosity kept things peaceful. "Peaceful" and "Woodstock" became synonyms and opened the door to the possibility of other large gatherings and music events that became part of American culture.

The movie caravan left San Francisco headed for Washington, DC. Along the way the hippies of the Medicine Ball Caravan met small-town Americans, in the Southwest, in the plains states, and in the Midwest. Some of the greats of the day, B.B. King, Alice Cooper, Joni Mitchell, Hot Tuna, Pink Floyd, Rod Stewart, members of Jefferson Airplane, and others, made appearances. The Grateful Dead had dropped out of the caravan before the first bus pulled out, but Tom Donahue and Warner Bros. had too much invested to pull the plug, so our wagon train started "Eastward Ho" without them. After the final concert in Washington, DC, the crew would fly to London for the final concert at Canterbury.

It was a reverse pilgrimage in which we set up camps of tie-dyed teepees, and threw big, free rock-and-roll concerts in the middle of nowhere. To many we were the first live hippies they had ever seen. But there were only a few clashes of the *Easy Rider* kind. We were there to spread the joy of Rock and Roll and with some dramatic exceptions, most were happy to receive us. To the good folks in Placitas, New Mexico; Boulder, Colorado; and Yellow Springs, Ohio, we were weird, but we were not boring.

To Wavy and the Hog Farm, I must have seemed pretty square. Despite my growing involvement in the counterculture and the Movement, to them I was still Dr. Brilliant, a professional, an adult. I had long hair, but Elaine and I had no intention of staying with the caravan for the trip they planned to take overland to Asia after the final concert in Canterbury. We were one of very few married couples. I wanted to get my parathyroid surgery over with and get back to finding a residency program, and Elaine was slated to start law school at the University of California immediately after the last concert.

After the final American concert in DC with Hot Tuna, B.B. King, and Stoneground, we boarded an Air India jumbo jet to fly to London. Warner Bros. insisted on Air India because it was one of the few ways the company could spend all the Indian rupees it had accumulated as the primary film distributor in the pre-Bollywood era. The company couldn't take the money out of the country any other way.

Halfway across the ocean the Indian captain smelled pot, left the cockpit, and marched straight toward the film crew in his crisply pressed uniform and white turban with the stern look of a policeman. He was tall, bearded, well-built, and we were intimidated.

"What are you doing?" he demanded to know.

"Smoking hash."

There was an awkward silence.

Then one chippy hippie blurted out, "Want some?"

"Of course," he replied and sat down with us. It was a hell of a lot scarier watching the pilot get stoned than worrying about getting busted by the captain. Somehow, we landed in London safe and sound.

Most of what I did as a doctor with the caravan between concerts was treat colds and flus, help people out whose trips had pushed their minds too far, and stitch up cuts from minor tumbles. It was an easy way to become friends with all these lovable characters. But it was a different story when I did my job as a Rock Doc at the concerts. The drug of choice was migrating from the gentler mushrooms to the dangerous methamphetamine. During one concert near Boulder the speed junkies were out in full force. A guy showed up with the metal teeth of a bear trap still stuck in his shoulder. He got into a knife fight, which started over two dogs who had been going after each other. Wavy brought both protagonists and their dogs onstage and praised each for protecting the honor of their dog; somehow, the clown got the two fighters to hug, and the audience responded with a standing ovation. That was Wavy Gravy, peacemaker. I will never understand how he pulled that off.

At the same concert in the Colorado hills, I had to help a woman who had been assaulted. Her labia had been sliced off by a crazed meth junkie with a knife, one of the saddest and most gruesome memories of my life. I kept her from bleeding out while we waited for the helicopter to medevac her to the hospital. I suspect she would have bled to death if we hadn't had the helicopter. Survival is one thing, but I have no idea of the emotional scars that followed her through her life. What kind of man could do something like this? I only know that he was on a long-acting amphetamine called STP—named after the automobile lubricant. I know this because he was wearing a shirt that read "STP" and he was part of an off-the-grid community from the woods outside of Boulder that called themselves the "STP family." What a fucking evil drug.

The freedom of the Summer of Love led to many wonderful things, but also to this. I learned the lesson that every society has had to learn: each emergent community must have rules. The pendulum swings between individual freedom and law. There are beautiful and ugly things about the human spirit, and we need protection from horrible people who commit horrible acts of depravity.

The peace movement was spontaneous, safe, generous, and free, until the murders: JFK, RFK, MLK, black and white civil rights activists. Kent State. And Altamont, the anti-Woodstock, where the Rolling Stones hired the Hells Angels for security and paid them in beer. Four people were killed, scores were injured, cars were stolen and abandoned. The days of pure peace and love were becoming complicated.

CHAPTER 4

Magic Bus Trip

The great morning which is for all
appears in the East.
Let its light reveal us to each other
who walk on the same path
of pilgrimage.

—Rabindranath Tagore

T he Americans are coming! The Americans are coming!"
Wavy loved running through the narrow lanes of Canterbury playing Paul Revere in reverse, announcing the arrival of the Medicine Ball Caravan. We were getting ready to put on our last concert, with Pink Floyd and Rod Stewart. One bus was now festooned with signs, "Free John Sinclair," who had been jailed in Michigan for possession of two joints of marijuana. By the measuring stick of two marijuana joints, nearly every one of the thousand Brits who attended the concert on August 31, 1970, would also have been jailed. However, the Brits preferred their cannabis in the form of hash combined with tobacco, and so both the smokes and the music were decidedly English.

The hippies on the other side of the pond were no less prone to the usual concert accidents, and I spent most of the day in the emergency area of the Rock Doc tent, sewing up minor wounds and caring for those who had imbibed too much of one or another substance. With or without herbal support, it was a great concert and a wonderful end to what would turn out to be, after editing, a really awful movie. Elaine and I packed up our gear and said some long goodbyes to the musicians, cameramen, groupies, roadies, assistant directors, producers, stage crews, and bus crews who had formed the accidental community of making this Warner Bros. movie. Elaine and I took a train to London and stayed in a hotel for a couple of romantic nights. It was the first time we had been really alone in months.

We planned to meet up with the Hog Farm crew to say goodbye. Wavy decided he wanted to drive on to India or Nepal. He persuaded Stoneground, the house band from the caravan, to do a benefit concert to raise money for the Hog Farm to buy a new bus to get the group through Europe and Eurasia, over the Khyber Pass in Afghanistan, and then inside India. Reality was catching up with us. Elaine needed to get back to law school; she returned home to San Francisco after Canterbury. I agreed to stay to help out with the concert.

The concert was held at the Roundhouse and brought out the cream of British rock and roll; even Beatle George Harrison flittered about backstage. Most important, it was a sellout, raising more than $10,000—enough to buy a very old British Leyland transport, christened "the Sterling Hog," that would be retrofitted into a mobile commune for a dozen or two to live on.

We decided to do a test run with the new bus in Arthurian and mythical England by celebrating the autumnal equinox at

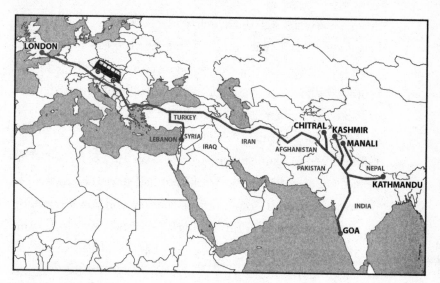

The Hippie Caravan

Stonehenge and Glastonbury. At Stonehenge, we camped in the middle of the monoliths, while Wavy performed Hopi and Huna ceremonies and chanted *Om*. There were no barricades then and we were completely alone. Then we took the bus the short distance to Glastonbury and climbed the Tor, an ancient druid religious site on top of which was built the Church of St. Michael, where the Holy Grail is supposed to be buried. We drank electric Kool-Aid and nettle tea in honor of Tibet's greatest cave saint, Milarepa, who, Wavy told us, lived on nettles while in meditation. Tripping on acid, the vision of the postmodern Hog Farmers joining hands with some ancient druid practitioners celebrating the equinox made me feel as if I had joined an eternal circle. I felt like I was amidst the Children of Light and would find my Knight's errand that would help hold off darkness. It was a very vivid experience. After it, I knew that I wanted to stay with the buses, join the Hog Farm, and go to the Himalayas. First I would have to go back to San Francisco and convince Elaine to join us. I had trouble leaving this wonderful communal family, but I had promised Elaine, so I stayed only long enough to drive with them to Paris and Amsterdam, where, in the back of the bus, I helped one of the Hog Farmers deliver her baby.

I returned to Elaine in our apartment on Turk Street. She had been there only a couple of weeks but had started law school as planned. We agreed to put off the conversation about rejoining the Hog Farm buses in Europe until after I had my surgery and she had a taste of what law school was like. While she was going to classes and I awaited my date with Dr. Richards's magical scalpel, I worked as an emergency room doctor to raise enough money to start paying off our debts. Presbyterian Hospital was kind to me and waived the costs for my surgery, even though I was no longer in the internship program. Dr. Richards also refused to charge for his fee, citing "professional courtesy." It was thrilling to think that someone as respected as he would consider me a colleague.

The surgery to remove my parathyroid glands went well. I suspect my body, like others Dr. Richards had operated on, cooperated with his deft hands. And best of all, the biopsy taken during surgery looked like an adenoma, not a malignant adenocarcinoma. The specimen was sent off to a specialty lab for confirmation.

I did turn yellow right after surgery—they never found out the cause of the jaundice but I suspect it was from the inhaled anesthesia. Whatever the cause, it extended my recovery. Wavy and Bonnie Jean also returned to the States and stayed at our apartment on Turk Street while I was recuperating, just long enough to convince Elaine that we should rejoin the Hog Farm. Wavy's idea for the "Journey to the East," as he called it after Hermann Hesse's book by that name, consisted of two parts. The first was to "Visit every Christian shrine, Jewish synagogue, Muslim mosque, Hindu temple, Buddhist vihara on our drive between Europe and Asia." The second part of the journey was to "Raise money, bring medicine and food to the people in India and East Pakistan who are starving and sick." Elaine was putty in his hands. No self-respecting hippie could resist an offer to join this loving commune on a magical trip like that.

The kicker came in early November: a historic cyclone hit Bhola Island, the largest of the East Pakistani (now Bangladeshi) islands at the mouth of a river that emptied into the Bay of Bengal. Early reports were that a half million mostly poor, rural people had perished when the storm laid waste to Bhola and western India. With the United Nations and other international relief organizations slow to get aid to the victims in the months following the tragedy, Wavy came up with the idea of delivering aid ourselves. It was easy enough for me to go to hospitals in San Francisco and get medical supplies donated. If a bunch of hippies could provide food for cyclone victims, Wavy figured, the United Nations and other relief organizations would be shamed into taking a more active role in feeding and caring for the displaced. Warner Bros. had thrown in some extra tickets and supplies for the continuation of the trip. Somehow an Éclair 16 movie camera from the caravan and a cameraman materialized and joined us to document the hippie relief effort.

The transformation for me and Elaine from radical doctor and law student to hippies-in-a-commune was complete. I wouldn't be looking for a residency when I recovered from surgery, and Elaine was going to be doing her law school reading overseas.

During the time I was recuperating, members of the counter-culture royalty came by our Turk Street apartment to wish Wavy and Bonnie Jean bon voyage and to offer help in raising money for "Earth People's Stomach," the campaign to take food and medicine to Bhola Island. Hog Farm commune members from Woodstock, or the farm in New Mexico, or from earlier bus trips came by. Elaine organized her law school courses and books. The apartment was filled with interesting conversations and high spirits. It was a nice way to spend post-op time.

One night Ken Kesey, the original Prankster, author of *One Flew over the Cuckoo's Nest,* and captain of the Merry Pranksters bus Further came over. Kesey was larger than life. He had been a champion wrestler in high school and college, nearly making the U.S. Olympic team. He had the bearing of a jock, the heart of a mystic, and the timing of a street magician. As a creative writing student at Stanford, he had been an accidental early user of LSD when he volunteered to be an experimental subject for seventy-five dollars per day in what he later found out was a CIA-financed study of psychedelic drugs. Legend has it that the military wondered whether the drug that was opening the minds of young people in Haight-Ashbury and around the country might make soldiers more pliable, perhaps even compliant. No one, least of all Kesey, could have imagined what would come after one dose of Ken Kesey was mixed with several government-sanctioned doses of LSD: it gave birth to the Merry Pranksters, hippies, the

Hog Farm, and the counterculture. And to many who came later, Kesey was our culture's pied piper.

Amidst bearded, beaded, slumping hippies, Kesey was clean-shaven and athletic with an almost military bearing, a broad open face, and an easy, deceptive smile. His body looked powerful, like that of a fireman or policeman or ex–special forces, but his eyes were wise and mischievous. If there had been an opera of the gods and goddesses of the increasingly pantheistic 1960s, Kesey might have played the role of the Norse god Loki or the Native American trickster Coyote. Each time I met him I was struck by how he so quickly snapped from the "fade-into-the-crowd everyman" to riveting his piercing blue eyes on you, prizing open a higher, deeper person inside the looker and lookee alike.

Paul Krassner, editor of the underground magazine *The Realist,* was there, as was David Crosby, who had been living on a houseboat in nearby Sausalito. Paul and Laura Foster and others from the Merry Pranksters joined us too. I lost track of all the people who rang the doorbell. Lots of buds were lit and beer appeared. I brought up a nitrous tank that I had left over from the Medicine Ball Caravan. When blow-up pillows and clear plastic breathing tubes materialized, the nitrous dispensing began.

The phone rang and Kesey answered. It was columnist Herb Caen asking, "Is there a Brilliant person there?" Kesey responded, like it was scripted, "You want a Brilliant person? You are speaking to him," and thus flowed enough material to fill many columns for weeks.

An impromptu string band started up in our living room. Kesey spied the nitrous tank. "My favorite fruit drink!" he proclaimed and wrested control from me. He doled out the

nitrous, checked the tubes and blew up the pillows, telling outrageous stories and making sure everyone had a safe and soft
landing. He gave a pillow to Wavy, but when I approached
him for one—a little in awe, for Kesey was a bit of a messianic
figure—Kesey hesitated, even seemed to refuse. He tilted his
head, his eyes drilling into my soul as if seeing me, judging
me, with the eyes of God. "What makes you think you are . . .
worthy?" he asked.

A confusion of feelings about joining the Hog Farm, leaving
America to run away with the mystical circus, being doctor to
the pilgrims danced around my head, and I did not feel worthy.
Not in the way I felt Kesey was asking.

"Cheer up, Larry. You are worthy. We all are," Wavy inter-
vened, his eye lasers locking with Kesey's. "Ken! Don't play with
him so rough! He's new."

Everyone laughed. It was only laughing gas, right? Nothing
mystical or magic here, nothing profoundly spiritual. It wasn't
as if there were some kind of deep magic. Was there? As with
Wavy, you had to always be on guard with Kesey, lest a magical
moment break out.

During that wonderful evening with Kesey and Wavy at
our apartment on Turk Street, I caught one of the guests in
my office, rummaging through my little black doctor's bag,
tossing aside antibiotics and bandages, looking for narcotics. I
stopped him, but I could never again be so casual with my little
black bag. I decided then and there never to be in a position to
prescribe narcotics, and though I've kept my medical license
active for forty years, I have never had a narcotics license nor
prescribed them.

Wavy and Bonnie Jean flew to Europe to join the caravan a few days later while Elaine and I stayed behind to finish packing. Elaine's law books filled more than one suitcase. "Get well quickly and come have Thanksgiving turkey in Turkey," Wavy said. The follow-up tests on my tumor were reassuring. I was warned that I might have some residual effects as my body adjusted to the absence of parathyroid hormone. From time to time I did need help walking; my legs took months to figure out how to work again after surgery.

Elaine and I flew from San Francisco through Germany and met with the Hog Farm in Istanbul, where they had set up tie-dyed teepees in a gypsy-like campsite right on the Bosporus Strait. I brought a new Whole Earth flag from Stewart Brand, who had, some say, inspired NASA to release the photo of the entire Earth because of his nonstop badgering. Stewart felt sure that when people of all religions, nationalities, ideologies, tribes, and races of the world saw our common home, a tiny island of blue and white and green against the black void of space, peace and harmony would descend overnight as everyone realized that we are all in this together. That was the flag we flew over our tie-dyed rainbow-colored teepees on the narrow strait that separates Europe and Asia, where East meets West, the perfect symbol for Westerners journeying to the East.

When Elaine and I joined up with the two buses, we were given sleeping space in the Sterling Hog in the next bunk over from the Gravys. I got a new name, "Doctor Larry," as one of the two family doctors on board. Butch, our intense and beloved driver, was the "transportation commissioner." Lou was the "money commissioner," and Fred the Fed was the "police commissioner." In addition to my medical responsibilities, I was made the "guru commissioner." My job was to meet, interview, and report back on any of the Sufis and gurus, saints and sadhus, lamas and rabbis, preachers and mystics we met along the way to figure out whether they were legitimate or not. I barely knew what a guru was. My attraction to the counterculture had been strictly political, not at all spiritual. Because of my deep skepticism, I was either the best or the worst person for the job.

We drove the buses from Istanbul to Ankara and to the old Roman town of Trabzon on the Black Sea. Driving through a torrential rain, one of our buses broke an axel and a water pump, leaving us stranded in Turkey for two months while we waited for parts to arrive from Germany. We learned to say "Our water pump is broken" in Turkish, and every time we did, we were stunned by the hospitality offered to a bunch of poor hippies in a broken bus. We put the bus up on blocks near the shore, and during a terrible storm, when the tide threatened to wash the bus away, Wavy stood on the roof with a trident daring the storm to do its worst.

Because Warner Bros. had paid us in plane tickets back to the States from Delhi, we had to make it to India and get back to America before the tickets expired at the end of the year. We thought a year was plenty of time to go from London to Turkey to India, but we hadn't planned on being stranded thousands of miles away from the nearest American Express office, where most of us had money waiting for us. But instead of panicking, we explored. We visited nearby villages, went out to dinner, got friendly with locals. We were skinny and nearly malnourished but happy to be in Turkey together.

When the parts finally arrived and the bus was fixed, we headed to Tehran, where we found the only American Express office between Turkey and India. A quick look at the map helped us realize that we could, with a slight detour, make a pilgrimage to Mount Ararat, supposedly the site where Noah's ark landed and he saw the first rainbow after the flood. We could honor our Abrahamic tradition and celebrate the birthplace of the ubiquitous hippie symbol in one trip.

But because it was a cloudy day, we couldn't see the mountain as we approached it. All we could see were small houses and surrounding vegetation. A local family of Kurds invited us to tea in their backyard while we waited for the sun to appear. Within a few minutes, the sun came out, revealing a breathtaking panorama of green trees and snowcapped mountains, including Mount Ararat. The Kurds didn't get why we were so excited, but they said they had never been visited by strangers like us— we might have been space aliens, given how odd we must have looked to them. They could not have been more kind.

Next, we drove through Iran. Under the shah, Iran was a suffocated police state. Omnipresent was the Savak, Iran's secret police, intelligence service, and domestic security all wrapped up into one enterprise. Possession of hashish in Iran was a capital offense, so we double-cleaned the buses to make sure we had nothing. There had been public executions for smuggling or carrying drugs; even a young American had been executed. We stopped for one clandestine *zikar* ceremony performed by a half dozen whirling dervishes; their meditative dance brought us a sense of peace during the tense trip through the country. We picked up our badly needed travelers' checks at the American Express office in Tehran and hightailed it to the Afghan border.

At the border, the Iranians had held up six or seven hippie buses. Some were large like ours, others minibuses or VWs with two or three kids following the same siren call to the East as we were. When it was our turn to cross Mashhad into Afghanistan, the first town was the old city of Herat. The legend is that Alexander the Great himself conquered this Zoroastrian town on his way to the Indus.

Two customs officers welcomed us, stepping jauntily into the bus. Their eyes grew big when they saw the hippie decals, rainbow-colored ceiling, and the twenty or so makeshift beds. "Where is your hashish?" they asked me. In addition to being guru commissioner, I was given a sideline of customs and immigration; as "Doctor Larry," I could, when called upon, act as straight as an arrow.

"We don't have any illicit drugs," I insisted.

"Today we have many buses painted like yours. Every one so far had some hidden hashish they were bringing into Afghanistan," they retorted. There were lots of young people traveling over land to find spiritual awakening in India and Nepal. The old Silk Road was becoming the new Hippie Trail. In front of me was a line of hippie buses that had already entered Afghanistan. Behind me was another line of buses waiting to enter on their way to India. They all looked just like us. Each was painted with wild colors and carried passengers dressed in tie-dye or leather. The pull of spiritual India was strong on my generation, though I can't say we really understood what that meant.

"You need to tell us where your drugs are hidden. It will be harder for you if we find them on our own."

"We have none, zero, truly."

"Then why not?" the more senior officer pushed forward, challenging me.

"We are just coming from Iran. Carrying hashish is a capital offense there. Honestly, we may be hippies but we are not idiots. No, we do not have any hashish!"

"Oh, okay, okay. If this is true, you are unusual hippies."

These stern, mustachioed, crusty and macho guards exchanged glances and giggled.

"Yes. If you have no hashish, you must become our guests. Come, we must give you some of ours! Come in for tea and smoke some with us!" They laughed, slapped me on the back, and nearly forty hippies followed. The Afghanis seemed to know us so well, and we knew them so little. In that respect, not much has changed.

Compared with Iran, Afghanistan felt like a burst of freedom, macho freedom certainly, but even though more women wore burkas in Afghanistan than in the shah's modern Iran, more women in Kabul came up to our buses to find out who we were—boldly entering and taking off their headscarves. There was pixie dust in the air. In Herat, horse-drawn carriages adorned with tinkling bells carried passengers down the avenues, and the streetlights glowed like they had captured fireflies. We half expected Tinker Bell to pop out of a flower.

Just as Wavy had promised, we stopped to pray or meditate or just be silent at every place of worship—mosque, church, or temple—along our route, just as Hesse's protagonist did in *Journey to the East*. Wavy Gravy was our poet laureate and spiritual elder, and Bonnie Jean was the heart of our commune. Wavy read aloud to us every night. In Afghanistan, he read Rumi and Kabir. Some of us visited the huge statues of Buddha, the ones that the Taliban has since destroyed. We were on the Silk Road, witnessing the lasting influence of Alexander the Great, the meeting of Western philosophy, Buddhism, and Hinduism. We watched more Sufi dancing and hung out with the *malang,* the free-spirited cousins to the Sufis, who dressed in rainbow-colored robes like Joseph's from the Old Testament. The *malang* keep no material possessions, hold no doctrine, and follow no caste system. Some call them shamans, intoxicated by God. The *malang* still exist, although their numbers, never large, dwindled every year under the Taliban.

From Afghanistan, we drove over the Khyber Pass. Butch mastered steering our forty-foot-long bus into and out of the strangest places. To add to his legendary status, he decided to drive the Khyber Pass while yo-yoing out the bus window. We moved on to Pakistan, where we hoped to get visas to cross India and transit Calcutta to the newly named Bangladesh to get food and medicine to the cyclone victims and embarrass the relief agencies. But we were months late in our charitable endeavor, and our feeble efforts would not have embarrassed anyone. We arrived amidst a war of independence between Pakistan and Bangladesh. Pakistani officials didn't want us to go through their country to India, but they let us in after we proved that we had no hashish or other drugs. This time, however, no one offered us a shared smoke.

We drove the buses to a spot near Islamabad and Rawalpindi, where a dozen horses had been rented for us to ride into the hills with a guide so that we could learn the history of the Kushan Empire along the way. The coins of the Kushans bear witness to a time in the second century C.E. when parts of Pakistan and Afghanistan were the most religiously inclusive and liberal spots on earth. One coin has an image of Buddha on it; many show the gods and goddesses of Persia, Egypt, India, Greece, and Rome.

One is labeled "Adono," which is said to honor Adonai, the God of the Israelites, as they understood from Jewish trade caravans that passed through. Some historians believe that the Kushans were just smart merchants, who cared little for which god was stamped on a coin, as long as the gold or silver was pure. Others believe that this was a great period of enlightenment and tolerance, and that anyone was free to worship any of those gods. This most tolerant multiculturalism existed almost two thousand years ago in a land between India and Persia that is today Pakistan and Afghanistan, dominated by the Taliban and religious intolerance. The coins imprinted with dozens of gods and goddesses from a half dozen faiths remain in museums around the world, testimony to what was once a welcome to practitioners of every kind. Whether their motives were fiscal or spiritual, it gives me hope that such a place ever existed and may yet again.

Our first stop in India was the Sikh Golden Temple in Amritsar. Sikhism is a new religion, by Indian standards, founded in Punjab by Guru Nanak in the late fifteenth century. Amritsar is their Rome or Jerusalem; we had blundered into their holy of holies, dropping in one day in the middle of rituals like aliens from the sky. Yet the Sikhs adopted us and quickly took to our psychedelic buses. It was part of their religion to feed every traveler in a common kitchen called a *langar*. We were skinny and had been running out of supplies, eating mostly bulgur wheat, living off the little we had left. "Hunger is the best condiment," goes the Indian saying, and we had that sauce in abundance. The food was wonderful: large fluffy naans and delicious, satisfying tandooris. We might have come for the temple, but we stayed for the food. They taught us whatever we could handle about their monotheistic religion, created in part to provide a safe zone between the bitter enemies of Muslims and Hindus. And then it was on to the capital of India, New Delhi.

As in Tehran, our first stop was the American Express office to pick up mail and money we hoped had been sent from back home. There were too many Hog Farmers to all go in at once so we took turns going in while the rest of us waited in the bus. While Wavy was in line, he bumped into Ram Dass, who had flown back to India to see his guru and was retrieving the first printed copies of his new book, *Be Here Now*. Without missing a beat, Ram Dass took one of the unopened copies of the book and inscribed it, "To Wavy Gravy and the Hog Farm Family, the Hanumans of the 70s."

I was sitting in the Sterling Hog, in front of the American Express office in New Delhi, waiting my turn as we passed the brand-new copy of *Be Here Now* around. This was one of the books credited with bringing the East to the West. It stopped violent political activism dead in its tracks for millions of young people all over the world who shifted their focus to the inner life.

If you're a person of my generation, you know where you were when you heard that JFK had been killed. I was walking across the diagonal on the campus of the University of Michigan when I heard a crying girl scream out that JFK had been shot in Dallas. The world stood still and it seemed the tears would never end. Many of us also remember where we were when we first heard about *Be Here Now*. I certainly do.

The serendipity of bumping into Ram Dass in New Delhi was astonishing. Elaine and I had gone to hear him speak during my internship in 1970, when he delivered a series of three lectures at San Francisco's Unitarian Church on three consecutive Thursdays in February of 1970. Also serendipitously,

Thursdays were my only night off from the hospital. San Francisco had its share of false prophets, yet Elaine and I, skeptical, used up one precious night to go to the first lecture. We had no idea that Ram Dass had been a professor at Harvard who was fired for giving psychedelic drugs to undergraduates—one of the events that would lead to Ram Dass playing a major role in catalyzing a spiritual revolution.

"There is an old story from mystical India," he had said to begin his talk back in San Francisco. "A young man was told by his village leader to take a chicken and kill it for supper. There were lots of children around, so the leader told the young man to kill it where no one could see. After a very long time, the young man came back and the chicken was still alive. The village leader was angry because the chicken was supposed to be for dinner. 'Why didn't you kill it?' he asked. The young man answered: 'You told me to kill it where no one could see. But everywhere I go, the chicken sees. And so does God.'"

"God is omnipresent," Ram Dass said. "God is watching you all the time, not because you're a big deal, not because you are something so important, but because God sees all. So live as though you know this."

There was something about Ram Dass's resonant voice, his spiritual demeanor, the holiness he had encountered in India that spoke to a place deep inside of both me and Elaine. My memory of this more than four decades later is that it was as if a light were coming out of his eyes or from his forehead. Whatever it was, that night, without drugs, sex, or earthquakes, it felt like the earth had moved.

"Be. Here. Now." As he said this, stillness came over the room. "Quiet the breath, be still, be silent, be here. Take in all the love around you, feel the love." A baby in the front row screamed. Ram Dass said, "And take that in too. Take in all of life, the pains of childbirth, the wailing of infants, the death throes, the happiness, the agony and the ecstasy. Be here now; be part of all the world." As we left the church, there was a sign-up table for a new book that Ram Dass was going to write. For $3.33 when it was finished, he would mail a copy. It was going to be called *Be Here Now.*

Whatever was bringing Ram Dass that much peace, Elaine and I wanted more of it. Neither Elaine nor I were yet hippies or devotees—but both of us were very curious, very moved by Ram Dass during those talks in San Francisco.

And now we were to have dinner and some spiritual and hippie talks with both Ram Dass and Wavy together at an art gallery here in New Delhi. It felt perfect. This encounter between the Hog Farm and Ram Dass's group was *beshert,* blessed, destined.

Later that night, these different branches of the extended counterculture family gathered at the Kumar Gallery. We all—Hog Farm and satsang alike—knew it was a special moment. The Hog Farm was in tie-dyed pants and Haight-Ashbury overalls; the ephemeral devotees were all dressed in white cotton ashram attire. The devotees folded their hands, bowed, smiled, and said, "Namaste." They sat calmly with their eyes closed in the middle of the gallery. They smiled as if in on a shared secret. We in the Hog Farm were more frenetic. Ram Dass and Wavy each spoke to the crowd. We sang and danced and it was a magical meeting.

Bonnie Jean's brother, Brook Beecher, who had joined us on this latest leg of the journey, was a large and physically powerful man who towered over everyone. Brook had been born with a hearing impairment, and while very intelligent, he also suffered from behavioral issues—he was sometimes difficult to control.

Out of nowhere, Brook grabbed Ram Dass by the neck, screaming, "You're a fake, Ram Dass!" He picked up a rock to hit Ram Dass and kept saying, "You're a fake!" Ram Dass was turning colors, and a little blood had appeared on his head. It took several Hog Farmers to pry Brook off of him, alternately carrying and dragging him out of the gallery as he yelled a half-mad, half-profound *cri de coeur:* "Holy men are full of holes! Holy men are full of holes!"

Ram Dass continued with equanimity; he seemed a sea of tranquility, just as he had been in San Francisco. No one was mad. Ram Dass spoke with compassion, forgiving the assault by Brook. Elaine was completely taken. I was too.

Without a word, these two distinct branches of a common psychedelic tree began to celebrate together. Almost in trance, we lifted our leaders, Ram Dass and Wavy, onto our shoulders and carried them in a circle singing, "Swing low, Sweet Chariot." The resonance of our combined voices, the peace and forgiveness the devotees showed toward Brook, made me feel drawn to whatever had made them like that. I remembered hearing the same power behind Martin Luther King's voice as well.

After a week in Delhi, the buses were cleaned, repaired, and ready to move again. But we were never going to get to what was now Bangladesh. We could get visas for Nepal, however, so we changed direction and planned to go to Agra, Benares, and then north over the mountains to, as my fellow Detroiter Bob Seger sings it, "K-k-k-k-k-k-Katmandu."

With medical supplies and food still in the bellies of our buses, we camped inside the grounds of the Taj Mahal. There were no barricades then, no threat of terrorism. The crowds were sparse, and there was so much open space. Elaine and I loved walking alone in the light of the moon. Some hippies slept out in the open, others in tents or in the buses, and still others actually crept inside the crypt, which housed the tomb of Mumtaz Mahal, the favorite wife of the Mughal emperor Shah Jahan. It is said that this is the greatest monument to love ever built, and of all the romantic times on our journey to the East, the most romantic of all were the nights making love in the shadow of the Taj Mahal.

A few days later, on the new moon of February 23, 1971, the Hindu festival of Shivaratri began. It was Shiva's night, and our buses had reached Benares, the holiest city in India, where the dead are burned every day in the ghats or piers by the sacred Ganges River. Shiva, the god of destruction, is one part of the Hindu "trinity," along with Brahma, the overseer of creation, and Vishnu, the god of preservation. Shiva is the heart and soul of Benares and on his new moon, it is said that hungry ghosts roam the streets of the city. By the banks of the Ganges, you can feel the ghosts in the marrow of your bones. A daily tide of beggars is drawn to Benares, perhaps to die, perhaps because wealthy Indians who are about to die are more generous with their daily handouts. On Shiva's night in Benares, virtually every drink, every chapatti or rice dish or vegetable or cake or sweet is baked with a form of marijuana called *bhang*. Shiva loved to smoke his hashish-filled pipe, or chillum, just as do the wandering mendicants devoted to him. So on the new moon of Shiva, everything edible is cooked with added pot and *bhang*. Whether tourist or pilgrim, you could hardly consume anything that was not intoxicating. The celebration made Woodstock look dry in comparison.

About twenty of us were living on the Sterling Hog, the forty-foot-long bus with psychedelic paintings, rainbow-colored cushions, and a grand kitchen, at least for a hippie bus. Wavy, Bonnie Jean, Ruffin, Dolphin and Goose, Claudia, Butch, Fred the Fed, Red Dog, and Gypsy were among our sisters and brothers on the bus. When Wavy saw all the hungry beggars in Benares, he wanted to organize a massive dinner to feed everyone on the night of Shiva.

A dozen bus mates wandered through the bazaars and shopped for veggies to cook in this most vegetarian of cities. We settled on a site for the bus in Assi ghat, or "Pier 80," as we might think of it, a residential area on the Ganges that had become a meeting point between colorful Indian sadhus and equally colorful European hippies and travelers. Wavy went through the crowds with a papier-mâché megaphone announcing "Free dinner" in English; a few bilingual sadhus translated. One of the sadhu-translators was a *naga baba,* a naked "snake man" covered only with ritual sandalwood paste and ash.

It was only March, but the Indian heat was excruciating. The Hog Farm cooks kept the stoves on the bus fired up all day. We had planned to serve two hundred, although we figured we could stretch the food to feed four hundred if we were careful. But we underestimated Wavy's marketing prowess and the hunger of the beggars. Thousands came. Lepers, beggars, amputees, sadhus, elephant mahouts, *naga babas,* chillum *babas* smoking hashish, hippies, and travelers all waited in an ill-formed line that snaked around the bus in concentric circles. When it became clear that we didn't have enough for everyone, the crowd turned unruly. They surrounded the bus and rocked it.

That was the night I learned that you can't feed the hungry of the world with only good intentions, a lesson that has stayed with me forever.

To really make a difference, it takes much more than goodwill; it takes the dedication to learn something to offer, a skill or profession. It also takes perseverance. Charity that is not sustainable is over in the blink of an eye. The old adage attributed to Maimonides is right: "Give a man a fish and you feed him for a day; teach a man to fish and you feed him for a lifetime." To really change the world requires deep understanding and humility, doing the hard work of systemic thinking, a keen awareness of how a particular system operates, and—perhaps most important—an unwavering sense of what you, alone, are uniquely fit to do that will do the world a world of good.

As the crowd circled the bus, I was on top of it because I had some kind of awful dysentery. All day I had stayed out of the kitchen so I wouldn't contaminate the food. As other members of the Hog Farm served the meal, I had to get away from the bus, and the only place left for me to go was up on its roof. I lugged with me an old thin mattress, a bottle of water, and the last of the toilet paper. Elaine was with the rest of our Hog Farm bus mates beneath me, doling out ever-smaller portions of food, hoping and praying for a modern version of the miracle of the loaves and fishes.

I felt like a piece of meat sizzling on a grill. When I tried to stand up, I almost fell off the roof into the crowds. I called for help, but no one could hear me over the din of the hungry crowd. I was wearing a kurta, a pajama-like top, and a white Indian dhoti, a cloth wrap popular in North India and long enough so that in case of death it could double as a shroud or burial cloth.

I could see in the distance the funeral pyres near the Ganges, and as I ran out of toilet paper I had to use strips of cloth from my dhoti until only the barest of coverings remained. I had no water and no Lomotil, the pharmacological cork. That left only a few rupee notes, my passport, and my medical license. Since I needed my passport to get home, I considered my medical license and remembered that, back in San Francisco, a psychotic patient had once told me to shove my medical license up my ass. Before it was over, I would have no choice but to do just that.

I collapsed in a sick, dehydrated clump on top of the bus, wound myself into a fetal position, and drifted into some kind of altered consciousness. The crowds were rocking the bus; I think Butch started the engine and slowly moved us off like a mahout moves his elephant. I hung on to something and prayed to all the gods and goddesses of Hindu and Buddhist lore and to the God of Abraham, Isaac, and Jacob to make the bus go and my diarrhea stop. Rocked by the movement, I fell asleep.

As painful as it was to run out of food, it was tremendously satisfying to feed the hungry. We kept doing it for the rest of our journey. We tried to find ways to distribute food and medicine in every poor pocket we encountered in India and Nepal. We visited Tibetan refugee camps along our pilgrimage to the Buddhist holy sites—gave out food and medicine, sometimes buying or trading watches for carpets. We took turns sitting under the Bodhi tree, the sacred tree under which Buddha twenty-five hundred years earlier had reached enlightenment. We drove north through the towns of ancient Hindu kings and relics of the third-century Licchavi kingdoms, through the border at Raxaul and into Nepal. On the ride into Kathmandu, half a dozen Hog Farmers were stoned and buck naked on the roof of the bus, hooting and cheering, waving Nepali and Tibetan flags and banners as the long pilgrimage along the Hippie Trail and the Silk Road from London to Kathmandu was about to be realized.

Hippies were in love with Kathmandu, and Kathmandu reciprocated with streets named "Freak Street" and places like "Tashi's Trek Stop," "Big Mac Buffalo Burgers," and Krishna's Hashish House. "We take higher" was the slogan on its ubiquitous hash-and-coffee house advertising posters. The English was flawed but the meaning unmistakable. And then there were the pie shops. It did not take our Nepali friends long to realize that nothing satisfied the cannabis sweet tooth like "Chai and Pie Shop" and shops along Pie Street in Durbar Square, where Hindu, Buddhist, and hippie culture seemed to merge so seamlessly.

We applied for trekking permits to Upper Mustang, the former mystical Kingdom of Lo, and were rejected. I cut my long hair, trimmed my beard, rented some mountain climbing clothes, and reapplied for a trekking permit for forty young people to climb from the flats through Pokhara and up to Jomson on the border of the legendary kingdom. While we were waiting for the permits to clear, we parked near the Tibetan Swayambhunath temple complex just outside Kathmandu where a famous golden stupa has the eyes of Buddha painted at its top.

The haircut and cleanup partly worked; we would be the first bus allowed to drive to Pokhara on the new Chinese-built road. We camped by the Fishtail Lodge on the shore of the lake in Pokhara, gathered the family and our gear, and then everyone scattered into the hills. The last party to leave for the mountains consisted of Wavy and Bonnie Jean, Elaine and me, another Hog Farmer named Ruffin Cooper from the Medicine Ball Caravan who had the camera to document our journey,* and two Tibetan porters—one to carry Wavy's toys, and one to carry my medical supplies.

We began the trek out of Pokhara on a gorgeous day, the white peaks of Machapuchare—a mountain named for its fish-tail twin peaks—shining brightly over green hills and a riot of colorful wildflowers. Just for us, it seemed, a cartoonishly vibrant double rainbow appeared, inviting us to begin the ascent to the sacred mountains.

Hardly a day into our trek, just before we reached the first town, we met two Tibetans who had gotten into a drunken fight at a bar. Each man had wielded a broken beer bottle and cut off most of the other's cheek. They were bleeding profusely. I set up my impromptu operating room by the side of the road and stitched their faces back together, while Wavy sat on a stone outside, blowing soap bubbles to keep onlookers from crashing my sterile operating area. One of our porters—either Dawa Tundrup or Sanya Mandu—acted as translator while I sewed the Tibetans' wounds. I had needles and surgical thread but no way to anesthetize them. They were so stoic throughout the procedure; when I finished, both men thanked me profusely and then bowed to each other as they said, *Om mani padme hum,* which translates roughly as "Hail to the jewel of the lotus, symbol of awakened humanity." When I finished doing the surgery, I found a line of new patients waiting for me to treat them, nearly a quarter-mile

*This footage showed up in the documentary about Wavy Gravy called *Saint Misbehavin'.*

long, snaking down to the river and across a bridge. I did the best I could with the tools I had while Wavy blew more bubbles and exchanged stories and jokes. For a moment, we had quite a loving open-air hospital in those sweet hills.

Every patient who received a pill or suture or cream thanked me by saying "Hare Om" or "Om mani padme hum." Either way, the "Om" made me feel at home. Hippie culture back in San Francisco, and even on the Hog Farm buses, was powered by chanting *Om*. Indeed, the values we found trekking in the hills of Nepal remain with me today. I still remember the names of the little villages—Pokhara, Goropani, Tatopani, Marpha, Jomson—because they felt so comfortable then, and yet so exotic. Every step, every sacred ritual—the ganja, the prayers, the way that people looked each other in the eyes with respect, the idea of community—they all mirrored much of what the counterculture aspired toward, the raison d'être for the hippie movement.

We must have looked like Martians as we walked past their homes, in our patchwork, tie-dye, fancy backpacks, watches, and radios; Wavy in his all-orange jumpsuit, pointed jester's hat, and rainbow-colored teeth. And we must have looked like klutzes as we crawled on our bellies over the bridges they danced across. We paid them less than a dollar a day for room and board, yet they welcomed us as intimate members of the family. We played with their children, held their most sacred objects. Wavy and Bonnie Jean, Elaine and I, made a promise to each other, that if ever we became richer than the poor hippies we were then, we could give back something to those wonderful people in Nepal. That promise became realized less than ten years later when the four of us and our friends from the smallpox program started an organization with the Hindi and Nepali name for service, Seva, and the eyes of Buddha from the Kathmandu stupa as our logo. The mission has been to give back sight to blind people in Nepal. And while the Seva Foundation started in Nepal, it has grown to more than two dozen countries, and our programs and projects and friends have given back sight to more than four million blind people. There are many wonderful and varied reasons Seva has succeeded, but it began when poor Nepali families shared everything with four Martians who happened to walk by.

CHAPTER 5

Renunciation

However convenient the dwellings,
You shall not remain there.
However sheltered the port,
And however calm the waters,
You shall not anchor there.
However welcome the hospitality that welcomes you
You are permitted to receive it but a little while.

—Walt Whitman, "Song of the Open Road"

B y the end of our trek, we were metaphysically healthy but physically wrecked. We were all undernourished, beaten up, and broke. Bonnie Jean, who was pregnant during the trip, had pushed on even when there was little food. Elaine developed hepatitis and was malnourished.

But no one had it worse than Wavy. He liked to call himself the "Temple of Accumulated Errors," but he had become the temple of accumulated diseases. Wavy was fearless. In India he would plop himself into any muddy body of amoeba-ridden water. At ninety pounds he had lost nearly half of his body weight. I was concerned about his survival, so I put him on a plane in Kathmandu for the United States. Upon arrival at Roosevelt

Hospital in New York City, in typical Wavy fashion, he won the dubious distinction of having the most illnesses at the same time. But after a couple of months' convalescence, he was almost as good as new.

While everyone else wanted to continue exploring the outer world, Elaine was more interested in exploring the inner world. She and Linda, one of our friends from the Hog Farm buses, stayed in India to take Buddhist meditation courses. At one course she recognized Mirabai from the night at the Kumar galleries. Mirabai was an American meditator and Ph.D. student close to Ram Dass. She had been with us the night Brook had yelled "Holy men are full of holes" in Delhi. It didn't take much to convince Elaine to go with her to the mountains to meet Ram Dass's mysterious, secret guru. From descriptions in *Be Here Now,* the guru hardly seemed real.

While Elaine went north to the mountains, Hog Farmers who stayed in India went to Goa, the pot-smoking hippie paradise in South India. I took off on my own, first sleeping in ancient jungle temples in Burma, then taking a trip through Thailand where I found myself trekking near U.S. Air Force bases and getting into arguments with pilots about the U.S. bombing of Cambodia and Vietnam. I trekked through Laos and spent nearly a month there before leaving for Japan, Korea, Hong Kong, and a quick visit to China until I finally returned to the States—a very different person after more than a year of wandering across the world.

In the fall of 1971 most of the crew of the bus trip to Nepal had gathered in New York. We hung around Greenwich Village waiting until Wavy was well enough to travel again, gathering supplies and readying the old Hog Farm bus we had left behind after the

Medicine Ball Caravan filming had wrapped in DC. The plan was to take the now very pregnant Bonnie Jean from New York to San Francisco, where she wanted to give birth. Our itinerary included a stop in a suburb near Cleveland to see my mother.

Butch, still wearing the beaten-leather hat he had worn over the Khyber Pass, drove the commune on wheels across the New York Thruway to the Ohio Turnpike, through towns and suburbs of the Rust Belt. American roads were not a challenge after navigating the tiny villages and winding roads of Nepal and India. Most buses we passed had familiar destinations like "Chicago" or "New Jersey" on their marquees; ours was more aspirational: "OM." After ten hours on the road, Butch eased the OM bus into the parking lot of my mother's condo, blocking three or four parking spots.

Since my dad had died, Mom had been living on her modest income as a jewelry saleswoman. Compared with the Kurdish mud villages in Turkey and huts clinging to the sides of the Himalayas in Nepal, the marble and brass of her building's lobby and the crystal chandelier hanging above us were over the top.

"You can't come in, Larry!" she said, when I buzzed her apartment.

"Come on! Mom!" I shouted back through the intercom. "I've been gone a year and I've got a busload of tired and hungry people. Why can't we come in?"

"Because I'm crying and my mascara is running."

"Why are you crying, Mom?"

"Because you're a doctor, but you're living like a filthy dirty hippie."

She wasn't completely wrong, but I wasn't living *like* a hippie, I *was* a hippie.

"Please, Mom."

Bonnie Jean badly needed the bathroom. I intensified my pleas.

"The police are going to come and take that bus away, Larry! You're blocking everything. You gotta get out of here!"

After ten minutes of negotiation, my mother relented. She dried her tears, touched up her makeup, and put on some of the jewelry she used to wear when my father's jukebox business was flush. Twenty or so hippies coming up at once would have overwhelmed her, so Bonnie and I went up first. Mom greeted us at the elevator. I had not seen her in almost a year. There were big hugs and lots of tears.

Mom took one look at Bonnie Jean and said, "Oh honey, you're the most beautiful girl I've ever seen. And the dirtiest! What are you doing riding on that bus when you're this pregnant?" Mom drew a bubble bath for Bonnie Jean and gave her an oversized sequined dress from Miami, which suited Bonnie Jean just fine. Then Mom got out her gold-rimmed plates and finest silver to show off what we were missing by living the anti-materialist life she imagined we did.

So that Mom wouldn't feel overwhelmed, the rest of the crew came up one by one to shower and eat. She laid an outrageous spread on the table. In the middle of dinner, Mom piped up, out of nowhere, "Larry, I'm really so sorry to hear that Elaine is living with another man!"

I was incredulous. "What are you talking about, Mom?"

"She left you, Larry. Elaine left you. I saw it in the telegram."

"What telegram, Mom? Where's the telegram?"

"She's living with a guy named Maha-something. And someone named Ron is there too."

Ah! *Relief.* Telling me that my wife was living with Maharaji, pictured in *Be Here Now* as a fat old guru wrapped in a blanket, and his student Ram Dass did not worry me, though it would have been entirely possible that Elaine was living with someone else. She and I hadn't had much contact since India—the primitive communications of the 1970s limited us to telegrams and letters to set up appointments for short, expensive phone calls. There were no phones in the ashram. "Write me in Nainital," she said, but I didn't know where that was. I was sending letters to her at the American Express office in Delhi. She sent me telegrams, all of them saying the same thing: "Come back to India. You have to be with Maharaji." But I never received most of them.

Yes, she could have been living with someone else. We did not establish rules about who was with whom when we went our separate ways in India. We had more relaxed definitions of relationships back then. There were times on the buses when it seemed like everyone was sleeping with everyone else. But there were also times in the temples and monasteries when nobody was sleeping with anybody. Elaine and I had both slept with other people on the Medicine Ball Caravan. Neither she nor I considered this a big deal. Our relationship seemed to transcend all that. But I missed her so much during the six months we were apart. I noticed how Elaine's message sparked feelings of jealousy and loneliness, all while I was surrounded by friends, family even, from the commune.

After two days of hot baths, food, and recuperation, Mom began to let her guard down. She had a moment of wide-eyed astonishment when she entered the tie-dyed, psychedelic bus, especially when she realized what the sleeping arrangements meant; but she did love the color scheme. She came to adore the hippies. The next day, we said goodbye and got back on the road for San Francisco.

Outside of Denver, we stopped for gas at a Chevron station at the Tomahawk Truck Stop, parking there for the night, right under the sign. In the predawn hours, Bonnie Jean went into labor. As Dr. Larry, I had planned for the "imponderabilia"— the unexpected risks that befall travelers—by shopping in New York for extra medical supplies, including an emergency home delivery kit, clean sheets and forceps, and especially some nitrous oxide if needed as an anesthetic. I had helped deliver babies in much more difficult settings—Wovoka on Alcatraz, another Hog Farm baby on the bus in Europe, and several babies in the hills of Nepal. Bonnie Jean's labor in the back of a clean bus was thankfully without complications. She named her son Howdy Do-Good Tomahawk Truckstop Gravy. "He was born under the sign of Chevron, with Texaco rising," she said. As soon as he was old enough to be legally able, Howdy Do-Good Tomahawk Truckstop changed his name to Jordan. Wavy, who had flown ahead to San Francisco when his back was hurting too much to stay on the bus, came back for Bonnie Jean and his new son in Denver.

Bonnie Jean, Wavy, Howdy Do-Good, and I arrived in San Francisco to a complete mess at our Turk Street apartment where we planned to stay. Elaine and I had departed in haste, and *The Body Politic* subscription money, which arrived in small checks in the mail, was left in the hands of a friend who managed to blow it all, along with the last of his neurons, on drugs. It was the beginning of my longtime hatred for some of the poison being peddled on the streets.

Everything we had left in the apartment was trashed or gone. Now we had to figure out how to close up shop and repay the thousands of dollars in subscriptions we had collected from nearly five thousand readers. But I knew I could raise the money by working as an emergency room doctor if I had the time, and I was in no hurry to go back to India.

Elaine and I suffered through agonizing phone calls: "Come to India," she said. "Come home to San Francisco," I replied. Stalemate. While neither of us was giving ground, I was more and more aware of how much she meant to me. In the end, Pakistan's air force settled our standoff by bombing Indian army bases near the ashram where she was staying, heating up the third or fourth Indo-Pakistani war. "They have planes and bombs headed for us, and Maharaji is sending all the Westerners away," Elaine told me just before Christmas. I could barely hear her voice, which was cracking over the crackling phone line.

"Come home, now, please," I said again.

"Maharaji said I should go back to America and return when the war is over and bring you with me. He said, 'Bring the doctor.' Larry, I'll come back by Christmas if you promise that as soon as the war is over and you can clear up our debts, you'll come back to India with me and see Maharaji."

I feared losing both the phone connection and my Elaine connection so I shouted "Yes!" more out of panic than conviction.

When I picked her up at the San Francisco airport, it was like we had never been apart; it was love again. We now call those six months of separation time off for bad behavior. We went straight to Mount Shasta, a dormant volcano in northern California, to contemplate what it meant to put our marriage back together, what it meant to go back to India. The radio DJ Wes "Scoop"

Nisker used to end his show by saying, "If you don't like today's news, go out and make your own." I took him literally—I was pulled by that desire, by the force of politics, the urgency of current events, the drama of the daily news. To participate in full, I believed I needed to be in America, where the change was most likely to happen.

But Elaine wasn't "Elaine" anymore. She had a new name: Girija, which means "daughter of the mountains" or "daughter of the Himalayas." In Indian mythology Girija was Shiva's wife, also named Parvati or Uma. Maharaji gave a new name to her as part of her initiation. He was apparently a new, but different, love of her life. It was a little weird.

She dressed differently too. She was wearing flowing cotton robes, draped scarves, loose pants, and sandals—what I imagined to be the ashram uniform. She tried to keep to an ashram-like routine of meditation and prayer. I felt the financial load on my shoulders as her new spiritual demeanor—and her jingling ankle bracelets—turned off prospective employers. Going back to India to sit at the feet of an old Indian yogi wrapped in a Scottish plaid wool blanket was not my idea of a good time. But to save my marriage, I had agreed.

To pay off my medical school debts, I signed up for an eight-week contract as a weekend emergency room doctor in Los Angeles, where doctors were in short supply. I also did a locum tenens for about a month, taking over a medical practice that covered several hundred square miles between Las Vegas and Reno after a Nevada-based doctor broke his leg. For one month, Girija and I lived in Tonopah, Nevada. We were vegetarians in the middle of cattle ranches and steakhouses. I traveled hundreds of miles around Nye County making house calls in a Winnebago, which I liked to pretend was my hippie bus, an extension of my experiences with the Hog Farm. Many patients came to see me at Nye County Hospital, including all the local prostitutes, who, by law, had to have a weekly vaginal exam and blood tests. Every Monday morning, I did two dozen vaginal exams before noon. It was an unusual way to get to know some of the kindest people I have ever met.

Elaine, I mean Girija, prayed every day that I would find God. That was not happening yet, but at least I found the money to get to India. I still needed to make good to the subscribers of *The Body Politic* whom I had abandoned, and to that end, my friend Stewart Brand donated five thousand copies of the Whole Earth Catalog that I could mail as a thank-you and goodbye for our subscribers. In an anti-materialist purge, Girija and I got rid of everything and prepared for our lives as renunciates.

We moved out of the Turk Street apartment into the basement of a house in tony St. Francis Woods owned by the Levitans, doctors who had welcomed me in my internship. We shared the space with Wavy, Bonnie Jean, and little Howdy Do-Good. Wavy was recuperating from spinal surgery—one of many spinal fusions he would undergo because of the number of times he had been beaten by cops at protests. He was in a full body cast that Bonnie Jean turned into art, decorating it with currency notes from the Hog Farm pilgrimage—British pounds, Turkish lira, Pakistani and Nepalese and Indian rupees, as well as more than a few canceled checks. Wavy christened it his "Cast of Thousands." When space got tight, we borrowed a camper bus from a Hog Farmer named Lois and parked it in front of the house.

One night, Wavy heard that a famous Tibetan lama named Chögyam Trungpa Rinpoche would be speaking at "God Hill," part of the graduate school of theology at Berkeley, where the churches stood and most religious groups held their ceremonies. We'd seen a few Tibetan lamas in India and Nepal, and the chance to hear Trungpa, who spoke excellent English, in our own backyard was cool. Waddling like a duck in his awkward cast, Wavy accompanied Girija and me to the lecture in his first venture out of the house. Bonnie stayed home with Howdy.

For the occasion, Girija wore her sari, and I put on a pair of overalls onto the bib of which Bonnie Jean had sewn an exuberantly beaded rainbow with a medical caduceus. I was proud of that rainbow-beaded caduceus. It was a symbol of my acceptance as Dr. Larry of the Hog Farm.

About one hundred people packed into the room, most sitting cross-legged on the floor. While Girija and I settled in the back, Wavy made his way awkwardly to the front past the formally dressed ushers, whom we called the storm troopers; he looked quite out of place in his Cast of Thousands and jester's cap. He was in a lot of pain and asked to lie down near the elaborate British club chair and table that had been set up for Trungpa. Lying down in front of a makeshift altar adorned with a Tibetan *dorje*—a ritual scepter—a bell, candle, incense holder, and Trungpa's private pack of Marlboros and bottle of Drambuie, Wavy looked like a decorated mound. To most of the hippies there it was as if the spirit of Woodstock had arrived.

Trungpa's devotees chanted as he limped into the room; he had been partially paralyzed after crashing a car into a practical joke store in England with another man's wife in the passenger seat. He was dressed in a three-piece suit and tie. In the back of the hall, I blew up balloons that read, "From your doctor for being good," and tossed them into the room. As Trungpa settled into his seat, Wavy reached over to the altar, snatched the lighted candle, and set it into a puddle of wax on his cast just over his belly. Trungpa eyeballed Wavy, who muttered *Om mani padme hum* over and over until Trungpa began to speak. When Trungpa paused to light a cigarette, Wavy picked up the glass of Drambuie that Trungpa had brought in and took a sip, eliciting an audible gasp from the devoted. After Trungpa took a drag off his Marlboro, Wavy picked it up to take a puff.

"I'm very happy," Trungpa began in perfect, almost Oxonian English, "to be here in Berkeley where so many important events have taken place."

And then he got into the meat of his talk. "I know you are all well-intentioned, whether you are already Buddhists or you are devoted to another religion or even if you are hippies or anti-war and civil rights activists. I know you mean well and I know you want to do good in the world. But I want you to know that you can't do anything of lasting benefit for anybody until you first reach a level of spiritual awareness that brings you enough wisdom so that you don't go one hundred miles per hour in the wrong direction and end up doing harm. Before you can really help with anyone else's suffering, you first begin the path toward your enlightenment by addressing your own suffering. You want to do good in the world, but you must first meditate so that you really know how to help others with their suffering."

"What about the starving people in Bangladesh?" Wavy bellowed, interrupting.

Refilling his drink, Trungpa replied simply, "Meditate first."

Wavy reached over and took a sip of the lama's drink and let it rest on his tongue. "You're right, Boss, but while we are meditating, let's feed the people who are starving in Bangladesh."

Trungpa took back the glass from Wavy, smiled and said, "Feeding the people is meaningless without intentionality. You must first clean your mind, find balance and direction, and start the path toward enlightenment. I say first you practice these three levels of Buddhism—Hinayana, then Mahayana, then Tantrayana—so that you can become a Buddha yourself, so that you will know how best to help others. Become a Buddha before you act, or your actions will only add to the suffering and muck up the world."

During the next hour while Trungpa spoke, Wavy continued to puff from Trungpa's Marlboros, which were burning slowly in the ashtray, and also to sip from his tumbler of Drambuie. He parried each thrust. "I agree with you, Boss. Let's meditate. Let's do nothing except seek enlightenment. One hundred percent. But, along the way, let's feed the people. During every one of those stages to enlightenment, Boss, we must feed the hungry of the world. We meditate, then feed, chant, and then feed, pray, and then feed. The Hog Farm commune took buses with food and medicine to feed and treat Tibetans in refugee camps in India and Nepal. They were hungry—so we fed them."

"It's meaningless," Trungpa replied, "unless you have the right motivation and wisdom. Feeding people doesn't end their suffering. It doesn't cut it out by the root. Only wisdom gained through meditation and spiritual practice can do that." I was on Wavy's side, but the memory of the near riot we had caused trying to feed people in Benares because of the lack of wise planning stung a bit.

Trungpa was extremely intelligent, adapting the practice of his esoteric Buddhism to the moment and his audience. But Wavy kept pushing back against his dogma. If Trungpa seemed patronizing, Wavy chanted "Om mani padme *hung*" in a mocking, singsong voice. When storm troopers moved in to carry Wavy away, the crowd in the room chanted, "Wa-vy, Wa-vy."

The stalemate ended when Wavy declared, "Of course you are right, Boss, we will meditate first and do nothing else." In a stage whisper he added, "But while we are seeking enlightenment, how about we all get together just a little bit and feed the people in Bangladesh because they're starving!"

Trungpa got up and left. Everyone left. Some, not all, stopped to congratulate Wavy on challenging Trungpa.

As Wavy navigated through the well-wishers and balloons still lying on the floor, I realized something. Since my days in Ann Arbor, I had been part of a political movement for change, freedom, equality, and the end of poverty. During that time, there was a gradual, though unmistakable, shift in the movement toward spirituality, but I didn't want to retreat to a cave, unable to alleviate at least some part of the suffering of others while seeking spiritual development. Even if I couldn't eradicate all suffering, I wanted to do something about it. Wavy, himself in pain in his body cast, had reminded us that we can do both at the same time: seek personal spiritual growth *and* change the world—integrate hospitals and schools, march to stop wars, and work to end poverty. We didn't have to choose between the inner and the outer work, nor surrender to the inevitability of war and injustice. We did not need to be passive spiritual observers. But at the same time, Trungpa also spoke to me: few of us had confidence that what we were doing as political activists was working. In order to be more effective, we *did* need more wisdom, more spiritual development.

San Francisco was not only the epicenter of communal living and spiritual experiments in the early 1970s; it was also home to many of the most radical political organizations. I had considered myself a radical until the intellectual and theoretically minded SDS picked up guns and morphed into the Weather Underground. When Wavy and Trungpa were debating the nuances of nonviolent social activism versus contemplation, left-wingers began bombing the U.S. Capitol, the Pentagon, a townhouse in Greenwich Village. The radical politics we had embraced was becoming a New Left terrorism. While I was not attracted to the strict teachings of Trungpa personally, his warning about how even the best intentions could go terribly off track without a firm moral compass and spiritual grounding resonated with me—in much the same way as had Dr. King's call for justice and nonviolence.

Trungpa encouraged us to read Buddha instead of Marx, the *Dhammapada* instead of Mao's *Little Red Book*. "Read how the great spiritual teachers of history dealt with injustice and poverty and the struggle for freedom and equality." He asked us to not get caught up in the costumes of spirituality, as he did in his aptly titled book *Cutting Through Spiritual Materialism*. Putting activism into a spiritual context, he advised, would help us understand how to be more effective in the world. To which Wavy added, while we're reading and studying, let's get out and do some good.

It seemed to me that Wavy and Trungpa were re-litigating one of the oldest arguments over how to live a good life: how one can boldly act to bring about justice and civil rights and at the same time withdraw from the world to seek communion with God—whatever name and in whichever language you commune. The union of the two paths was clear in the actions of the spiritual followers of Mahatma Gandhi. His nonviolent activism, *satyagraha,* had far more impact on the British leaving India than hundreds of Weather Underground bombs would ever have on the American political system.

I was still considering this paradox on the eve of our departure for India. Girija and I made a final pilgrimage to Mount Shasta, the place where, just a few months earlier, we had recommitted ourselves to our marriage. Its white peak was an echo of the highest white peaks of the Himalayas, where the ashram of Maharaji sat nestled in its foothills. Near the top of snow-covered Mount Shasta, Girija and I prayed that our journey to India would transform us. We prayed that, like Ram Dass, we too would go to India and return as better people, more enlightened souls, by retreating from the spinning-out-of-control world of politics and taking a break from the seductive hedonism of American life. Girija was returning to the ashram she considered her spiritual home, and I was leaving my crazy wonderful Hog Farm family and my radical politics for a new life. We drove back to San Francisco, resolute, joyful, ready.

After taking our little borrowed bus to a car wash prior to returning it to its owner, we parked it in front of the house in St. Francis Wood. On the dashboard, Girija placed a photo of Maharaji wrapped in his Scottish plaid blanket, waving his finger, like a berobed Saint Francis. We slept in the bus that night.

"Larry, wake up!" Girija was shaking me. The bus was full of smoke. We rushed to the house to call the fire department. We were inside when we heard the explosion. I ran out to a surreal tableau of hypodermic needles from my doctor's kit stuck in the trees and the medical supplies we were taking to India scattered across the yard and the street. The bus was on fire—its propane furnace, the flue to which had been bent at the car wash, had exploded. We rushed in to salvage what we could. I grabbed what was left of the medical supplies. Girija ran right through the flames to rescue the picture of Maharaji, which was barely touched—burned only in the corner where his finger was pointing.

"Maharaji woke me up," Girija said. "I was sound asleep. I could feel his hand on my shoulder and that's when I smelled the smoke. Larry, he saved our lives." We took it as a sign to get on with our pilgrimage to India.

CHAPTER 6

Initiation

What lies behind us and what lies before us are
tiny matters compared to what lies within us.

—Ralph Waldo Emerson

W e were soon to become every Jewish mother's worst
nightmare.

Girija and I abandoned our careers as a lawyer-doctor couple for the career path our parents most feared: hippie renunciate, whose offices were in a Hindu monastery at the foot of the
Himalayas.

We boarded the plane in San Francisco in matching orange
parkas, the closest color we could find to the saffron worn by
holy men, sadhus, with all our possessions in one orange backpack each. It was not that shucking off our material possessions
was the only way to God; it just seemed simpler. As Ken Kesey
had said, "You can fly to God in heaven with a Cessna or a 747.
The 747 just requires a lot more skill and a helluva lot more fuel."

Our first stops were in Detroit and Cleveland to break the
news to our families.

"Why are you always running away from everything?" Girija's mother said when we told her our plans in Detroit. She was intellectual, a voracious reader, but always seemed to find the worst in the day's news and, more troubling, in us. She blamed me for dragging her daughter away to San Francisco and the hippie circus, and now to an ashram. She did not know it was Girija who was the ringleader this time.

Grandma Ida in Cleveland was more understanding. With her white hair pinned up and wearing a printed cotton smock and round granny glasses, she greeted us with so much love. "Come in, let's eat," she said. She cooked an unending series of potato latkes and rolled cabbage, as if having one more meal to eat would prevent us from leaving. I loved Grandma Ida so much. She had the adventurer's wanderlust—she fled Russia for Cleveland on her own as a teenager—and a wonderful, mischievous laugh. I was a symbol of the completion of the family odyssey to becoming real Americans by being first to graduate high school, first to go to college, and first to become a doctor; I was afraid my leaving would break her heart. But she blessed me as only a grandmother can, assuring me, "God will take care of you and he will take care of me too." We both knew it was the last time we would see each other.

My mother, meanwhile, had fallen in love with a Jewish businessman named Newton, from Marathon, Ohio, which distracted her enough from fully absorbing what Girija and I were up to.

We picked up our cheap ticket, Pan Am flight #2, to India via London and Frankfurt in New York, where I had one last goodbye to say. I needed to check in with Ben Spock and let him know we were leaving again.

Ben was a New England Brahmin, with the heart of a political revolutionary; his Brooks Brothers three-piece suit and antique watch fob made him always easy to spot in the antiwar crowd. He was open-minded and curious, but he never approved of the hippie lifestyle of my generation, which he saw as a distraction from activism. He disliked Tim Leary, whom he thought had co-opted the civil rights and antiwar movements by redirecting activists to a cynical practice of tuning in, turning on, and dropping out. Though he knew other students who had gone on spiritual trips with gurus, Ben didn't know any doctors who had, at least not any who went at warp speed from political activist to hippie to renunciate in less than two years. I wanted to say goodbye, but I think I was really looking for his blessing.

He lived in a beautiful prewar building on the East Side, just off Park Avenue. A white-gloved doorman greeted Girija and me, ushering us quickly into a waiting elevator. He made us leave our orange gear with him in the vestibule, lest our appearance trouble the other residents. Upstairs, Ben was waiting for us with some tea. "Larry, I know you haven't forgotten how bad the war is, how much work there is to do on civil rights and poverty. I know what Martin Luther King meant to you and to all of us. So what are you doing?"

I tried to explain. "I hate the violence, Ben. We had an intellectual and moral passion when you and I marched with Dr. King. The New Left was a nonviolent left. Now it has become enamored of bombs, guns, kidnapping, and violence. I know we are better than the bad guys, we care more. We know we are all in this together, but I never dreamed my friends would pick up guns. Is it as confusing for you as it is for me?"

"But what are you after?" he asked. "Drugs? Asian religion?"

"The psychedelic experience," I told him, "did something to me. I connected to, I don't know, God? A higher being? A different plane of consciousness? A door has been opened. I don't understand it. I find it unnerving. Exciting. I hope we can come back from India the next time and tell you that we found the true destination of this New Age culture." Ben seemed unconvinced. We left on a strange note.

The first trip to India overland on the Hog Farm buses had taken almost a year. Asia revealed herself slowly to us, like in the imaginary dance of seven veils Oscar Wilde invented for Salome. We had time to adjust to the gentle cultural shifts from Big Ben to the Taj Mahal. Air travel condensed that experience of discovery and transformation into a single twenty-four hours. Girija and I had spent so many days imagining living in the ashram, embarking on our mystical adventure. But when this dream suddenly came to life, it was as real as the riot of color and sound, the clamoring crowd of beggars and drivers at the Delhi airport. We donned our faux saffron attire and embarked on the long journey to the ashram, making our way north from Delhi on a rickshaw, an overnight bus, and another rickshaw through the arid plains and the cool foothills of the mountains, where our orange down jackets were put to good use. We were moving toward the Kainchi ashram, which was pulling us in like a homing beacon.

We arrived finally at the point on the map where the borders of India, China, Tibet, and Nepal converge. The bus dropped us by the lake in Nainital, the capital of the Kumaon region on the top of the world, and off we went on the first of what would become daily hikes to the Evelyn Hotel, where waves of the Western satsang camped out between visits to Neem Karoli Baba's ashram.

I had met a few of these followers of Neem Karoli Baba the night Wavy Gravy's brother-in-law had attacked Ram Dass at the Kumar Art Gallery in Delhi. They all had Indian spiritual names: Dwarkanath Das, Krishna Das, Ravi Das (Michael Jeffery), Balaram Das, Kabir Das, Tukaram Das. And the women: Sita, Gita, Draupadi, Mira, and Sunanda. They greeted Girija like a long-lost sister. They didn't pay much attention to me.

At the hotel, Girija and I took off our orange parkas and unpacked what we thought were the appropriate clothes. Girija had a white sari she had purchased on her last trip. I wore a *khadi kurta* of homespun cotton that I had purchased at the Gandhi ashram in Delhi, near where his cremated remains are guarded by an eternal flame. Girija and I had visited Gandhi's shrine and prayed in honor of the man who combined the mystical life with political work on behalf of the oppressed. He was the inspiration for Martin Luther King Jr. and Cesar Chavez on their own paths of nonviolence. Young Americans frequently conflated the many-thousands-of-years-old Indian spiritual traditions with the more recent struggle against British colonialists. They were not the same thing. But that unique combination of inner and outer struggle certainly felt right as a model for those of us in the States who were also pulled in both political and spiritual directions.

The next morning four or five of us piled into a taxi for the thirty-minute ride to Kainchi. Coming down from Nainital we followed the serpentine undulations of the Kainchi River. Nainital is filled with legends of mystics, seers, gurus, *rishis,* Sufis, and lamas—a wonderland of magical mountains and the fabulous tales of the mystical powers of saints and the miracles they performed. It was a clear blue September sky, with a high sun that shone on the mountains' white peaks and a riot of wildflowers—geraniums and chrysanthemums, orange, almost ochre, the saffron color of sadhus' robes, symbolizing the purity to which Girija wholeheartedly aspired and that I approached tentatively.

Our taxi turned a corner and the ashram suddenly appeared looking just like the photo in Ram Dass's book, on the far side of an arched stone bridge painted in vibrant Technicolor, a rainbow bridge to what looked like the mythical Norse land of Asgaard.

The Kainchi River was ten feet across; wood and brick walls surrounded the ashram on the other side. A large arc over the gate was painted in deep red and white, with Devanagari script proclaiming, "This is the Temple of Hanuman the Reliever of Suffering."

Girija was relieved and excited to be back; I was apprehensive. From the taxi I followed her across the vibrantly painted footbridge to the main temple, which looked as if it were hewn out of the steep mountain behind it. The smell of incense and burning butter lamps wafted from the entrance.

About twenty-five people, half of whom were Westerners, filled the temple. It was a big crowd for that time of year, according to Girija. Musicians chanted *Sita Ram,* or *Ram, Ram, Ram* (God, God, God) or *jai, jai, jai* (victory, victory, victory) in a constant drone accompanied by a harmonium, a keyboard instrument that looked a bit like an accordion. Girija sang along; I didn't know any of the words. The music and beat of the tabla went morning to night: *Sri Ram jai Ram jai jai Ram* (hail God lord God). People greeted each other with "Ram Ram."

I only knew that "Ram" meant "God." I didn't yet understand all of its different meanings or the connection between the historical King Rama and the god Rama, the sacred incarnation of Vishnu. Nor did I yet grok the purpose of repeating the name of God over and over and over again.

We took off our shoes and made the rounds, paying respects to each deity in their separate alcoves. In front of each of the idols, some devotees reached for a brass bell that hung from the ceiling, ringing it every time they sang out the name of Ram or Hanuman, the monkey god who served Rama and to whom Neem Karoli Baba was particularly devoted. Others threw flowers into each idol's alcove, toward Ganesh, the elephant god of luck, or on the Shiva lingam, the god's divine phallus. Each idol was fully clothed and decorated with jewels. Hanuman wore a crown, as did Rama and Sita. Each temple scene looked like the most colorful crèche I'd ever seen.

Devotees bowed—some from the waist like the Japanese, some on their knees. Others were completely prostrate, stretched flat on their bellies with fingers outstretched. I copied Girija and bowed at the waist at each alcove.

The monsoons had just ended, so everything was vibrant and green and alive, as if the jungle had woken up to drink moisture from the rains, growing so fast you could see it inch upward toward the sky. *Arti,* or morning prayers, had begun. The temple priest, the *pujari,* who led the prayers, wore an old white dhoti and a white thread curled from shoulder to hip, showing he was twice born. In Hinduism, if a young man is from the upper castes, he goes through a coming-of-age ceremony like a Hindu bar mitzvah or confirmation during which he's given this sacred thread, which he never removes. The *pujari* moved the thread aside as he leaned over to pick up a sacred brass lamp; he put clarified butter, or ghee, into each of the half dozen openings in the lamp, placed wicks in each, and lit them. While people sang, chanted, and rang bells, he walked to and fro swinging the lamp in a circle. Everyone he passed hovered their hands over the lamp, waving the flame of the burning ghee lamp toward them as if to bathe their faces in the light. They gestured toward the *pujari*'s feet. After blessing everyone, he put down the lamp, picked up a red cloth, and waved it in front of each idol to catch the god's attention. Then he offered food and water to the idols. Everyone sang. He poured water from those offerings into our outstretched hands and we drank it. He made a *tilaka* mark on the men's foreheads with a bright red powder and sprinkled it on the women's palms for them to place the mark on themselves, as a priest should not touch the forehead of a woman who is not his wife. This marked the end of morning prayers.

I followed the group out of the temple to the courtyard in front of Neem Karoli Baba's room to wait with Girija to see him for the first time and to receive what Indians call *darshan,* the blessing of his presence. As was the custom, we had brought some gifts to offer him—bright orange marigolds, a bag of oranges and apples, and a box of *laddus,* sweet, cooked round balls about an inch in diameter made with chickpea flour, milk, and sugar that are favored by the monkey god Hanuman. The shutters on Neem Karoli Baba's doors and windows were painted yellow. I could feel the comfort of this color. And yet, I squirmed for about fifteen minutes trying to meditate, trying to find my place in this crowd, fussing with a gray shawl, pulling it over me to keep warm.

Maharaji burst through the doors like an opera star taking center stage. A huge bustle ensued as everyone leaped to help him sit down. I pulled away and stood with my back pushed against a post in the rear of the courtyard, about ten feet away. Maharaji sat down with one foot dangling over the simple cot, or *tucket,* he sat on. Devotees jockeyed for position, trying to grab his foot to touch it or massage it. Sometimes he'd allow it; other times he'd pull it away.

I had never seen anyone like him, he moved in a way that was electric but like an ebullient child, laughing, smiling, giggling as he watched the dancing, singing Western devotees—some longtime meditators, some young hippies fresh off the bus from Delhi— prance around him, some gazing at him with lovesick eyes.

It was like watching a movie—but everything around him looked as if it were in black and white, with Maharaji alone in vibrant color. He glowed. When he opened his eyes wide, they were lighthouse beacons playing over the ocean of devotees. He reached under his blanket and took out what looked like a ro- sary of flowers. He started playing with it, like a Catholic with a rosary, saying the Hindu name for God over and over, a practice called *japa,* his eyes closed, his mouth soundlessly forming *Ram Ram Ram.* A quiet came over the group; they stopped talking and wrestling for his foot. We closed our eyes, sitting with him while he prayed. The *Sri Ram jai Ram jai jai Ram* chanting con- tinued in the background along with the drone of traffic and trucks rumbling by on the ramshackle highway outside the ash- ram walls. My insides were also rumbling from this emotional roller coaster.

When we arrived in Kainchi I had been so excited. I was hop- ing for the kind of mystical experience Ram Dass had spoken and written about, in which I would discover my higher self and feel at one with God. At the same time my head was filled with Wavy's tales of meeting gurus, getting zapped by them, and blissing out as the heavens opened. Like a lot of people of my generation, my mystical experiences to this point had been psychedelic, and mine had mostly happened around Wavy. I attributed the magic of them to pharmacology or to Wavy's ability to evoke peaceful transcendence as he had with the four hundred thousand people at Woodstock. The rainbow-painted bridge at the entrance to the ashram felt like a gateway to this kind of experience. I loved the singing and the chanting, so soothing, so familiar, like Jewish prayer, also in a language I didn't understand. But I got queasy about the idols and the Westerners bending down to touch the feet of the *pujari* during morning prayers. I was told that this was a sign of respect—like washing Jesus's feet. *I will take the dust of the guru's lotus feet to wash the mirror of my mind* is the prayer that accompanies the gesture. The lotus of purity grows out of the mud of delusion, which can be dispelled by the guru. *Gu* means "dispeller," and *ru* means "darkness." All this made sense to me in theory. But in practice, when the Westerners tried to touch Maharaji's feet in a kind of feeding frenzy, pushing and shoving to get to him, it was to me like chaotic idolatry. It gave me a stomachache. This part of the experience just looked to me like any other cult.

If I have to touch his feet to be accepted here, I remember thinking, *I just won't do it.*

And yet when Neem Karoli Baba turned his intention to God, his eyes drifting to the sky or his fingers playing out the name of God on beads or flowers, everything stopped. As he stayed in conversation with God, it felt like he was talking to an old friend.

He seemed to go in and out of different states of consciousness. He put down the flower rosary but continued mouthing *Ram,* counting the repetitions by touching the tip of his thumb to the joint of each finger, beginning with the tip of the little finger. When he finished his meditations, he started tossing apples and oranges to the gathered devotees, engaging and laughing with everyone. He warmly welcomed Girija. I waited for him to notice me, "Doctor America," as Girija said he called me. I half hoped he would say, "Welcome, Doctor America, we have been waiting for you." But he didn't ask about me at all. He never even looked in my direction.

As dusk approached, the Westerners scattered from the ashram, some to rented houses dotting the nearby hills and the rest of us for Nainital by bus or taxi.

The second day was a repeat of the first except that Maharaji asked the Westerners to sing a particular prayer 108 times. It was called the *Hanuman Chalisa,* forty verses dedicated to the monkey god. This recitation took most of the day, with breaks for tea, lunch, and an afternoon nap. I sat in the courtyard trying to memorize it. A group of us broke off to read the story of Hanuman, the *Sunderkand,* the "beautiful" chapter of the *Ramayana,* which features the history of King Rama. In this chapter, Rama's brother was dying from a poison arrow. One specific herb, *sanjivani,* would save Rama's brother, but it grew only on mountains hundreds of miles away. Hanuman flew to the mountain, but he was only a monkey and could not tell the difference between *sanjivani* and a poisonous weed. So Hanuman lifted the entire mountain and flew with it in one hand, back to Rama, who picked the right herb to save his brother's life.

I felt like an anthropologist listening to these stories, watching the devotees pray, studying the varying numbers of arms on each idol. This Hog Farm guru commissioner wasn't convinced. But the story of Hanuman was very moving: if this monkey could serve God, maybe I could too, despite the strangeness I felt in Kainchi.

By the third or fourth day, I was still trying to figure out my place. I wasn't backed up against the pillar at darshan anymore; I was sitting next to Girija. Every day Maharaji would talk to her, but not to me. As he continued to ignore me, the other Westerners, with whom I had enjoyed conversations, began to ignore me too. I thought perhaps a silent signal had gone out that I was not one of them. I became more alienated, confused, even frightened.

Compounding my misery was the fact that Girija was getting more drawn in. Maharaji warmed more to her every day. They had long, intimate conversations about her life, about giving up smoking *beedies,* thin cigarlike Indian cigarettes tied with a string, but he said nothing about me or to me. He asked about the minutest details of many of the others' lives—"Did the package from your mother arrive?" "How was your pilgrimage to Benares?" I could sense that they experienced magic in the place, but I felt excluded.

I started to leave the ashram during the afternoons, crossing the street to talk with the family of the *chai wallah* (tea seller) while the satsang studied their texts. I tried to make myself useful as Hanuman had, so I treated the villagers who needed medical help. I fixed cuts and bruises when they fell. I stitched and

Left: Joe and Sylvia Brilliant, Detroit, c. 1943.

Detroit Mafia Enters Senate Jukebox Probe

Gangsters Listed For Testimony In Rackets Hearing

WASHINGTON ⋯—The Senate Rackets Committee opens hearings today on its charges that Mafia mobsters have gained a powerful and sinister influence in the jukebox business in Detroit.

Witnesses from other cities have told of ties between gangsters and corrupt labor union officials in what the committee says is a nationwide plot to dominate jukebox and some other coin operated machine enterprises.

Robert F. Kennedy, committee counsel, said that is the pattern the evidence will show in Detroit, too. He said witnesses will include underworld big shots, among them men whose names appear on a chart already placed in evidence and captioned "Partial Mafia (Syndicate) Relationship Study."

Used Last Year

The chart was used in hearings last year to illustrate testimony that there is a secret international society of criminals with branches in the big towns of this country, with many of its members related by blood or marriage.

Angelo Meli and Dominick Corrado, whom Kennedy termed Detroit underworld figures named on the chart, were listed for quizzing about their dealings with various union officials.

Meli already has been named as an important figure in the Detroit jukebox business. Milton Hammergren, former sales official of the Wurlitzer Company, testified he had employed a firm headed by Meli as a distributor of his company's jukeboxes.

First day witnesses, Kennedy said, will include Joseph Brilliant, a former Detroit jukebox distributor and operator. Kennedy said Brilliant "will testify about gangster run companies and a union."

Other Witnesses

Kennedy listed other first day witnesses as Neil Holland, a television technician from New York City formerly active in organized labor circles in Detroit, and Roy Small, former head of the United Music Operators Association in the Detroit area.

Also on the witness list are William Bufalino, president of teamsters Union Jukebox Local 985 in Detroit, some of the local's business agents, and Eugene (Jimmy) James, a former head of the local before it was reorganized into Local 985.

Above: Larry with his brother, Barry, at Larry's fifth birthday.

Left: Article in Detroit newspaper about Larry's father's testimony before the McClellan Committee, which investigated the Mafia's involvement in the jukebox industry, U.S. Senate, Washington, DC. Larry's father appeared before the committee at the request of Robert F. Kennedy, committee counsel.

Below: Larry and Elaine's wedding, Detroit, May 25, 1969.

Below: Larry and other radical MDs on the cover of the *Medical World News* published a few days before the start of Larry's medical internship at Presbyterian Hospital in San Francisco.

Above: Elaine and Larry, San Francisco, 1969.

Below: Dr. Martin Luther King Jr., University of Michigan, 1962.

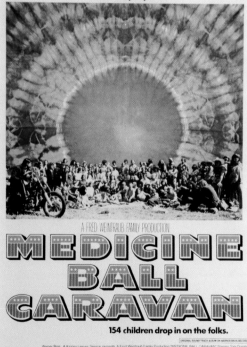

Above: Larry arriving on Alcatraz to help deliver the baby Wovoka, 1970.

Left: Poster for *Medicine Ball Caravan,* the Warner Bros. movie the Hog Farm appeared in.

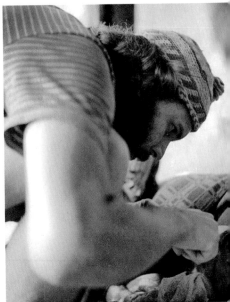

Below: Larry performing surgery on a local Tibetan, Nepal, 1971.

Above: Larry's best friend, Wavy Gravy.

Below: Wavy and Jerry Garcia, early 1970s.

"NUCLEAR WAR IS BAD FOR BUSINESS"

Right: Ram Dass and Maharaji, Kainchi, 1971.

Below: Wavy and Jah (Bonnie Jean) in Amsterdam, 1970.

Above: Larry and Elaine with Hog Farm bus, Khyber Pass, Afghanistan, 1971.

Left: Girija at Kainchi ashram during polio program, post-2000.

Left: Larry and Girija at the Taj Mahal, holding photo of Maharaji, 1972 or 1973.

Below: Girija at Kainchi, 1972.

Below: Maharaji with Western devotees, with translator Ravi Khanna standing far right, Kainchi, 1972.

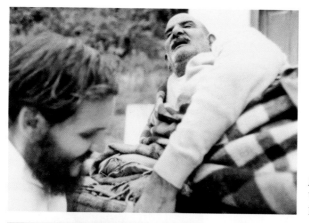

Left and below:
With Maharaji,
Kainchi, 1973.

Above: Front of diary Larry kept
during smallpox campaign. The
handwritten note, written in
Hindi, is from the *Ramayana:*
"Until I have completed God's
assigned work, I cannot rest."

Below, right: Front of postcard with
Maharaji's prediction, printed and
distributed in 1974, six years before
smallpox was declared eradicated.

"Smallpox will
be quickly
eradicated. This
is God's gift to
mankind because
of the hard work
of dedicated
health workers."
—July, 1973

Left: Hanuman statue at Maharaji's temple.

Below: Maharaji with Li Gotami and Lama Govinda, Almora, India, 1960s.

Above: Sixteenth Karmapa (back left), tickling Jamgon Kongtrul Rinpoche, Rumtek, 1974.

Right: Girija with Maharaji, Kainchi, 1971.

bandaged wounds or got a taxi to rush someone with chest pains off to a hospital. I read the *Bhagavad Gita,* walked in the mountains, and talked with families near the ashram. In my primitive Hindi, I learned who bought their homes and who rented, how they felt about Westerners coming to the ashram, and whether they thought of Maharaji as a great saint or just as a tourist attraction helping them sell tea or sweets.

Girija was at the ashram faithfully every day for *arti,* meditation, and darshan. But after a week of watching these other smart, educated, modern young people stampeding to touch this old man's feet and gaze at him as though he were God himself, I started to hate the whole setup. I wanted to run away. I was ready to give up and go home, or maybe travel, but Girija implored me to be patient.

The first of the Ten Commandments is, "I am the Lord thy God and thou shalt have no other gods before me," and yet all over the ashram idols were being worshiped—not just respected or loved, but worshiped. It's a big deal for Jews. While I had been looking for spirituality elsewhere—in Buddha and Jesus and all over India—I never worshipped stone idols and I was skeptical of anyone who wanted me to worship an idol, stone or human, or touch his feet. Maybe my skepticism is the reason I had been named guru commissioner on the bus, tasked with inspecting holy people and reporting whether they were genuine or whether, as Brook Beecher had charged, they were "full of holes." Indians had two lovely words for this: *nuckli* or *suckli*—counterfeit or genuine, fake or the real deal.

As guru commissioner I was beginning to worry that my wife's ashram was another cult, which like all cults emotionally entangles with psychological barbed wire. Broken glass at the top of the ashram's walls began to take on a more sinister meaning. I was told it was there to keep thieves from the temptation of breaking in and stealing, but I was beginning to wonder whether it was there to keep us in instead.

When we woke up at the Evelyn Hotel the next morning, I told Girija I needed to be alone to think. Seeing how sad I had become, she hugged me and went off to the ashram while I stayed in Nainital. I went out to the lake and rented a small flat-bottomed boat, paddled out to the center of the shallow, dark green water, pulled up the oars, and drifted. I felt awful. So alone. Wildflowers of many colors covered the hills; the sun played over the snowy mountaintops that peeked through the clouds and nearby foothills. So much color, such an exotic land. I should have been happy. But this trip was not turning out as I had hoped. I had already lost Elaine, and now I felt Girija slipping away.

I was sure I did not belong with this cult, but I could see that Girija did. This inscrutable man had captivated her. There was no doubt that I would lose her if I made her choose between him and me. I wanted to shove the beauty that I saw all around me into the hole in my heart: the mile-high lake, the snow-capped mountains, and the tranquil scene of wildflowers. I was desperate for a way to make myself feel better, but I had no inner resources. Nothing dispelled the darkness. My mood matched the algae-clogged, muddy, gross, polluted water I was floating on.

At the edge of the shore the trees reflected in the dark water, beneath yet another red-roofed pagoda, another Hindu temple, Naina Devi Temple, at the northern edge of the lake. I did not know then that *naina* means "eye." In one story, Shiva's wife, Parvati, also called Girija, was so distressed at this very place, she set herself on fire, and her eyes were said to have fallen at this spot. That image of Parvati's dead eyes falling into the lake would have been too much for my poor spinning brain to absorb. I am glad I did not then know the myth of the name of the lake and town of Nainital. The ashram was already too weird, too pagan. I just wanted things to be the way they had been. I wanted my wife back. I wanted to know whether this guru was a fake or a saint; whether my wife and her new friends were on to something, had found God, or had gone nuts.

Girija wanted me to find God. That's why she had brought me here. If I left, she would continue her inner journey without me. My journey was about putting science and medicine to use in order to help ease suffering. We had had such an auspicious reunion in San Francisco. We turned our lives upside down to come to India. I would do anything to keep from losing her now, even in this godforsaken place. I tried to put my rational scientific mind in neutral, set aside my deep hurt, and reach out to what I thought was God. I tried to pray but really didn't know how. I had memorized some prayers, and I could recite a few, mostly in other languages, but I barely knew what they meant.

"Amazing grace, how sweet the sound . . ." we had sung during marches with Martin Luther King Jr. and others during the civil rights campaign. I loved that song, but today it was not working. *Om mani padme hum* is what Trungpa and the Tibetan refugees and some sherpas in Nepal would say. Then there was my Torah portion from my bar mitzvah: *"Vidabar Adoni El Moshe b'har see mor namor . . .* then . . . something else . . . something else." "And Jeremiah said, 'The Lord God came unto me and said, "Buy thee my field in Anathoth, which is in the land of Canaan; for the right of redemption is thine to buy it." '" For their Torah

portions, most of my friends had gotten what seemed like serious, deep spiritual verses: "Lord God is One," or "Follow these my commandments." But what did I get? "Go buy some land." In the land of Canaan of all places.

I dug deeply into my religious upbringing. *Sh'ma Yisrael Adonai Eloheinu Adonai Echad. Hear O Israel the Lord our God the Lord is One.* I felt no door opening the way it had with psychedelics. I was still on this ugly, smelly, polluted lake floating with an overwhelming sadness that I had come this far, only to lose the woman I felt destined to be with for the rest of my life. I was begging, pleading, hoping for a sign, anything that might provide a bridge to this spiritual world Girija had found, anything that would tell me I should stay.

"Dear God, it does not have to be a big sign. Just a small sign, even a little rainbow in the oil on the polluted lake. Nobody else has to notice, just a tiny sign between you and me." The trees with big white flowers were still standing high in the hills, the startlingly bright red bougainvillea still cascading along the shore, the snowcapped mountain peaks still glistened.

The silence was my answer; as hard as it was to accept, as sad and broken as I felt, it was time to leave the ashram. It was time to leave my wife to her guru and his cult. We had only been married for three years, but we had known each other for half of our lives already—since we were teenagers. I could barely imagine being without her.

I brought the boat around. My arms were almost too tired to row. It seemed to take forever to get back to shore, to haul the boat out of the lake, to pay the few rupees, to go back to the Evelyn Hotel and walk up to our room. I stared at our few possessions that would have to be divided. I started to cry.

That night, after dinner, I tried to find the words to tell Girija, but she already knew. We both knew. If Maharaji was the real deal, then I might have lost my chance for entrance into the Kingdom. If he was a fraud, Girija was going to stay with him anyway. Either way, this was how it would be. She had faith; I did not. I wasn't sure I even wanted it. That night, she asked me whether I would come to the ashram to say goodbye to Maharaji.

"Of course," I replied. I was devastated, but not without manners.

Early the next morning, Girija and I divided our meager possessions. I put my orange backpack and travel gear in a taxi outside the hotel. We arrived at the ashram before anyone else. I asked the taxi to wait because I did not expect to be long. Girija and I passed through the gate, crossed the bridge to the temple area, removed our shoes, and walked through the public yard. We settled in front of Maharaji's tucket. As we waited for his entrance, Girija looked at me with such deep love, deep sadness. She had been asking Maharaji, "Will my husband find God?" He hadn't answered her either.

We held hands while we waited. I scanned the ashram, the temples, the statues of the gods and goddesses, the red roofs, the yellow windows and doors, the deep green forests, the soft, gurgling, winding river, the line of Westerners arriving by foot, by taxi, and by bus beginning to congregate by the front gate.

Devotees from the neighboring houses had left flowers and fruit offerings on Maharaji's tucket arranged in a design that spelled out the name of God, Ram, in Hindi script. One of the apples in the "M" of Ram had fallen to the ground, which made God's name incomplete. God's name should not be incomplete or imperfect in any language.

I got down on my hands and knees to pick up the apple and replace it to repair the name of God. At just that moment, Maharaji burst through the oversized double doors from his room, and before I could look up or move, he seemed to lunge at me, deliberately stepping on my fingers, pinning my right hand to the ground just as I grasped the apple. I was stuck. He seemed to weigh hundreds of pounds. I couldn't free my hand from under his foot. My worst fear in the ashram. I couldn't get up off my knees. It was weird.

Maharaji looked down at me, giggling. "Where were you yesterday?" he asked in simple Hindi that even I could understand. "You were not here. Were you sick?"

I twisted my hand, trying to get free but could not.

"Were you at the movies?" he asked.

"Were you at the library?" And then he paused. "Oh, yes," he said, "were you at the lake?"

Up to that point, he had said everything in Hindi or the local mountain dialect, Pahari. But when he said "lake" in English, I felt exposed, naked; a strange buzzing feeling started at the base of my spine; my whole body began to tingle.

"What were you doing at the lake? Were you horseback riding? Did you go swimming?"

My stomach lurched. I began to shiver. The tingling intensified, rising up my spine like mercury in a thermometer. I could barely feel my fingers.

He leaned down and whispered in my ear, "Doctor America! Doctor America! What were you doing by the lake?"

He paused and then put the back of his hand on his forehead, his eyes darting between Girija and me.

"Oh, yes. I know. You were talking to God."

I stopped struggling to free myself. His voice echoed inside my head.

"Doctor America! Did you ask God for something?"

Looking up, I saw him, as if for the first time, clear as day. It was like he was on fire. I could not catch my breath. My spine buzzed; so did the paint on the doors and windows of the ashram. My skin hurt. My eyes hurt. *Was the light always this intense?*

Time slowed, then stopped entirely. But my heart still pounded like a jackhammer. The sparks in my spine became a four-lane highway of lightning bolts, moving from my sacrum up to my belly, to my chest and neck. I could feel my neck veins bulge.

I was terrified. *I might die!* I was filled with love. *I might live!*

Maharaji sat down and released my hand. He was as massive as a Himalayan peak. He smiled the most loving smile I had ever seen, his eyes filled with lifetimes of compassion. He pulled me closer to him.

"Did you ask God for a sign?"

Maharaji twinkled. He reached over to my face with his fingers and tugged and twisted at my beard, caressing my tear-drenched face. He opened his eyes wide and our gaze locked. Light seemed to pour out of him into me and I felt like I was being filled with love upon love. It became too much, my container too small to hold everything he was beaming my way. When he saw that I was full, he broke the contact like nothing had happened, giggled, and tugged harder on my beard.

What little was left of my skepticism vanished. I felt utterly at peace. *He knew. He knew. I do not know how. But he knew.* I felt loved like never before, completely understood, naked and yet unashamed. I felt accepted. Tears streamed down my face.

Girija wrapped her shawl around me and hugged me, and so did the rest of the Western satsang. Maharaji twinkled once, twice more, and then released his spell.

I was home.

Maharaji sat back on his tucket and began doing japa on his fingers, repeating the name of God again, his thumb again counting the names of Ram. His eyes half closed as he mouthed the words of his own mantra: "Ram, Ram, Ram." It felt like the whole world converged on him while he was radiating out love for everyone, every being in the world.

In that moment, I was not surprised that he loved everyone. *That is his job,* I thought, *if he's a saint at one with God. He's supposed to feel that way.*

What astounded me more than anything then was not that he loved everyone; it was that in that moment, *I loved everyone too.* I loved Girija for her patience with me, the Westerners in the ashram who had annoyed me, the colleagues who had stuck a hypodermic needle in my picture the first day of my internship in San Francisco, my parents in a way I never thought I could, politicians, antiwar protestors, the cops who had beaten Wavy in Chicago, friends and enemies, myself and all others. I was in love with the love, with the moment, with Maharaji, even with my own bursting heart.

Maharaji had lifted the veil of *maya,* the illusion that makes us all feel separate and alone. When he did, he took me to a place where I forgave everything and everyone, including myself, and found nothing but love. This was real magic. I didn't worry about being accepted or whether the ashram harbored a cult or my marriage with Girija.

And then without a care, I touched his feet. I do not know what prompted me to do it, but I felt like I was connected to electrical cables that were plugged into the wiring of the universe and it triggered something in me. This was the first time I felt that powerful love—certainly the first time I felt it without a psychedelic like LSD coursing in my body—and I've felt it many times since with no drug other than love. It blew away my intellect and blew my guarded heart wide open.

That moment in which I found myself awash in a tsunami of love for every being in creation became the touchstone by which I measured every future experience, and a state to which I constantly yearn to return. At the heart of it is Divine Love. That moment of pure love has driven everything in my life. That is what I keep coming back to—love, love for everyone. I fail hundreds of times each day. But the aspiration alone changed everything about me. It made me act unpredictably. I was governed by love. It made me ambitious in a different way. I had no context for the experience. I knew it was a gift, but I didn't yet know what I was supposed to do with it.

CHAPTER 7

You Are No Doctor

You might be a rock 'n' roll addict prancing on the stage
You might have drugs at your command, women in a cage
You may be a businessman or some high-degree thief
They may call you Doctor or they may call you Chief

But you're gonna have to serve somebody, yes indeed
You're gonna have to serve somebody
Well, it may be the devil or it may be the Lord
But you're gonna have to serve somebody.

—Bob Dylan

There is an expression that when the flowers open, the bees
come uninvited. Maharaji was the flower. We were two
of the bees—the expanding group of young seekers who had
come from everywhere around the world. Girija and I moved
into a small white detached stucco house that hugged the hills
across the river from the ashram. We shared the "White House"
with four or five other devotees of Maharaji. For the next several
months we settled into the ashram routine.

Most days began with *arti* in the early morning, followed by
some combination of chanting, praying, meditating, reading
scriptures, darshan with Maharaji, napping, drinking tea, and

eating sweets and deep-fried food. Days usually concluded with another darshan just before evening, when those who had to catch the bus for Nainital and the hotels left the ashram. Those of us who did not have to catch the bus stayed as long as Maharaji let us.

No two days were the same. Tuesday was Hanuman's day, and with it came the chanting of the *Hanuman Chalisa* and a light fast. All grains were prohibited, but we were allowed to eat sweets and fruit, so it wasn't a very demanding fast. We studied the *Ramayana*, especially the *Sunderkand*, the chapter on Hanuman. On other days we might read the *Mahabharata*—the great Indian epic of the battle between good and evil, especially the chapter that has come to be known as the *Bhagavad Gita*, the "Song of God." We were avid readers of a variety of spiritual texts: the *I Ching*, the Koran, the Bible, the *Tao Te Ching*, the Buddhist *Dhammapada*. Someone around the ashram was always reading the *The Tibetan Book of the Dead*. Practitioners of every stripe, Muslim, Sikh, and Jain, came through as well.

Maharaji took responsibility for me the way a parent takes responsibility for a child. I had gone from skeptical observer to devotee; I had become his *chela*.

One evening, Maharaji called to me. "Doctor America, I have a headache. Do you have medicine for me?"

I knew that he liked Tiger Balm, a pungent ointment Indians thought alleviated muscle pains. It came in a small round red tin with Chinese characters on it. I handed it to him. He took it, balanced it on his head, and laughed. "I feel much better. My headache is gone. See, Doctor America has fixed my pain." With an impish smile, he looked at me, the red tin balancing on his bald head, and giggled. He asked me whether everything was okay. "Girija okay? Food okay? Do you want to run away from the ashram again?"

Maharaji, I quickly discovered, loved to play. He laughed continuously, saw humor in everything, even the most serious relationships between guru and *chela,* doctor and patient, God and human.

Indians call this play *leela.* It's something like the manifestation of the divine in a human performance. Rama, an emanation or Avatar of the god Vishnu, plays out his *leela* in the *Ramayana.* Krishna plays one *leela* in the *Mahabharata.* I think of Jesus and his parables, the lessons of which have lasted millennia. Gurus have their own kind of *leela.* It is their way of teaching. Maharaji taught in parables, through *leela* and joyful improvisation. It felt like a divine version of how Wavy Gravy and the Hog Farm and Ken Kesey and the Pranksters improvised performance art, filling a gray day with paisley, tie-dye, and rainbows—the *leela* of the counterculture. Maharaji imparted wisdom by keeping us off balance. I never knew what to expect.

One morning after prayers, we gathered around Maharaji for darshan as usual. He was sitting on his tucket, wrapped in his usual plaid wool blanket, surrounded by a dozen Western devotees. He was deep in concentration, his eyes half closed, while he silently mouthed the name of God, *Ram, Ram, Ram.* Girija and I sat down, which seemed to wake him with a start. He smiled and said, "Doctor America, Doctor America, my good friend Lama Govinda is ill. Please go visit him and care for him."

Lama Anagarika Govinda was one of the spiritual heroes for my generation. Born in 1898 in Waldheim, Germany, as Ernst Lothar Hoffmann, he became a Buddhist at the age of eighteen.

He studied in Sri Lanka, traveled with the poet Rabindranath Tagore, and spent nearly two decades in Tibet, where he studied the habits of Tibetan lamas, many of whom he described as being able to fly or walk across the entire country in one night. On the Hog Farm buses, we had passed around his spiritual memoir, *The Way of the White Clouds,* marveling at the supernatural tales.

Maharaji's driver, Habibullah, drove Girija and me to Almora, where Lama Govinda lived with his wife, Li Gotami, a Parsi artist. It was about a one-hour drive northeast toward the white caps of the mountains—just up the street in the context of the Himalayan foothills. Almora was home to decades of English eccentrics, mystics, and writers during the British Raj, their simple hill station houses lined up along a hilltop known affectionately as Crank's Ridge. It became part of the Hippie Trail in India after Timothy Leary reportedly ran naked across the clearing, and was later dubbed Hippie Hill. Among the many visitors to Lama Govinda were Bob Dylan, Cat Stevens, and Gary Snyder. When we arrived, Li Gotami stood in front of the gate trying to shoo Girija and me away, but I told her that Neem Karoli Baba wanted me to check in on Lama Govinda. She was surprised that Maharaji knew Lama Govinda was ill.

Together, we walked up the hill to the modest old British house. Gray-bearded, thin, and slightly stooped, Lama Govinda got up slowly from a chaise longue. He had a long nose, high cheekbones, pale skin, and a serious mien that exploded into a wide grin at the best moments. He wore a pointy Tibetan pundit's maroon hat, with earflaps that made him look sweet and impish. He wore several *malas,* or Tibetan prayer beads, around his neck; a dark maroon shawl was wrapped around his shoulders. Li Gotami was dressed in colors matching Lama's—maroon hat, shawl, and a blouse of yellow cotton or wool.

A few days earlier, Lama Govinda had become dizzy and fallen. His arms and legs were weak, his blood pressure inconsistent. His description of the light-headedness and brief loss of consciousness matched the symptoms of a transient ischemic attack, a "warning stroke" as it used to be called, caused by a momentary tiny clot in the cerebral arteries that dissolves within a minute or two. The experience is usually very alarming, but Lama Govinda seemed quite at peace. He didn't want me to fuss over him. Instead, he wanted to talk about Maharaji and Girija's and my spiritual path. I examined him under protest. His pulse was good, his heartbeat sound. He was a little dehydrated, which could have contributed to his dizziness.

I wanted to take him to Delhi, where he could get a full checkup, but he wouldn't hear of it. I gave him the phone number of the teashop across the street from the ashram in Kainchi and promised to return in two weeks.

After the examination, he served us dark, bitter, salted Tibetan tea, thick with sour yak milk. "What is Maharaji teaching the Westerners, Larry?" he asked. "What kind of meditation? What kind of *bhakti* [devotion]? Are you all reading the *Bhagavad Gita* and the stories of Hanuman?"

Yes, I told him, and we were also reading his book *The Way of the White Clouds*. He laughed and encouraged us to read the works of his friend Walter Evans-Wentz, especially his translation of *The Tibetan Book of the Dead* and of the works of the great Tibetan saint Milarepa.

Soon, it was time to go. "But I have not paid you for the house call," Lama Govinda said to us.

"I have never taken payment for a house call, let alone one for a lama. I didn't do anything anyway," I replied.

"Well then, let me bless you," he responded.

I stood in front of him. He put his left hand on Girija's head and his right hand on mine and started to chant. As he repeated his prayer, all I could catch was *Om mani, padme hum,* softer and softer. I felt pulled into a meditative state in which we were there and nothing was there at the same time. It was pure bliss, pure consciousness, pure being, completely free of time and space. It was the second time since I had come to the Himalayas that a spiritual teacher had unexpectedly opened my heart.

We remained in silence. Girija's eyes lit bright with joy.

We drove back to the ashram from Almora—we felt so light we seemed to fly—and reported on Lama Govinda's health to Maharaji. I mentioned we'd gotten the better of the bargain, a routine house call in exchange for one of Lama Govinda's blessings. Maharaji laughed and pulled my beard and kept repeating to everyone who came for darshan: "Look at this! Doctor America has healed Lama Govinda." I realized then that we were the ones being healed; Maharaji had sent Girija and me to experience Lama Govinda's blessing.

Every day after that I found myself trying to figure out how the gentle touch of my guru or Lama Govinda could unleash something that opened my heart so expansively to the world. In those moments of dissolution, I loved everyone; I was love, unconditional and unlimited, full of compassion. I wanted to ease the suffering of everyone. Was this what it had been like for Ram Dass, a love so pure it fundamentally changes what we were trained to think of as reality? I wanted to spend the rest of my life in pursuit of this feeling, willingly throwing myself into its wonderful addiction, while at the same time trying to figure out how to put such an explosion of love into practice, in life, in the world. It was different from the experiences I had with LSD and psilocybin.

When Maharaji requested that Ram Dass give him a strong dose of LSD, Ram Dass remained in his presence for an hour. He expected some reaction from Maharaji, but nothing happened. Maharaji seemed unaffected by it. Maharaji called LSD "yogi medicine," and many people say he told them variations on the same theme about it: "LSD puts you into the room with God or Christ. It allows you to bow down to Christ, but you are there like a thief sneaking into the presence. It will wear off and you will be back where you started." Other times he asked, "Why sneak in to the presence of God like a thief when you cannot stay? Why not earn your way in through spiritual practices?"

Maharaji taught us that there are many paths to God, many forms of yoga—the "yoking" of one's soul to God—and that all paths are equal. About the different religions, Maharaji often said *Sub ek,* all one, "there is only One. All religions are the same. You should think there are no differences between Ram and Christ. God allows them to serve in different ways. They all lead to one-pointedness." But the Hindu belief that all yogas and paths to God are equal is complemented by the belief that there is a path best suited to every soul. Your individual fate, your karma, determines your customized path, your own way to God, your own dharma, your own unique path to enter into the kingdom. Through a combination of study, practice, and discussion, we would each discover our own way.

———

Maharaji was sometimes gone from the ashram for reasons that were mysterious to me at the time. During those periods, we read, studied, meditated, chanted, and talked about dharma. At other times he sent us off as pilgrims during the autumn, when it became too cold in Kainchi, to visit other famous spiritual masters near his winter ashram in Vrindavan: Sai Baba and Krishnamurti, Muktananda, the Dalai Lama, Ananda Moyi Ma, and Pugal Baba (Crazy Baba). Girija and I took S. N. Goenka's Buddhist meditation course in Benares and visited Maharaji's devotees in Allahabad.

On one of his long periods away from Kainchi, we spent a month in Orissa and rented a house by the Bay of Bengal in a town called Puri. We swam in the ocean, hired a car, and spent a couple of weeks touring the tribal communities. We met the native inhabitants of India, called the Adivasis, the First People—the Ho tribe, the Santhals, and the Gonds. As successive invaders had come to India—Aryans, Mughals, and British—these dark-skinned peoples had been pushed into more remote and hostile lands, like our own Native Americans or the Aborigines in Australia. The Adivasi were among the poorest people in India. On one trip to a village, Girija and I visited gatherers who lived off only what they found or foraged. They smashed nuts and berries and then mixed them with water. They did not have a word for cooked food; they used the same word for "eat" and "drink." Their life expectancy was about thirty years. Half their children died before the age of five from diseases that held no mystery for modern medicine; many women died during childbirth. There was nothing noble or mythic about their lives. The suffering was overwhelming.

Ram Dass tells the story of visiting Benares, where he came across lepers, beggars, amputees, and children with twisted, deformed bodies. He asked himself what a good person does when confronted with such suffering, how one can allocate resources, deciding, in a hell realm like this, who to help, who should receive the largesse of a few coins from one's pocket. He started giving out rupees and quickly realized that the suffering was an unquenchable fire. No matter how many rupees he gave out, it wouldn't make a difference. It was like the spiritual contest between Wavy and Trungpa. One needs a spiritual grounding to figure out, as Ken Kesey had said, how to put one's own bit of good where it will do the most good.

Watching the Adivasi children die from common diseases triggered something in me. I found myself thinking like a doctor again. The mystical experiences had reawakened the certainty that God was real and that I had some duty to find out how I could both serve God and keep that feeling of love I had experienced. I wanted to ask Maharaji for guidance toward some service, some action, something I could do for the people who were suffering in service to them and my soul. I needed to find my own dharma, my own customized path. But I was in no hurry.

When we returned to Kainchi, we discovered that Maharaji had decamped to his winter ashram in Vrindavan, so we turned around and headed back to the lower and warmer environs between Agra and Delhi. As at Kainchi, the highlight of every day was the same—to spend as much time as possible sitting with Maharaji in darshan and asking him questions. He had given different members of the satsang quite different instruction. To some he said they should deepen their meditation practice: "Worldly people go outward, but you must go in like the tortoise, withdrawn, within your shell." And to others he said they should always keep their thoughts only on God: "If you remember God, then He takes care of everything. He who knows God knows everything." And when he was asked, "What is the best form to worship God?" he answered, "Every form." As we sat on the veranda where Maharaji's tucket was placed, I would try to sit up straight, slipping in and out of meditation, in and out of sleep if it was a hot day. Maharaji would start to give darshan to Westerners, handing them apples or oranges or flowers. Sometimes, seeing me trying to meditate, especially if I had nodded off, he threw apples to me or at me—aimed just at my testicles, it seemed. I felt confused.

A few days later, Girija and I were drinking tea in the rear of the temple complex. Maharaji sent his translator to get us. We came quickly to the veranda where Maharaji was sitting, wrapped in his blanket on his tucket surrounded by several Indian devotees. We *pranam*-ed, palms together, bowing low.

"Doctor America!" Maharaji yelled. "How much money do you have?" He turned toward me and looked up at the heavens, peeking at some invisible timeline that stretched through permutations and combinations of events into a possible future that I could not see.

"Doctor America," he repeated, louder this time, "how much money do you have?"

"I have about five hundred dollars," I answered in Hindi.

"Doctor—Doctor America! Five hundred dollars! Is that all you have? *Jut ne bola?* Is this not a lie? Are you telling the truth? How much money do you have?"

"Five hundred dollars. That's it."

"Oh, you mean that's all you have in India, right? How much money do you have in America?"

I figured how much money I had left from my internship and the movie caravan and the weekends I had worked as an emergency room doctor in Los Angeles.

"I have another five hundred dollars back in America," I said.

"*Hare bo!* [Wow!]," he said, laughing in a singsong kind of way. "That is not much money for a doctor. Five hundred here, five hundred there. You no doctor. Doctor America is no doctor. No doctor."

He smiled at Girija. "Will you have to get a job?" he asked me.

A job? No one in the satsang held a job in any conventional sense. And how could we get work permits? I could not practice medicine in India even if I wanted to. We were expats, living in an ashram, on tourist visas. Our work was being with Maharaji.

"You are no doctor," Maharaji said in English, putting the back of his hand up to his forehead, impersonating a carnival fortune-teller, giggling, rocking from left to right.

"You are no doctor, you are no doctor, you are no doctor, you no doctor, you-en-oh doctor, you-en-oh doctor . . . ah . . . you-en-oh . . . Doctor America is going to go to work for the you-en-oh and be a doctor for the United Nations. You will go to the villages and give vaccinations."

I didn't understand what he meant. "You want me to give a shot to someone here?"

He began chanting again. "Doctor America is going to become you-en-oh doctor, you-en-oh doctor. United Nations Organization doctor."

Ahh. U-N-O. What we call the United Nations—U-N in English. Much of the rest of the world calls it UNO, pronounced "you-en-oh." United Nations Organization signs were all over India.

"You will work for the United Nations," he said. "You are going to go to villages and give vaccinations against smallpox."

"Smallpox?"

"Smallpox, this terrible disease, this *mahamari,* this great epidemic, is killing our children. You will go to Delhi, join the United Nations, go to villages and give vaccinations against smallpox. It will be *unmulan,* eradicated from the world. This is God's gift to humanity because of the dedicated health workers. God will help lift this burden of this terrible disease from humanity."

Throughout India and Nepal, I had seen people with terrible disfiguring scars from old smallpox. I'd never seen an active case and only dimly remembered something about Edward Jenner and cowpox and a vaccine in the eighteenth century. But I did remember giving smallpox vaccinations to Wavy and the Medicine Ball Caravan crew. I also remembered driving by the WHO building in Delhi, across from the Yamuna River. I presumed that's what he meant by UN or UNO, the specialized agency of the United Nations, the World Health Organization.

My mind traveled like crazy. My mind could go to work for the United Nations, for smallpox, to give vaccinations—but I couldn't. It would have been easier to accept Maharaji's saying I would fly on a magic carpet or be in two places at once than his telling me that I would work for the United Nations. I had no experience in public health.

This crazy idea took my breath away. Later that night, Girija and I walked back to our room, through the peacock gardens, toward the old city of Vrindavan. It was all we could talk about. I didn't know what to do. I didn't know where to start—so I decided to ignore what Maharaji had said, hoping he'd eventually forget about it.

CHAPTER 8

Prophecy

The heart has its reasons, which reason does not
know. We feel it in a thousand things. It is the heart
which experiences God, and not the reason. This, then,
is faith: God felt by the heart, not by the reason.

—Blaise Pascal

Time stretched out like the first long summer away from
home at camp. Every hour seemed a day, every day a week,
every week a new adventure. Girija and I were staying in a rest
house, a *dharamshala,* provided free to religious pilgrims by a
merchant family from Jaipur. Every morning we walked about
a mile to Maharaji's ashram in Vrindavan. The languid daily
routine had at first repelled me, then captivated me, then bored
me. I tried to find my niche, something to keep me learning and
going deeper. I redoubled my efforts to find meaning and joy in
the hypnotic devotional chanting and singing. I could not tell
whether I was feeling equanimity, or just tranquilized, sitting
around swatting flies.

Like everyone else, I was almost always sick. The water in
Vrindavan is notoriously contaminated. Indians would tell us

Westerners that we would get used to it, and that may have been true for digestive troubles caused by E. coli, but not for parasites and worms. I handed out the antibiotic Flagyl each day like it was candy. Maharaji would always remind us that suffering can make us closer to God. I wanted to be closer to God, but not to amoebas.

Nothing at all happened after Maharaji proclaimed that I would go to villages and give vaccinations. Nothing at all was mentioned about becoming a UN doctor. It seemed that the far-fetched idea was dropped. Perhaps it was a dead end. I did not mind, really. Well, maybe a little bit. It was such an unrealistic, magnificent idea. Working on a UN team that might eradicate a disease was out of my league. Maharaji had a reputation for predicting the future. There was a story I heard many times about the 1962 Chinese incursion on the Indian border. It was said that Indira Gandhi, as president of the Indian National Congress at the time, consulted with Maharaji on a course of action. He told her to do nothing, to wait, and that the Chinese would go away of their own accord. Just as Prime Minister Jawaharlal Nehru was considering a counterattack, much of the Chinese army turned around and went home. No one ever knew why. Maharaji was known in India as having the spiritual power, or *siddhi,* for predicting the future, so I was embarrassed that he'd made a prediction about me that seemed like it would not come true.

We settled into the routine of Vrindavan, which was much like that in Kainchi, the chanting of morning prayers followed by darshan. At midday, when Maharaji went into his room, the Westerners read as much as we could—from the *Ramayana,* the Old and New Testaments of the Bible, the *Gita,* the Koran, biographies of saints and mystics and gurus.

Girija and I resumed our studies together of the Hindi language and history of Hinduism. The Vishnu tradition is the source of two sacred books, perhaps the greatest books in Indian literature, the *Ramayana,* or spiritual journey of Ram, and one of the longest epic poems in the world the *Mahabharata*—or *The Great Epic of Bharat (India),* which is much about Krishna, another incarnation of Vishnu. Since Vrindavan was where the historical Krishna had lived, we paid special attention to the chapter in the *Mahabharata* known as the "Song of God," or the Song of Krishna. This part is known to most of us in America as the *Bhagavad Gita.*

The sweetest activity, however, was doing our daily *parikrama,* the meditative circumambulation of Vrindavan's hundreds of ancient temples, most of which were devoted to Krishna or Krishna's consort, Radha. Vrindavan is sacred in India because it was the town in which the young Krishna, the dusky-colored (sham) avatar of Vishnu, cavorted with his lovers, the milkmaids, and Radha, his consort. Despite his erotic frolicking with so many milkmaids, Krishna and Radha were seen as a divine pair. The mixing of generalized eroticism with a lifelong fidelity may have made some orthodox Brahmins uncomfortable, but it made sense to American hippies. We loved yelling out the local greeting "Radhe sham!" which meant something like "Hail to Krishna-and-Radha." It was like saying "good morning," "good evening," "hello," and "goodbye" all rolled into one—just as Radha and Krishna were also rolled into one.

Vrindavan was becoming the center of Krishna worship, housing the global headquarters of the Hare Krishna movement and making it an unlikely place for a temple to the monkey god Hanuman. The Hindu pantheon can be daunting, but differences were not a problem for Maharaji, with his common phrase *sub ek* attesting that all gods are one, all religions are one. He built his temple in Vrindavan on a side street called Hanuman Nagar, or "Monkey God City."

One of Maharaji's closest devotees, Dada Mukerjee, a Bengali professor of economics from Allahabad University, had come back to the ashram from his teaching job. While he was in Vrindavan, he translated for Maharaji. One night, right before sunset, Girija and I set out to our rooms. Cows meandered in the stillness of dusk. Monkeys scampered around the temple, and bells rang in nearby shrines. Like a call to prayer amidst this pastoral scene, Maharaji bellowed, "Doctor America! Doctor America!" I thought someone might be hurt, so Girija and I rushed to the back of the ashram where Maharaji was sitting. "Have you got your job at WHO yet?" he asked in Hindi as we approached.

"No, Maharaji," I answered.

Then he asked Dada to translate: "You will go to work for the United Nations. God is going to give humanity a gift. The terrible disease, smallpox, will be pulled out by the roots. You will see. You will see."

Dada emphasized, "Pulled out by the roots." Then he added: "There are two different ways of saying in Hindi that a disease will be conquered. *Katam karna* means to simply end it, while the expression Maharaji used, *unmulan,* means to uproot it. *Muli* means radish, and it is the Sanskrit word for root." It was the same in English. *Radic,* in eradicate, like the word radish, also means root.

I murmured something and hoped he would drop the subject again. Girija and I joined the cows walking home toward our *dharamshala,* still confused.

Because the ashram was so close to the Taj Mahal, it was often filled with Indian tourists in addition to Indian devotees and a dozen or two Westerners. Some days, Maharaji would receive political leaders, like Shankar Dayal Sharma, then head of the Indian National Congress, and later president of India; or Akbar Ali Khan, governor of the state of Uttar Pradesh. Maharaji would then hide us elsewhere in the town so they wouldn't notice that many of us had overstayed our visas. Sometimes he'd send us to visit the Taj or make a pilgrimage someplace else in India.

When the president of India was coming, he sent us all to Kausani in the Himalayas, where Mahatma Gandhi had gone on retreat to contemplate his plan to win independence for India. There, Gandhi had made his own translation of the *Bhagavad Gita* into English. Girija and I stayed near the site, reading Gandhi's translation in the same place it was generated. His version is a powerful guidebook for living a life that combines a spiritual path with social activism.

Since Girija and I had been in India for more than the six months permitted by our tourist visas, it was time to face the visa renewal dance. We went off to the district magistrate's office in Mathura to ask for a visa extension. Our first request was denied and a deportation order, called a Quit India notice, was stapled to our passports.

I typed a long appeal to the district magistrate, about being a Western physician in love with India, reading the *Bhagavad Gita,* living in the ashram in the very town where Krishna had grown up. I peppered my letter with Sanskrit phrases and flowery couplets in the local Brijbassi dialect to show off my knowledge. "Please let me appear in person and make the case for me and my wife, who has taken the Indian name of Girija, to request a visa extension." Eventually, we were granted an appointment to appear in person before the magistrate. To further impress, I wore a white dhoti, the same type Gandhi had worn to meet the king of England at Buckingham Palace. Gandhi was later asked, "Didn't you feel rather underdressed wearing only that loincloth in the presence of the king?" Gandhi replied, "His majesty was wearing sufficient clothes for both of us."

Dressing that morning, I wound the dhoti carefully under and between my legs and then tucked the end into the waistband to secure it, making sure it covered my lower body. Fifty or more Indian supplicants—young and old, men and women—waited for the magistrate to settle matters of landownership and government subsidies. Girija and I were the only Westerners. After several hours of waiting and pacing, the magistrate called out. "Lorrie?" he said, like the British word Indians use for "truck." Realizing he meant "Larry," I leaped out of my seat, catching my dhoti on a nail protruding from the bench. It immediately unwound and plunged to my ankles, leaving me bare-assed in public.

There was an audible gasp from the Indians around us, a moment of awkward silence, and then laughter. The district magistrate, dressed in a proper English suit, turned away out of modesty, waited while Girija helped me cover my nakedness, and then said the Hindi equivalent of, "Nice try. I would give you an A for effort if you had not embarrassed everyone. You had better learn how to tie that thing before you come here again—or go anywhere else in India." But he also stamped both of our visas with the six-month extension. The embarrassment was a small price to pay.

A week or two passed uneventfully as we celebrated being able to stay another half year in the ashram. But then Maharaji started up again, asking me every day, "Did you get your UN job yet? Has Doctor America become UNO doctor yet?" During darshan, if I sat to meditate while he engaged with others, he would giggle and continue to throw apples or oranges at me, his aim improving every day.

Maharaji rarely said "do this" or "do that" or indicate that one thing was right or another wrong. He taught by parable or by having us focus on a verse from the *Gita*. "See how Krishna tells Arjuna that not even God can take time off and not work," he would say. "God must be in the world. You must be in the world, not hiding away in a cave. Work to help relieve suffering, but don't get a big head." I took this to mean that I wasn't good enough for spiritual development through meditation, or *dhyana yoga*. I did not understand that Maharaji was teaching me about another form of yoga, *karma yoga,* working to be one with God through work in the world.

"Wake up, wake up," he would say in a high-pitched staccato. "Meditation, devotion, and worship are all good. Very, very good. Do these *upaya*—these methods. But for you, not only meditation or devotion or *asanas* [postures]. Your yoga is *nish kam karma* yoga. You will do service, but avoid praise, and give the fruits of your labor to God. Don't get excited about your role. That is your dharma. Your path is working in the world, not in meditation. You will find your dharma when you get your UN job. Don't get a big head."

Weeks passed and I remained as puzzled as ever. Then one day, Maharaji shouted across the courtyard, "Doctor America. Now! Go to Delhi. Go to WHO. You'll get your job. Girija, go with the doctor. Today. Right now!"

Girija and I took a pedal rickshaw from Vrindavan ashram to the Mathura train station, where we boarded a train to Delhi.

We asked the station attendant when we arrived two or three hours later where the WHO office was located. "Indraprastha Estate," he said. We jumped in a taxi, yelling at the driver, "WHO, the UN building in Indraprastha." A few minutes later, we arrived at the WHO office, a five-story pastel blue structure everyone called SEARO, for South East Asia Regional Office.

I was still wearing my homespun kurta and Girija her sari. We walked to the entrance, and the *chowkidor,* the guard, asked us to wait in the reception area. The receptionist, a fifty-something Anglo-Indian woman named Mrs. Edna Boyer, took her seat and asked me to approach the counter. She was wearing a dress, not a sari; she wore lipstick, had plucked and penciled eyebrows, and a wide open face framed by a short haircut. She was one of the few modern-looking Indian women I had ever seen.

I began with what would become my regular spiel: "Hello. I'm here to get a job with the World Health Organization. My guru, Neem Karoli Baba, who lives in the Himalayas, said I would work with WHO and go to villages to give vaccinations for smallpox. Smallpox will be eradicated, because of God's gift to humanity and the effort of dedicated health workers."

I will never forget the expression on Mrs. Boyer's face. There was not a hint of cynicism, just pure delight. Years later she confessed that a long-haired kurta-wearing hippie was a breath of fresh air for her, a welcome relief from the parade of stiff diplomats and unhappy local contractors with whom she usually dealt every day. Without hesitation, she went into the back room and returned with UN application forms. I filled them out as best I could. I had to leave blank the section where I was supposed to list all of my scientific publications. I struggled to deal with the requirement of a reference from "an internationally renowned physician not from your own country." I couldn't use Ben Spock. Maybe the English neurologist and poet Dr. Martin Bax, who had been my summer preceptor at Guy's Hospital in London, but I had to approximate his address. Mrs. Boyer asked me to come back the following week to meet with the WHO personnel officer, Mr. Katri.[†]

Katri was from Lucknow, the capital of the state of Uttar Pradesh and the city of one of Maharaji's most famous temples. Every Tuesday, the day dedicated to Hanuman, students at Lucknow University would come to the temple, usually to pray for good grades. Katri had been one of those students. Though he knew of Neem Karoli Baba, he did not buy my story. He told me I looked like a crazy hippie who had wandered off a movie set. In fact, he told me I looked *exactly* like one particular crazy hippie in one particular Bollywood movie, *Hare Rama Hare Krishna*. Which, in fact, was true.

When the Hog Farm buses had been parked outside Kathmandu, the Indian filmmaker Dev Anand was filming his latest project there, a Bollywood movie about hippies. He wanted to cast the colorful Hog Farm hippies as extras in the movie, which he described as a film about the deep spiritual quest that brought the stream of young Westerners to India. For our services, he offered us each twelve rupees, or about twenty-five cents, per day plus all the hash we could smoke, which he hoped we would do in front of the cameras. About a dozen of us, including Wavy, Bonnie Jean, Girija, and me, were extras for a couple of days. The film became a cult sensation in India; the only problem was that instead of a film about our coming to India to search for God,

---

[†]A few names have been changed in the book, and they are noted with a dagger.

Dev Anand sensationalized the hippie lifestyle of sex, drugs, and rock and roll, painting us as every Indian family's nightmare. For the next decade, whenever any of us walked through a village or met someone for the first time in India, they were likely to break out into the movie's theme song, "Dum Maro Dum" ("Puff After Puff"), about smoking hashish from morning to night. Sometimes it was cool to be recognized, but sometimes that song, which was a huge hit, came back to haunt me.

Thankfully, Katri didn't break into song, but he didn't give me a job either. WHO had no openings, he explained. The organization hired only expert consultants from medical schools and academic institutions outside of India. That was the rule. They had never hired an American who was in India on a tourist visa. WHO would hire experts only from a learned academy such as the National Institutes of Health or the Centers for Disease Control (CDC), not from some Monkey Temple in the mountains that proper modern Indians didn't even go to anymore. To further complicate matters, I was younger by at least a decade than any foreigner SEARO had ever hired.

At Maharaji's insistence, however, I kept going back to WHO, more than a dozen times by taxi, bus, rickshaw, and train. Mrs. Boyer and Katri always treated me kindly, registering only mild irritation whenever I appeared at the doorstep bucked up by Maharaji's confidence and his prediction.

On my ninth or tenth visit, Katri softened and changed the subject. "Bearing in mind that hiring you is quite impossible," he said, "and confused as I am as to why you want to work for WHO, there is one important program that, if they could ever get it going, they would have to staff up quickly in order to achieve their goal."

"Which program is that?" I asked.

"It's the smallpox program," he answered.

A gentle, familiar buzz went through me.

"The Government of India," Katri continued, "is adamantly against expanding the WHO program to fight smallpox. India has bigger problems, such as malaria, infant mortality, even diarrhea. Each of them kills many more children every year than does smallpox. And then there is Prime Minister Gandhi's major priority: family planning. Smallpox may be the top priority of other countries, but it is not India's priority at all. There are WHO smallpox programs in twenty other countries, but there is no such program just for India, not really. There is one valiant French woman doctor, Dr. Grasset, who works with missionary zeal, in charge of smallpox for the SEARO region, but even she has trouble getting permission to go to the remote areas of India. You can meet her. It won't do any good, but if you come back next week I'll take you to see her. She is also the only lady doctor here in WHO."

After the conversation with Katri I began to realize I needed to look a lot more presentable. Maharaji's devotees in Delhi, the Barmans, graciously lent me a suit. It did not fit well, but it was an improvement over the ashram clothes. To complete the look, which felt like a disguise, I bought a terrible-looking tie, pulled my hair back into a ponytail, and tucked it into the collar of my white shirt.

Dr. Nicole Grasset was an urbane, elegant, and charming French-Swiss epidemiologist, sometimes called the "Hurricane on High Heels" because of her fashionable style and irrepressible spirit. She was a public health hero from her time in Africa when she left her job at the Pasteur Institute to violate no-fly zones in order to take vaccines to people who needed them during the war in Biafra. She was kind but quick to disabuse me of any hope that she would even read my application. "I'm sorry," she said. "We really don't have a job for anyone like you."

By this time, Maharaji had moved back to Kainchi. When I returned, he asked, "Did you get your job?"

"No, Maharaji. I'm not going to get this job."

But I kept going back anyway, every time he asked me. Trips to Delhi from Kainchi were grueling, a dozen hours if everything went right. Trains were late or canceled regularly; bus rides on mountain roads were terrifying. Delhi was an obstacle course of beggars, with the craziest drivers in existence and cows and other animals wandering the streets. It would have been great if Maharaji could have sent me there just once, on the right day to see the right person so I could land the job.

But mystical traditions are filled with stories of teachers testing and training and sometimes tormenting their students. A classic example is the story of Milarepa, the eleventh-century Tibetan saint Wavy had told us about who subsisted on nettles during meditation. Milarepa had been a robber and a murderer, so his teacher, Marpa, made him build and tear down tower after tower—a humiliating process that lasted years but would purify the obstacles to spiritual development, that is, Milarepa's inner stew of rage, violence, and revenge. I am not Milarepa and I am not a saint, but walking into the WHO office over and over again and explaining that my guru had told me to come work for them might have altered my biochemistry. I think Maharaji wanted me to gain nonattachment to success. A spiritual apprenticeship can be confusing, even counterintuitive. Those long, exhausting trips, constant rejections, and the daily reminder of my unworthiness, the roller coaster of doubt and the balm of Maharaji's reassurance, were all part of the preparation. What developed in me during that time was faith—delicate, wavering, tenuous, but faith nonetheless.

Sometimes people say that faith is the opposite of doubt, but I don't think that is true. To me, the opposite of faith is rigid certainty. Doubt is the constant companion of true faith; like God, it is more verb than noun. Faith is the ride, not the station, as Indians describe it. No one can avoid doubt, skepticism, fear, and uncertainty on the journey to faith if they are honest with themselves. Obstacles are the training ground.

"Go back to WHO," Maharaji said again.

So I took the twelve-hour trip back to Delhi.

Dr. Grasset let me down as gently as possible. "No, I'm sorry, there is no job available. I know your teacher said you would work here, but I can't help you right now. We will keep you in mind."

"Did you get your job?" Maharaji asked as soon as I returned.

"No, I didn't."

"See the French doctor again." This routine was getting embarrassing.

This time, I skipped the taxi-bus-rickshaw-train trip and phoned Dr. Grasset from Nainital. I had to book the call a day or two in advance from the county post, telegraph, and telephone office. The connection crackled as she explained that there was no expansion of the smallpox program and no possibility of hiring American doctors, but she thanked me politely for my continued interest in the work.

Days passed. At morning darshan one day Maharaji sat up straight and commanded, "Immediately! Go to WHO!"

I jumped on the train to Delhi reluctantly, unhappy to leave the ashram. I waved to Mrs. Boyer when I entered. She was talking to an American man I had never seen there before.

"Oh, let me introduce you to a fellow American," she said to me.

"What are you doing here?" he asked.

Here we go again. I recited my story: "I've come to WHO to work for the smallpox program. My guru, who lives in the Himalayas, told me I would work for WHO."

"Are you a doctor?"

"Yes. I just finished my internship in San Francisco."

He smiled and left the room, and I talked with Mrs. Boyer.

Dr. Grasset did not answer the phone when I called from Mrs. Boyer's desk, but Mrs. Boyer suggested I be patient and wait. After a while, Dr. Grasset called back and said there was still no expansion of the smallpox program, but the chief of the global smallpox program, D. A. Henderson, was there from Geneva, Switzerland. "He is upstairs here with me. Why don't you come and meet him?"

Henderson turned out to be the man I had met in reception. He confirmed that Prime Minister Indira Gandhi had still not given WHO permission to bring a team of medical officers into India for smallpox eradication. This was the purpose of his visit, and he was hoping to have a meeting with her the next day. At Dr. Grasset's insistence he agreed to interview me and wrote a note for the record that I found years later when he asked me to return to India to close down the smallpox program: "This young man says he is a doctor, and he seems to like foreign cultures and might do very good international work someday. But he appears to have 'gone native.' And he has no experience in public health, no training past internship. Although I wish him good luck in the future, we have no job for him."

"Listen. We can't hire you," he said. "For starters, you have no training in epidemiology."

He was right. And I had never even seen a case of smallpox.

"Second, the Indian government doesn't want Americans working here," he said. In fact, the government had been kicking Americans out after India accepted Soviet aid to go to war with the United States–backed Pakistan. I don't remember whether it was before or after I started at WHO, but there was talk of the Indian government kicking out of India all workers of the U.S. Agency for International Development (USAID) after the organization, in a brazen act of arrogance, released millions of irradiated male mosquitoes without the permission of the Indian government. The intention was understandable, even admirable. They were trying to figure out a way to sterilize mosquitoes in an attempt to eradicate the vector that carried malaria, but doing this as if India were the organization's own private lab was such a naked act of neocolonialism that the Indian parliament convened a special meeting and nearly tossed out both the malaria and the unrelated smallpox eradication programs in protest.

"And third," Henderson said, "we are not ready to fully launch a program in India. We all know that India will be the most difficult place to work; this is where we expect to see smallpox make its last stand. India may wind up being the last place on earth that has smallpox. We will need to finish the eradication process in other countries first, then redeploy all our resources here in order to wipe smallpox from the world."

I returned to the ashram disheartened, and when Maharaji asked how it went, I reported dutifully about meeting Dr. Henderson and what seemed like a final "no."

"Call the lady doctor again!"

I telephoned WHO with great hesitation.

Dr. Grasset was gracious and amused as always. "Dr. Henderson has not met with the prime minister yet about the status of the smallpox program. If there is any change I will telephone you, but it is unlikely."

Girija and I had had very little contact with our families since arriving in India with our orange backpacks. Girija's mother, Ann Feldman, was the only family member on either side who traveled abroad. The daughter of Russian immigrants, Ann was born in Detroit in 1916. Her parents, like my grandfather Louis Brilliant, died in the great influenza pandemic of 1917–1918, leaving Ann in the hands of her five older brothers. I had never known her to be anything other than unhappy. We hoped seeing our life in India would change how she saw things, so I bought her a plane ticket to visit from Detroit. We got a telegram confirming the date Ann would arrive in New Delhi.

"Maharaji, we are leaving tomorrow, Tuesday, to pick up my mother at the Delhi airport," Girija said.

"Day after tomorrow, Wednesday," he replied without missing a beat.

"No—it is tomorrow, Tuesday," I countered, thinking he misunderstood. I had bought the ticket; I knew when Ann was coming.

"Day after tomorrow. Wednesday."

"We saw the telegram. It's Tuesday."

"She will be here Wednesday." And he laughed and giggled.

Certain we were right about the day of her arrival, we left for Delhi. But there was no Ann at the airport. When we got back to Vrindavan, another telegram had arrived saying, "Plane delayed one day. Now arriving Wednesday." Maharaji giggled.

Ann arrived safely, and after some sleep and sightseeing in the neighborhood, we got a car and took her to the Taj Mahal in Agra. When we thought she was getting used to the crowds and lack of sanitation, we drove to Vrindavan to meet Maharaji. It was only an hour away from Agra.

"I'm not going in there! I'm not going in! Take me back to Delhi! Get me out of here," Ann screamed as she was surrounded by a half dozen children begging and clinging to her dress outside the ashram gates. "This place is filthy. I hate you and I hate your cult!"

I tried my best to persuade her to come in and meet our guru, but got nowhere. Ann got back in the car and locked the doors. She never did meet Maharaji. Instead, we took her for more sightseeing—first, to the spectacular city of Jaipur in Rajasthan State. After that, we visited the white Lake Palace in Udaipur, which looks like a dream castle floating on water. It was one pixel of the millions of exquisite pixels on the map of India.

The palace had become a luxury hotel, where we had booked rooms. Ann's room was at the far end of the property. While she was moving into the room, we saw another Western woman, the only other Westerner, also checking into her room nearby. *No. Not possible!* Nicole Grasset was about to enter the room next door to my mother-in-law! This was just too much of a coincidence, the odds too great, but in my altered state in mystical India, it somehow made complete sense.

"Dr. Grasset! Nicole, it's me! Larry Brilliant! I'm here too with my wife and mother-in-law. She's staying in the room next door!"

"Oh, Larry, how remarkable to bump into you so far away from Delhi. It is nice to see you but please forgive me for not being social. This is my first vacation and my first day out of Delhi since coming to India and I only have one day. I am going to have a good rest," she said. "Have a lovely vacation."

After two months of running back and forth to Delhi's WHO offices, Girija and I were exhausted. The coincidence of seeing Nicole next door to my mother-in-law was followed by an emotional letdown. That had been the closest we came to feeling that there was any chance that I would ever work for WHO.

Ann returned to the States, and we went back to Vrindavan. Maharaji had gone traveling; he had sent everyone away, and the satsang was moving about. Girija and I decided on a trek in the mountains in Kashmir. We stopped at the Barmans' house in New Delhi and I used their phone to call Nicole at WHO and tell her of our plans.

"We will be in Kashmir. In case we happen to bump into you there I want you to know I'm not stalking you." Nicole laughed. "And of course if by any chance a job comes through," I said, "please call me in Srinagar."

"You know," she said, "a very strange thing happened last evening. I am not a person given to visions, and I am not a fan of gurus. But I had this feeling about you, about working with you, like a dream but it was not a dream. I don't know—maybe it was bumping into you in Udaipur, maybe it's your guru talking to me or something like that, which would of course be silly." She laughed and added, "But one thought does occur to me. Can you write?"

I told her yes, and that I had edited several magazines. I thought it best not to mention at that moment how politically radical they were.

"Well, you know we can't really hire you as a smallpox doctor, both because you have no experience and because the Government of India has not allowed us to have a full-scale program here, so thus far the entire program is just a Czech epidemiologist, me, and the Indian administrative assistants. But if you're really that determined to work for WHO, I was thinking maybe I could hire you as an administrative assistant, a secretary on the SEARO payroll for local hires. I don't think I need much approval to get that done. Would you be willing to type and file and answer phones? And of course your pay would be at the Indian level, not at the level of an international medical officer."

"I'll do anything!" I assured her.

The next day in the office, Nicole altered my application, switching it from "doctor" to "administrative assistant." She sent a telegram to D. A. Henderson, who had returned to headquarters in Geneva: "I'm going to hire Brilliant as a secretary."

Since D.A. had thought I had "gone native," I can only imagine the expression on his face when Nicole's telegram arrived. But one thing about him: D. A. Henderson was the most supportive boss and he was a great manager. If Nicole wanted to hire a crazy hippie kid to file and type, he would let her.

While all of this was going on, Girija and I floated on a houseboat on Dal Lake in Srinagar. It was a lovely, sweet reprieve from hustling for a job, a nice break from the daily prayers and satsang struggle as everyone jostled to get closest to Maharaji in the ashram. We exchanged the wakeup call from the *kirtan wallahs,* singing "Sri Ram, jai Ram," for the sound of the muezzin calling Muslims to prayer five times a day echoing peacefully across Dal Lake.

We'd been visiting sacred sites to Shiva and hiking most days during our reprieve. The day we were leaving, we heaved on our backpacks and started to walk the couple of hours to Srinagar. Twenty minutes into the trek, we heard a series of wails coming from a wooden building by the valley side of the road. As we got closer, we saw it was a doctor's office, shingle and all, saying "Dr. Ashraf Beg."

"Allah akbar hai!" God is great! we heard a patient shout. Curious, we knocked on the office door. A young, clean-shaven Muslim doctor was surprised to find two *Angrezis* standing on the other side.

"I'm a doctor from California, living in India," I began in a conflation of Hindi, English, and Urdu. "I heard the shouts and wondered whether everything was okay."

"More than okay," came the reply. "Come in, have some tea. Let me show you." Dr. Beg was operating on people who had been blinded by cataracts, restoring their sight. "My patient was totally blind. He hadn't seen his grandchildren in years." His joy upon seeing again was the source of the cry we'd heard. Dr. Beg let me remove the bandages from another man, who also cried, "Allah akbar hai!," thanking God for his gift of sight.

This was my first view close up of sight-restoring surgery. The procedure took only a few minutes, cost less than a meal in Srinigar or Delhi, and was easy to perform. It was breathtaking that something so debilitating, so dire as blindness could be conquered so quickly and cheaply and sustainably. As it would turn out, after smallpox, this easily reversible blindness that plagues so many in developing countries would be our target. For that, Girija and I helped establish the Seva Foundation less than a decade later.

"Did you get your job yet?" Maharaji asked when we returned to Kainchi.

I told him that Nicole Grasset had come up with a way to hire me, "But it's still complicated."

"Go back to Delhi." So it was back and forth again, like a yo-yo. I put on the Barmans' suit and braced myself for more teasing and humiliation at SEARO.

But this time Mr. Katri, the personnel officer, called me in and closed the door behind me. "There is good news and bad news," he said. The good news, the remarkable news, in fact, was that Nicole's idea had worked and the application to be an administrative assistant had been approved. The bad news was that I would have to pass a U.S. government security clearance.

That was it. Probably the end of the road. There was no chance in the world that I could get a clearance. It was not so much a security clearance as a test of loyalty, required by only a few countries, Katri explained. President Harry Truman had signed an executive order creating the International Organizations Employees Loyalty Board to adjudicate the loyalty of Americans who wanted to work for the United Nations. The

Loyalty Board had been abused during the McCarthy witch hunts and during the peak of the Cold War; it had become more active recently because of the protests over the war in Vietnam. Any American who wanted a position with the United Nations had to undergo a full field investigation by the FBI. They would visit every place I had lived in the United States and interview neighbors and family and friends for evidence of "un-American" speech or activity.

I had plenty of reason to worry. I had been detained with Dr. Martin Luther King; I was a member of a radical medical student organization and involved with the MCHR, many of whose founders had been summoned before the House Un-American Activities Committee. Girija and I had joined another revolutionary group called the Venceremos Brigade and had signed up to pick sugarcane in Cuba, which we had naively conflated with opposing the war in Vietnam. Even though we never made it to Cuba because of the surgery to remove my parathyroid tumor, the mere fact that my name appeared on the list might be considered anti-American.

I returned to Kainchi feeling emotionally crushed. I tried to tell Maharaji that this fantasy ride was over.

"Oh," he said as if there were not the slightest problem. "Who is the person who is supposed to give you this security clearance?"

"I don't know."

"Who is the American who gives you the job?"

I mentioned that D. A. Henderson was the boss. Maharaji sat up straight and held his blanketed arm up before his face.

"How do you spell his name?" he asked.

"H, E, N, D—" I started.

"Wait." He repeated the letters slowly, in a deep voice. He peeked out at me through his fingers, like a psychic putting on a show at a dinner party, checking to make sure I was properly impressed, giggling with each new letter.

Girija and I were staying in the White House across the road from the Kainchi ashram. A few weeks later, we got to the temple early one morning and Maharaji called us into his "office." He was being uncharacteristically hospitable. He had tea and sweets brought in and hugged us. We were rubbing his feet. It was blissful. I thought he was trying to make up for our disappointment over the loss of the WHO job.

"Okay. Time for you to go," he said. We stood up, thinking he meant it was time for us to leave his room, time to leave the ashram and return to the White House. We bowed and walked out. But just as we approached the gate, the postman's car pulled up to the front of the ashram, and he handed me a telegram: "We have been notified today by Dr. D. A. Henderson from WHO headquarters in Geneva that you have received U.S. clearance. Come immediately to WHO-SEARO office in New Delhi to begin work."

My heart was racing. Girija was so happy. None of this made sense, but it did not need to. D. A. Henderson years later told me that around the time I was spelling out his name for Maharaji he had been attending a cocktail party at the American embassy in Geneva. The American ambassador and the U.S. surgeon general were there. The surgeon general asked Henderson how the smallpox eradication program was going.

"Great," said Henderson. "We have thirty-four countries cleared and only four are left."

"Are all the countries helping you?" asked the surgeon general.

"Yes. Russia's given us vaccine. Canada too. Sweden's given us a lot of money. Czechoslovakia is sending great epidemiologists. Many countries are helping."

"What about America? What are we giving you?"

"Well," said Henderson, "CDC is terrific with providing research, but otherwise the U.S. has not done so much."

"What do you need?"

"I don't know how I got into this, and I don't know why we're doing it, but my team in India wants to hire this young American doctor who has been living in an ashram in the mountains of India. They want to bring him on as a secretary and as a local hire, not a medical officer. We've never done anything like this before. But the kid was a hippie and war protestor and probably won't get a loyalty clearance, or at least the background check will take too long."

"Loyalty clearance? This doesn't seem like a high enough position to require that. Get him a temporary clearance and then if you hire him later get the loyalty clearance. Who gives him the clearance?"

Henderson said, "Well, the approval letter comes to me from your office so I guess you can do it."

"I can? Give me a napkin." He took the napkin, got out his pen, and wrote, "Brilliant—okay to start work for temp job while waiting for clearance." He gave the napkin to Henderson, who telegraphed WHO in New Delhi that I'd been cleared to work. Or at least that's the story D.A. told me over and over again. I would never be able to find out if it was true or if he was pulling my leg.

At certain moments, the ordinary rules of cause and effect are suspended. Living in a sacred space, surrounded by sacred images, following a guru, a teacher, or a prophet who seems prescient and nudges you toward a specific path—impossible things happen. Since you cannot explain them through reason, you must acquiesce to unreasonable theories. After that, everything begins to make sense again, but in an unexpected way: all impossible things begin to seem quite possible after all.

CHAPTER 9

Apprenticeship

Three Kinds of Souls, Three Prayers:
1) I am a bow in your hands, Lord. Draw me, lest I rot.
2) Do not overdraw me, Lord. I shall break.
3) Overdraw me, Lord, and who cares if I break!

—Nikos Kazantzakis

W e have to hurry," Nicole said, dragging me downstairs to the Monday meeting with the WHO regional director. The "Hurricane on High Heels" bounded down the steps from the fifth floor to the ground floor, her perfectly coifed hair bouncing behind her.

The formal meeting room at WHO was in the officer's decorous and stately board room, something straight out of an eighteenth-century British men's club. Some twenty doctors and various UN officials sat in large comfortable leather chairs around a long rectangular teak wood table. The view from the roof showed a dilapidated power station belching smoke in one direction and a sprawling slum of unimaginable poverty and filth in the other. The people in these slums earned their livings rummaging through garbage heaps in search of anything they could burn, sell, or eat.

The day's agenda was to prepare for the biannual report on the general health status for Southeast Asia. The countries represented were India, Nepal, Bangladesh, Sri Lanka, Burma, Thailand, Indonesia, Maldives, Mongolia, and Bhutan. Nicole and I entered as Dr. V. T. H. Gunaratne, the WHO regional director, a huge six-foot-five-inch Sri Lankan Buddhist, stood and scowled. He was ready to gavel the meeting to order. Nicole hated these meetings and thought they were a waste of time.

I felt too young, too inexperienced, too shaggy to be in that room filled with Asia's leaders in public health. When I scanned the faces at the table, it looked as if God had organized faces according to skin tone. The Mongolian health minister was first. Next to him was a golden Thai doctor, and on through the faces of Asia—Bangladesh, Japan, Korea, Indonesia, Burma, Taiwan—two African dignitaries, to the European staff members, a pale Englishman next to a tall blond Swede, next to a ruddy-faced Pole who was sitting next to an American. I had never been in a room with such diversity. It looked like a rainbow of humanity, a mystical convergence, a sign that I was in the right place. The room was a real-life example of what it looks like when the saying "we are all in this together" is translated into the practical, with representatives from so many diverse cultures, religions, and races, united in the fight to bring good health to all. That is what the words "World Health Organization" meant to me then.

The meeting began with presentations on the general mortality rate, or crude death rate, of regional member countries. India reported first: "India had fourteen deaths per one thousand

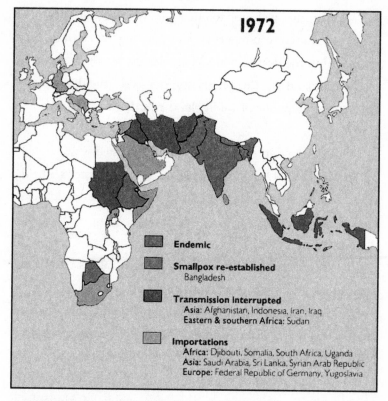

1972

Endemic

Smallpox re-established
Bangladesh

Transmission interrupted
Asia: Afghanistan, Indonesia, Iran, Iraq
Eastern & southern Africa: Sudan

Importations
Africa: Djibouti, Somalia, South Africa, Uganda
Asia: Saudi Arabia, Sri Lanka, Syrian Arab Republic
Europe: Federal Republic of Germany, Yugoslavia

Smallpox in the World, 1972

population last year compared with twenty-two ten years earlier," reported the Indian director general.

"Bangladesh, twenty deaths per one thousand population."

"Sri Lanka, eight deaths per one thousand," said the proud Sri Lankan health minister.

Gunaratne turned to the newly appointed Mongolian health minister, who a few days earlier might have been riding the steppes on horseback in traditional Mongolian garb, which he wore proudly during his first official visit to the WHO office, the first trip, in fact, out of Mongolia in his life.

"Mr. Minister, welcome to our Monday reporting meeting. It is our custom that you report various rates in your country. First, please tell us the death rate in Mongolia last year."

"Dr. Gunaratne," the health minister said, "the death rate in the People's Republic of Mongolia is exactly the same as it is in India."

"Sir, I need a number," Dr. Gunaratne insisted.

"In Mongolia, Dr. Gunaratne," the health minister said, "the death rate is exactly the same as it is in the honorable Soviet Union."

"Sir, I need a number in Mongolia."

"In Mongolia, Dr. Gunaratne, the death rate is exactly the same as it is in the People's Republic of China."

Dr. Gunaratne rose to his full six-and-a-half feet. "Sir, the rules of WHO are clear. You must report the death rate in your country each year so that we can measure your progress."

The Mongolian minister stood up and said again, "Dr. Gunaratne, the death rate in the People's Republic of Mongolia is the same as in the People's Republic of China, or in the honorable Soviet Union, and for that matter it is the same as it is in the wealthy United States of America. We have, in Mongolia, exactly and precisely one death per individual."

Everybody laughed.

The number didn't matter. He was expressing Buddha's First Noble Truth—that the suffering of sickness, old age, and death is inevitable for each one of us.

Like Gunaratne, the health minister was a Buddhist. He was not awed by the formality of the WHO clubroom. In the precarious geographical situation of Mongolia, wedged between the much larger and more powerful Soviet Union and China, he needed to not upset his oversized neighbors by reporting any kind of progress that surpassed them. He played the fool, speaking truth to power and displaying what it was like to inhabit the two worlds I was beginning to bridge, the metaphysical and epidemiological.

That was the only joke I would ever hear in that room. The light moment passed quickly. But I was in the right place, at the right time, the first day of my first real job. I may have been wearing a bad tie and ill-fitting suit, but I felt completely part of the plan and part of the great mystery.

I was giddy with anticipation that first day as a UN employee. I was the youngest expatriate hired by WHO, and certainly the first ever recruited from the Neem Karoli Baba Monkey Temple in the Himalayas. I was an enthusiastic recruit, the apprentice, the mascot, the kid who loved India, spoke Hindi, and thrived in an Indian culture that was not always inviting to Western outsiders.

But I did not know anything about smallpox or the United Nations.

So I switched on the part of me that was a good student and took copious notes through the tedious orientation, a short course in international law, UN history, and the rights and obligations of those who carry a UN passport. Plus a less formal, but equally important briefing about decorum and the high expectations of an international civil servant living in India. To top it off there were explanations on how to fill out WHO expense forms, monthly reports, and travel notes. Not a word yet about smallpox.

It was June 1973 in New Delhi, the rains had not yet begun, the summer heat seemed to build upon itself daily; dust storms made the city almost unbearable. Cows ambled slowly through the dry and dusty streets. Rickshaw peddlers cycled slowly over the steaming asphalt. The shops on Connaught Circus closed during the afternoon when demand for electricity peaked. The wealthy turned up their air conditioners, causing load shedding and brownouts, which made everything move even more slowly.

It was no accident that the British had moved their capital from Delhi to the hill stations of Simla and Nainital during the summer. Delhi was for working; the hills were for living and playing. Girija and I made the opposite move, coming down from the hill station of Nainital several days earlier on a quest neither lofty nor spiritual: we sought what every modern expatriate living in the Indian capital sought—a small apartment with a big air conditioner. We moved temporarily into a room at the Indian International Center, near the fifteenth-century gardens of the Lodi kings of Delhi. At least in those gardens one could find solitude, history, and cooling trees.

Mr. Katri seemed genuinely happy to hand me the new blue UN passport that meant I was really hired. I had a foot-tall stack of papers to sign: emergency next of kin, income tax exemption, retirement fund, rights and duties, and a form detailing what WHO would do if I died overseas. The discussion of what would be done with my body if I died in India was followed by a short ceremony—tea and biscuits—to celebrate my entry into the ranks of UN workers. It was a sweet gesture. Katri and I had been through a lot together—at least a dozen meetings after each trip I made from the ashram to WHO.

I thought about the first person to help me understand why, after World War II, so many people put so much faith in the United Nations. When I was wandering alone in Southeast Asia, after sending Wavy off to New York and to the hospital, I would often consult the *I Ching,* a Chinese book of divination, for guidance. John Blofeld, a UN diplomat living in Thailand, had written many books on Asian spirituality, including a popular translation of the *I Ching.* On a whim, while I was passing through Bangkok, I phoned the UN office and asked for John Blofeld. By chance, he was there and answered his phone. I told him about the Hog Farm bus trip and our use of the *I Ching,* and he invited me to lunch. His office was filled with exquisite Buddhist and Taoist images that rivaled those in any temple. He was the first person I'd ever met who was pursuing a spiritual path while working in what looked like a conventional job in a political organization. I asked him why he stayed at the United Nations instead of devoting all his time to spiritual practice. "Because the UN—nations united—is the best hope for humankind," he said. When the countries involved in the mass killings of World War I and II looked around at the carnage, they gave up a little bit of sovereignty in forming this organization in order to prevent such genocides from happening again. "And if we fail to see the UN live up to its promise," Blofeld continued, "it is difficult to envision a world where humans live up to our potential."

As the adopted new puppy of the WHO smallpox team, I got teased a lot. The younger Indians never stopped singing "Dum Maro Dum" when they saw me. And every time Nicole introduced me to someone new, she added in a conspiratorial stage whisper, "You know, his *guru* told him to come and work for WHO."

Invariably a scientist would ask me, "So if your guru told you to tie your shoes with green laces, would you?"

"Yes."

"Would you jump off the top of the Red Fort if he asked you to?"

"Yes, but he wouldn't ask me."

"But what if he did?"

"He wouldn't ask me to do anything to hurt myself."

"But if he *did* ask, would you jump?"

I started off with a sense of humor about this, but like all such taunting, it grew tedious. After all, we had bigger problems.

More than three-quarters of the smallpox deaths and cases in the world were now in the four countries on the subcontinent: Nepal, Bangladesh, Pakistan, and India. As the largest and most complex country on that list, India was the cause for most concern. But because Prime Minister Gandhi was focused almost exclusively on India's crippling poverty and near-disastrous population explosion—as she should have been—she did not support the transfer of resources from birth control and maternity and child health care to the smallpox eradication program. All across India billboards featured her smiling face with the headline "Two or three, that's enough," to encourage family planning. Sometime while I was in India I remember seeing a billboard with a document called the Twenty Point Programme, India's list of priorities. Building new roads, providing health for all, supporting women's rights, improving life in slums, and protecting the environment were among them. Although smallpox in India was on the top of the world's worry list, it was not on India's list at all.

There was good reason that smallpox eradication remained a global priority. The numbers of people killed during the twentieth century alone is staggering when compared to even the worst tragedies and atrocities of that century. World War I, the deadliest conflict in human history up to that time, was ended by the 1918 Spanish flu pandemic that claimed 50 million lives. World War II, whose conflicts and genocides nearly brought humanity to its knees, took 60 million lives. The Armenian genocide took 1.5 million, and the Cambodian, 4 million lives. Add to those figures the 20 million deaths during the Soviet and communist Chinese revolutions, and the war in the Congo Free State, and you have between 150 and 200 million deaths resulting from all the war, genocide, and disease in the twentieth century alone. That's roughly two-thirds the population of the United States.

Yet those 200 million deaths amount to less than half of the deaths caused by *Variola major,* the deadly form of smallpox. Between 1900 and 1980, smallpox killed half a billion people. Try to imagine anything else that could have killed 500 million in such a short period of time. We forget that over the course of humanity's ten-thousand-year history before vaccination, many human beings came into contact with smallpox, and it killed one of every three who contracted the disease.

Smallpox is a horrible disease and terrifying death. Small red bumps, accompanied by a fever, appear on the hands, feet, and face. They spread across the entire body both inside and outside, turning into painful, oozing pustules. They line the esophagus, turning even a sip of water into torture. They form on every organ, inside the colon, the mouth, the vagina, and in many cases the eyes, often leaving—if you are lucky enough to survive—blindness in its wake. Hemorrhagic smallpox, the worst form of the disease, has a cruel predilection for killing pregnant women. The victim will bleed from every orifice. It is fatal every time.

Smallpox might have been the plague of boils visited upon Pharaoh in the book of Exodus, and perhaps the cause of Job's lesions. Based on an estimate of the percentage of ordinary people with smallpox scars in the Middle East around the time of Jesus, some academics speculate that one-third of Jesus's twelve disciples had smallpox scars on their faces. As recently as the twentieth century no Indian mother would allow a daughter to marry a man who did not have scars on his face, because they signified that he had survived an infection. If the husband-to-be wasn't immune before marriage, contracted smallpox later and died, his wife might have to commit suicide, given the old Hindu tradition of *sati*.

In any effort to rid the world of a disease there is likely to be conflict between global priorities and the national needs of sovereign states. Indian priorities put the country on a collision course with the more than 150 countries that had already eradicated smallpox, making sanctions or even international quarantine a possibility. While Prime Minister Gandhi would have gladly settled for allocating modest resources to control smallpox, she was not willing to divert the massive resources called for by an eradication program, even if the long-term benefit outweighed the short-term costs.

Some skeptics believed that eradicating smallpox would increase the population explosion in India. But data show that though saving children's lives might increase population in the short term, in the long term, it is the single greatest determinant in population reduction. Parents decide how large their family will be on the basis of how many of their children are likely to survive into adulthood. National vaccination programs help parents opt to have smaller families, leading to lower population growth and fostering a robust society, because if you vaccinate a child, he or she will likely live into adulthood. This is known as the "child survival paradox"—that preventing childhood deaths, after a short lag, leads to an overall reduction in population. In Bangladesh and in parts of the Indian state of Bihar, 50 percent of kids were dying before age five. Parents who lost a sibling while they were themselves children are likely to produce more offspring, giving birth to twice as many children, so that they end up with enough children to work the family farm or contribute to services that might help the family earn a livable wage. As parents see their children survive longer, however, they no longer need to plan for replacement births.

When I first arrived in India, smallpox was still killing hundreds of thousands of Indians in a year. While that seems like an incomprehensible number, it did not seem so large to a planner in the Indian Health Ministry, who also had to consider that diarrhea, malaria, and respiratory disease each killed one million, mostly children, every year.

Add to this the fact that production of the vaccine, manufactured in India under WHO supervision, killed cows, a sacred animal in India, in the process. The vaccine or cowpox virus was implanted onto the belly of a cow and allowed to grow. Then the cow was sacrificed in order to harvest the vaccine. For Hindus, the gentle cow is the symbol of abundance and selfless giving. Killing cows, even in pursuit of a vaccine that could save millions of children, was too much for many Indians to consider.

The moment on May 14, 1796, that Edward Jenner injected the pus from a milkmaid's cowpox-infected fingers into the skin of his gardener's son was one of both inspiration and madness. The idea that that this process would someday stop a powerful plague from ravaging humankind seemed impossible. The inspiration for such inconceivable leaps of imagination is a sacred act. There are many such moments in public health—John Snow, the father of epidemiology, made the leap of imagination that connected one contaminated reservoir to the spread of cholera through London in 1854. He was seen as a radical for demanding the city government turn off a famous, trusted water supply, the Broad Street pump. Or when Bill Foege, short on supplies in Africa, realized that "ring containment"—selectively vaccinating those at greatest risk, in closest proximity to an outbreak, would be a more effective strategy for eradicating smallpox than mass vaccination. The very word *inspiration* means "to inhale the spirit." We think it means to inhale air, but *spiros* means spirit. When you die, you exhale *spiros,* or expire. I think of great moments in science—such as when we figured out that injecting children with a small amount of cowpox immunizes them against smallpox—as being intertwined with great moments of faith. I don't see how most truly profound scientists could ever believe that the things he or she studies could exist in the absence of intelligent design. At the same time, I find it hard to understand how any person of faith could believe that God can be diminished by the study of this glorious plan and design. Even Einstein himself believed both in an intelligent Creator and the approach of science as a method for unraveling the code of a master planner.

For the next few months, I worked as a clerk on weekdays at WHO. Girija and I would then drive from Delhi to Kainchi on Friday night, have Saturday and Sunday with Maharaji, and return Sunday night in time for me to go back to work on Monday. As a secretary, I had a stable and predictable schedule.

It was the best of all worlds—every day I inhaled reams of information about smallpox, epidemiology, how the Indian government worked, how the UN system worked, what treaties meant, and much more about public health. I typed up letters from Nicole to D.A., made *aide memoires* or notes to the record for each visit a WHO medical officer made to Burma or Indonesia or Nepal. I worked with the four other secretaries, all local Indians—Malhotre, Malik, Gupta, and Prem Gambhiri—to do the filing and bring supplies up to the SEARO team. I sat in most of the meetings on strategy and got to know the Indian counterparts, especially M. I. D. Sharma and R. N. Basu, who was the assistant director general of health services.

On the weekends, Maharaji exchanged ideas with me and Girija almost as if he were more consultant or coach than guru. "What are your colleagues like?" Maharaji asked me. "Do they believe in God? Why are they working so hard to stop suffering if they are not doing it for God?"

I told him about how Nicole Grasset was intensely devoted to her work but didn't talk about God. Bill Foege, an American who had been a missionary doctor in Africa and who helped devise our strategy, was motivated by a deep Christian faith. The Czech epidemiologist Zdeno Jezek was propelled by ideals of what we would call secular humanism. I could barely contain my admiration for these people. "But most of all," I told Maharaji, "I admire my Indian colleagues who have sacrificed time with family to work alongside us with so much generosity, warmth, and dedication."

Over the following weekends, Maharaji delighted in talking about the program's progress. I cannot understand how he knew about the seasonality of the disease, the mythology about the smallpox goddess Shitala Ma, the way smallpox is transmitted by breathing, how the disease clusters in certain Indian communities. But he always reminded us that beyond the science and logistics, behind the personalities of the smallpox warriors and the program management, was the purity of our motivation, which would make us worthy to do God's work. "Abraham Lincoln was the greatest president," Maharaji once said, "because he knew that the real president was Christ." My memories of those weekend conversations remain with me as lodestars for my life.

I spent most of my time at the SEARO office putting together the documents for what would become the Indian Smallpox Campaign. A search of all the municipal areas would begin in August 1973, followed the next few months by a door-to-door search of all houses in the highly endemic areas. After that, monthly searches throughout the country—"All-India Searches"—would begin, during which our teams would visit half a million villages, knocking on 150 million doors, making more than 2 billion house calls over the course of twenty months. But the search could only begin after Prime Minister Gandhi approved the full plan, which we hoped would happen any day.

One of the keys to the plan required pairing a foreign WHO epidemiologist with an Indian doctor counterpart in every single district of the badly infected states. It was easier to recruit Indians than foreign doctors. Dr. Muni Inder Dev Sharma, whose name combined the god Indra and a worldly sage, universally called M.I.D., was a tireless, grandfatherly epidemiologist who had headed the national malaria program. He now led the Indian National Institute of Communicable Diseases (NICD), and he had the idea of bringing back to work the older epidemiologists who had been forced into retirement at age fifty-seven, the age

CHAPTER 11

Escape from Central Prison

Faith is not a belief. Faith is what is left when
your beliefs have all been blown to hell.

—Ram Dass

The Central Team gathered Monday morning at WHO. D.A.
and Isao Arita came in from headquarters in Geneva. Zdeno
Jezek was back from South India. Bill returned from Lucknow.
Nicole brought our Indian counterparts, M.I.D., Dutta, Basu, and
the others, into the meeting room behind Mrs. Boyer's reception
desk. Everyone was studying the results of the urban searches, and
the first early case reports from West Bengal.

Smallpox had been surging; there were already forty-three
thousand cases reported and many believed that at least that
number were still hidden. More than one-third of all the world's
smallpox was in India. Tens of thousands of health workers
were brought in from every government department. The family planning, malaria, maternal and child, sanitary workers, and

junior doctors needed to be trained and carefully placed into the structure of the campaign. The largest peacetime "army" of health workers was assembling.

My job was primarily clerical: to draw up papers for the delegation of staff and to create the training manuals for the hundreds of foreign doctors we expected to arrive. After training the foreign doctors, I would get my first field assignment, to organize the search in the district where I saw my first cases of smallpox. The campaign was shifting into high gear. It had been a very long Monday. I left the office at midnight.

At 4 A.M. Tuesday I was awoken by a pounding on the door of our *barsatti*. It was the first time since we moved to Delhi that anyone had visited our tiny rooftop apartment. I staggered out of bed and saw an older Indian man I did not recognize. He looked like the night watchman.

"He is no more," the man said softly when I opened the door. "He is no more."

"What?" I think I said. "What?"

"Neem Karoli Baba is no more," he repeated.

I recognized him now. He was the driver for R. P. Vaish, a devotee of Maharaji, who was the general manager of Delhi Transport Corporation, the city bus system. When I began working at WHO, Vaish had been one of several Indian families that helped orient us.

"Who?" I continued. "Do you mean Maharaji? Has he left Kainchi?"

"He is gone, *mahasamadhi*," he said.

Mahasamadhi. The words mean "great enlightenment," but it is also a euphemism for death. The death of a great saint, the finality of the physical presence of an enlightened soul for whom there could be no finality was too much weight for a common word like "death" to carry.

I stood there talking a bunch of nonsense, asking over and over, "What do you mean Maharaji's no more? Do you mean he is not in Kainchi? He's moved?" When it hit me, I doubled over. The guru, my gateway to God, was supposed to be forever—not like my father and grandfather, who had died and left me. The center of our lives was gone.

Girija heard us and woke up. I could barely get the words out. "He says Maharaji has died."

Her body heaved. We held each other tightly. I thought back to the double rainbow that had reassured us after the weird night at Kainchi. It had been a lie. We looked at each other with empty and dejected eyes. Girija and I threw on some clothes and walked like zombies down the many flights of steps to the car. Only when we got into the car, where Vaish and his wife were waiting to take us to Vrindavan, did it really hit me. This was real; Maharaji was gone, dead. This wasn't one of his jokes.

Vaish was told that Maharaji had collapsed at the Mathura train station, perhaps from a heart attack. His translator Ravi Khanna and several bystanders got Maharaji into a taxi to Ramakrishna Hospital, where he died. His body had already been moved to the Vrindavan ashram. Despite his own grief, Vaish had driven out of his way to collect Girija and me. Intimate with death in a way we are not in the West, Indians have another gear for kindness in the face of loss.

The ride was silent except for our sobs, each of us alone with our thoughts. The sun was just beginning to rise when we reached Vrindavan. The car eased into the gate of the Hanuman Temple. The bright rays of the morning sun lit up the ashram like spotlights shining on an empty stage. No one had yet arrived on the buses coming down the mountains from Kainchi.

Maharaji's body, covered by a thin white sheet, lay on blocks of ice. Girija and I held each other while we stumbled across the same courtyard where he used to give darshan. Now, his body lay alone. Bright yellow marigolds lay on his chest, a garland around his neck. He looked serene, beautiful, dead. I sat on a block of ice and cried like a baby, harder than I ever thought possible.

Ravi told us that Maharaji's last words before he died were, "Jaya jagadish hare," Hail to the lord of the universe. The ashram was in mourning; everyone had blank stares and dead eyes. It was also in chaos; no one was in charge. The widows, called "the Mothers," who were always with Maharaji—attending to him, learning from him, caring for him, always dressed in white—hadn't arrived yet from Kainchi. His close devotee Professor Dada Mukerjee hadn't arrived from Allahabad.

With the sun reaching higher came more heat, and then the flies. For six hours, Girija and I stood, or leaned, or sat on blocks of ice, fanning flies away from our guru's body. I loved him so much, neither more nor less in death as in life. I thought of him neither more nor less Godlike, even with flies buzzing around his face, still vibrant in death. Death is the final common pathway of all flesh, as the Buddha taught, even for the holy ones. Sacred or secular, we take birth alone in blood and pain, and we exit in much the same way.

As the ice blocks melted, we replaced them. Bit by bit we stopped crying, sadness replaced with emptiness, sorrow with devotion, fear with duty. Eventually, the buses carrying Indian and Western disciples arrived from Kainchi. I tried to get myself together to help the newcomers who got off the bus in disbelief and moved through confusion and sadness and helpless wailing just like Girija and I had only a few hours before. When Dwarkanath and Ravi Das (Michael Jeffery) got off the bus, they looked into our eyes hoping to find something there that would tell them it was all one of Maharaji's long-distance jokes, a way to get everyone from all the ashrams together in one place. We kept asking one another, "Do you understand this? Do you know what to do next? Do you know what it means?"

When the Mothers arrived, their grief was physical, flesh and blood, deep, personal, and so thick it filled the entire ashram. They rushed to his body, caressing and crying, wailing and moaning.

Too soon, a shouting match began between Kainchi hill people and Vrindavan plains people—loud, harsh, plaintive—over where to cremate Maharaji's body. Some wanted to cremate him in the sacred Yamuna River, a few hundred yards from the ashram; others wanted to take him to Benares. Villagers and devotees flooded the ashram, each adding to the argument. Then a large entourage of yogis and pundits poured through the ashram gate in a disciplined single file. "You fools," Pugal Baba shouted when he arrived at the head of the line. He held up his hand to halt mourners who had been getting ready to move Maharaji's body. He was a venerated local saint and yogi whom Maharaji had loved.

"Stop it! You do not understand who he was—and you have no authority. A normal mortal, yes, when they die, you take them to the river ghats for cremation because the holiness of the river will sanctify and bless their bodies. This is no normal mortal. He was not a man! You don't know who he was. He was like God. You don't sanctify him by taking him to the river. If you burn him by the Ganges, his body will sanctify the Ganges. If you burn him by the Yamuna, his body will sanctify the Yamuna. Burn him here in the ashram, where people can visit. And then build a temple over the site of the cremation."

Pugal Baba settled the matter and ceremonial arrangements were quickly made. Brahmins and ashramites placed the body of Neem Karoli Baba onto a bier. He was wrapped in a simple white dhoti and covered with flowers. It seemed as if the entire city, already filled with thousands of widows who had come to serve Krishna, waiting to die among Vrindavan's sacred shrines, had been affected by an atmospheric change. The air was twinkly; it smelled different. Colors were more vivid. The heat made everything shimmer, the edges of objects blending into each other like a Monet painting. People and conversations moved in slow motion and seemed to be deeper, more meaningful, heavier with import. We held our breath. In each encounter, we would freeze the frame, expand, and share the moment so intimately that we were inside of each other. Everything opened, especially our hearts.

Vrindavan came to a halt. There was no commerce, no school, no city services. The ceremony began, transforming pain and loss into gratitude. Hundreds walked alongside the processional or followed in vehicles. Along the route peacocks released their strangely beguiling calls. Girija and I followed just behind Maharaji's bier, which was covered with red and yellow silk, secured by four posts on top of an improbable red 1955 Chevy station wagon with wood side panels. Any American car in Vrindavan would have been odd, but this one, for us at least, became part of Maharaji's legend. When we caught up to the vehicle, moving slowly through the winding narrow streets, we saw full-color stickers of Donald Duck, Mickey Mouse, and Minnie Mouse on its bumper. It was Donald Duck that floored me. From the moment we had met Wavy Gravy and joined the Hog Farm, whenever anyone died, Wavy would say, "Good grief," like Charlie Brown, and then add, "Death is Donald Duck," which made as much sense as death itself.

It was a little uncomfortable, a little magical, and very, very weird that our guru's corpse lay on top of that old Chevy plastered with Donald Duck decals. It was the only American car with Disney decals I would ever see in India. Maybe it meant everything. Maybe it meant nothing. We were in such an altered state of reality, nothing surprised us, nothing frightened us, nothing made us happy.

Jai, jai, jai, Neem Karoli Baba"—Hail, hail, hail, Neem Karoli Baba—or sometimes "One hundred and eight times honored is Neem Karoli Baba" echoed through the narrow caverns created by the ancient buildings lining the medieval streets. The traditional local greetings *Raday Sham* and *Jai Radha,* hail to the dark one, Krishna, the dusky blue-colored god, rang out. Victory to Krishna and his consort Radha, the goddess of the *gopis,* the milkmaids.

We followed the Chevy to, how could it not be, the levee, the ghats, the banks of the Yamuna River, through the Krishna peacock gardens, through the streets filled with ancient temples, and to Banki Bihari Temple where Maharaji loved to send Westerners to visit. We made a *parikrama,* a circumambulation of Vrindavan, and turned toward Maharaji's Hanuman Temple.

When the processional returned, the ashram was swollen beyond capacity. Brahmins, *pujaris,* and sadhus chanted Sanskrit prayers and mantras. There was a fire pit and a worship service for the fire god Agni, with pundits pouring ghee into the pit, raising the flames, bellowing "Swaha! Swaha!" So be it! So be it!

Maharaji's body was lifted onto an eight-foot-long pile of kindling and logs. It was covered with ghee. The cremation fire was set alight underneath him with a long stick wrapped in cotton cloth soaked in ghee. The torch was laid on top of the logs by someone I'd never seen; I was told his name was Dharm Narayan.

Maharaji's body burned for several hours while the fire puja was performed. When only the outline of a skeleton remained, Dharm Narayan picked up a long thick stick, light enough to lift but heavy enough to deliver a strong blow. He swung it overhead and brought it down hard, cracking open Maharaji's burnt skull, liberating his sacred soul from *maya,* the illusory cycle of birth and death, freeing him to merge into Brahma, the great consciousness of existence, the great mystery.

The sound of the stick cracking Maharaji's skull magnified the drugless psychedelic experience. The ceremony ended, my guru's remains smoldered. Although he had escaped from central prison, Girija and I and all the others who loved this man, cherished him, believed in him, depended on him, we all fell back to our earthly jails.

For the next two days, people stayed around the fire, crying, hugging, drinking tea, and, later, walking around the town, heading to bed if they had one or sleeping anywhere they could find a spot. Others were still arriving after hearing the news late.

When a new member of the satsang arrived to find out it was true that Maharaji had been cremated, each of us who was there relived the experience all over again.

The morning after the cremation, Girija and I woke, both still in a fog, and walked the short distance to the ashram to be sure the ashes had cooled. We filled a silver urn with many of his ashes. We did not know whether that was okay, but we wanted to keep him with us always. A saffron-robed sadhu with an eight-by-ten glass-framed photo of Maharaji dangling from his neck was walking around the smoldering bier softly saying prayers.

"Where do you come from?" we asked him.

"Akbarpur, where Maharaji and his children come from."

Children? It had never occurred to us that Maharaji had children. I don't think I had ever thought about it; I had assumed he was a celibate saint.

"You saw his son performing the ceremony to release his soul yesterday, when he cracked Maharaji's skull," the sadhu, Madrassi Baba, said, as we tried to comprehend this new set of facts. "He went back home to Agra."

"What?"

"Yes, one son, Dharm Narayan, lives in Agra and another, A. S. Sharma, lives in Bhopal. Go to Nib Karori station and ask around. It's the same station where Maharaji performed the first big miracle."

What miracle?

Maharaji's birth name was Laxshmi-Narayan Sharma. When he was young, during the Raj, he was on his way home when a British constable stopped his train at Nib Karori and ordered all

Indians to disembark. But Laxshmi-Narayan wouldn't budge. The police forcibly removed him. "Start the train," they said to the train's engineer once all the Indians were off the train. But it would not move. The engineers could find nothing wrong with the engine, and nothing the engineer tried could get it to move.

"Put me back on," Laxshmi-Narayan said. "Then it will go." After quite a bit of haggling, Laxshmi-Narayan returned to his seat and the train began to move. Thus he became known as Nib Karori Baba—or the "baba from the town of Nib Karori." Westerners bungled the pronunciation, calling him Neem Karoli Baba.

Girija and I decided we needed to go to Nib Karori to explore this mystery. We crowded into a taxi with four other Westerners. At the Nib Karori train station, we found many Indians with Maharaji's photo around their necks, wandering around with the same vacant eyes we had seen at the ashram. Some had shaved their heads, a sign of mourning. They guided us to the cave where we were told Maharaji had meditated for seven years. A Hanuman image seemed to emerge from the back of it. Locals invited us to see the tree near where he had lived and the temple where he had prayed. A man at a small kiosk was selling photos of a young Laxshmi-Narayan Sharma before he became Maharaji, photos that we had never seen. We bought them all to give to our friends at the ashram. At the tree a young man with a shaved head sat with one of the huge framed photos of Maharaji hanging from his neck. I asked in Hindi whether he knew the directions to the village where Maharaji had been born. Of course he did, and he jumped into our already crowded taxi and guided the driver the half hour to Akbarpur.

We walked up to the house where our new friend said that Maharaji had been born. His father had been wealthy—the house was made of brick, unlike the rest of the adobe homes in the city. Maharaji's father was known as the local *zamindar,* or "lord of the Earth"—he was a landlord and owned much of the farmland and the village itself. Maharaji grew up rich, but from childhood, he kept running away with the sadhus to sit with them at their fires listening to tales of mystical India. Trying to stop him, his parents married him off when he was still a child.

Thinking about Maharaji with a family was like imagining our own parents' primal scene. A young man sitting on the stoop saw us wandering and said, "You should meet his son in Agra." He joined us in the crowded taxi and guided the driver to an address in the center of that city.

Thus one day after the cremation, still in dismay, still in the same clothes we had left Delhi wearing forty-eight hours before, we pulled up to a house in Agra and knocked on the door. Three men, Maharaji's two sons and a grandson, looking like younger versions of him, each with a freshly shaved head, appeared at the door. Dharm Narayan recognized us from the cremation and welcomed us inside for tea. A woman rushed by, quickly covering her face with her sari. "That's Maharaji's wife and my mother," Dharm Narayan said. His brother, A. S. Sharma, added, "You have found us on this important day. Now you are part of our family, of Maharaji's family." After tears and tea, the elder son, A. S. Sharma said, "You are welcome to visit my son Dhananjay, Maharaji's grandson, and my family in Madhya Pradesh. We live in the capital city of Bhopal. Also, if you get to Dhanbad in the state of Bihar, please visit my sister Girija. That's where she lives."

Girija. Maharaji had named his daughter Girija. So casually revealed. My own beloved Girija burst into tears, overwhelmed that Maharaji had given her the same name as his own daughter by birth.

"Don't tell anyone about the family," Vaish advised the six of us when we returned to Vrindavan. Later that day the Barmans said the same thing. It was a secret that distanced those of us who had been in that taxi from the rest of the satsang for a while.

I have no idea where Maharaji fits on the hierarchy of angels and gurus and saints and mystics. It does not matter. He was more than enough for me, high enough for me, close enough to heaven for me, wise enough for me. He was my gateway to God. And he was so completely different from the rest of us. He had no personal possessions. He didn't care about what he wore or what he ate or where he slept or how he looked. He never talked about his accomplishments or powers. He seemed unaffected by the highs and lows of daily events. He was different from the rest of us in almost every way, except in death, in which we are all the same. Maharaji, Jesus and Mary, Mother Teresa, Buddha, Moses, Muhammad—all of these amazing beings—my father, my grandfather, and your mother and your grandmother each left or will leave behind a corpse around which flies will buzz in the heat. But while Maharaji's death and the pilgrimage to his family taught us more about his life, his corpse underscored Buddha's teaching of the truth of suffering and death.

One more lesson for me was to separate out the inevitable from the impossible. Even while knowing death and suffering are inevitable, many kinds of suffering could be ended. And while death itself was unavoidable, there was nothing at all unavoidable about death from smallpox. That could be pulled out by the roots, *unmulan,* eradicated.

My duty could not have been clearer.

I had come back to India to be "spiritual," thinking it was the next step after "radical political" and "countercultural." I thought it meant meditating, fasting, living in an ashram, and retreating from the world. Maharaji had shown me that my spiritual path, my dharma—no better than anyone else's destiny, no more or less exalted, no easier or more difficult, noble or venal— was to reach for God through karma yoga, doing good deeds without attachment. Mahatma Gandhi, in a conversation with his disciples about what constituted good deeds that would bring them closer to God, had said, "I will give you a talisman. Whenever you are in doubt, or when the self becomes too much with you, apply the following test. Recall the face of the poorest and the weakest man whom you may have seen, and ask yourself if the step you contemplate is going to be of any use to him. Will he gain anything by it?"

Now that I had been to villages with smallpox, it was clear to me that nearly all the rich people were vaccinated, but the poor were not; that the scars of smallpox were not on the faces of the rich, but on those of the poorest and most oppressed, who lived on the margins, in the shadows, the lowest classes, the lowest castes, the outcasts.

Eradicating smallpox would be consistent with Gandhi's talisman, with my adolescent search for the greatest good, the summum bonum, with Christ's Golden Rule, with the Jewish admonition of *tikkun olam,* to heal the broken world, and exactly what Neem Karoli Baba had told me to do.

Tomorrow I would go back to work.

CHAPTER 12

After-Death Experience

Lord, make me an instrument of Your peace. Where there
is hatred, let me sow love; where there is injury, pardon;
where there is doubt, faith; where there is despair, hope;
where there is darkness, light; where there is sadness, joy.

—St. Francis

L et's drop the rest of the leaflets on the roof of the WHO
building!" I yelled to the pilot over the high-pitched whine
of the plane's propellers. "Isn't that it right there?" It was two
months after Maharaji had died, Thanksgiving Day back in
the United States. We had taken off in the two-seater Cessna
that late November morning from Safdarjung airport in New
Delhi to fly thirty minutes northwest to drop leaflets on Meerut
in Uttar Pradesh. On the leaflets were a photo of a small Indian child with active smallpox lesions on his face, instructions
on where to report any case of the disease, and the amount of
the reward for reporting a new case. Just ahead was what looked
like the WHO office. *Yes, that had to be it.* Below was the bellowing smoke from the coal-fired power plant across the street. Just
to the south were mounds of refuse from the city's largest slum,

the rag pickers' *basti;* the smell of methane gas wafted up from the garbage heaps.

"Are you sure?" the pilot asked me with apprehension in his voice.

"Yes, I'm sure. We have to!"

"Won't you get into trouble if we do this?" the pilot asked.

If God did not want me to drop leaflets on WHO headquarters, why would he have located the WHO office right underneath our flight path? It was like saying to a hungry kid, "Don't eat this chocolate." As we had been doing all day in Meerut, we dropped the leaflets. I was proud of how effective the leaflets were and in defiant exuberance wanted everyone at headquarters to get a taste, especially those who had been so dubious of the efforts we were making.

The plane landed and I went immediately by taxi to the WHO office. I was late for a meeting with Nicole, but I was sure she would understand.

"Get upstairs quickly, Larry," Nicole said as soon as I walked in the door. "Gunaratne is going to have your head."

"What on earth were you thinking?" he bellowed the minute I got to the top floor. "Did you really do this? Fly in a plane? Over Indian airspace? Drop leaflets? On WHO?"

"Yes, I did, Dr. Gunaratne," I admitted. Suddenly it seemed like a very bad idea, and I didn't feel so, um, brilliant. But I was full of emotion. "I don't know what possessed me. You may think it's insane . . ." Gunaratne tried to interrupt me but I had a head full of steam, and although much time has passed, I think I said something like this: ". . . but you should see the faces of the parents as they watch their kids die in agony from a disease we can so easily prevent! Every other day a mother hands me a dead child asking me for a miracle because I have a WHO logo, a UN seal, on the door of my jeep. We can eradicate smallpox, but we are losing the battle. I don't know much about WHO, but I do know that in India most smallpox cases are still hidden from our workers. The smallpox team—both Indian and WHO—know that people are afraid to report cases to doctors because they fear getting punished or because they think Variola is a goddess or because they fear bad karma from a vaccine made by killing cows. But we found a way to get nearly all the cases reported: a small reward of only five rupees, less than twenty-five cents, recognition cards, and parades with elephants to bring out the children so that we can find the hidden cases. The district magistrates, the civil surgeons, everyone was so excited to see dozens, even hundreds of children coming out from their homes for the parade and the reward. We had an explosion of reports. Elephants worked. Parades worked. So I thought dropping leaflets from a plane would be even more effective!"

Gunaratne steamed. "Don't preach to me, young man!" Clouds as dark as the coal smoke across the street seemed to fill the room. He had a red pen in his hand—he was the only one at WHO allowed to wield a red pen; this way everyone recognized his comments, and his directives, which were the final word.

"Do not preach to me. What are you, twenty-five years old? Oh! You are *much* older—twenty-*nine* years old. You are not even a full staff member. You got into WHO because Dr. Grasset said you would just be a temporary clerk." He glared at Nicole. "Give me your UN passport, Dr. Brilliant. I can make sure you will no longer be burdened by the WHO logo on a jeep. You are barely a doctor. You could face serious charges for using UN money to drop propaganda posters on sovereign Indian land, let alone on the WHO building."

"This is ridiculous, Larry," Nicole said, pretending to be mad at me, but fighting back a giggle. "We have protocols. We know the protocols are going to work. You should follow them. Don't take this upon yourself."

We should have gone through our Indian counterparts, but at that point I hadn't yet been assigned one from the national government, so I had gone directly to the local magistrates. Ramesh Agrawal, the district magistrate I'd met on my first day in the field in Meerut, had mentioned that his brother was a member of the Delhi Flying Club and could get us a plane for distributing leaflets. He got permission from his superior, the divisional commissioner, and asked the Rotary and Lions clubs to kick in some money. They helped fund printing leaflets, hiring elephants, and, in this case, hiring a plane.

Nicole was hardly a timid bureaucrat, given her previous violation of a no-fly zone to get desperately needed vaccines to starving children in Biafra. She always said it was easier to deal with God than with his angels, and easier to seek forgiveness than permission.

Gunaratne held a crumpled red leaflet in his fist. He didn't care about the leaflets or the reward they promised. He was only concerned that he was about to get a phone call from a minister's office about an American flying in Indian airspace without permission and that in retaliation the Indian government would censure WHO, or worse, shut down the entire smallpox program.

"*Who* authorized *you* to spend WHO money on *this*?" Gunaratne demanded.

"Wait a minute. Wait a minute. Okay, I went too far, but not a penny of WHO money paid for the flight or the leaflets. Not a single penny. And of course the government approved. All of it was entirely authorized and paid for by Indian authorities. It was paid for by the district magistrate and commissioner! The district magistrate raised the money from his own budget and from local clubs. And the minister of civil aviation knows all about it. I have all the paperwork!"

"I don't believe you. You have five minutes. Go get the government order, bring it to me. Show it to me. Prove it to me! And," he thundered, "bring me your passport."

I raced down one flight of steps to our office on the fifth floor of the SEARO building to the desk of Mahesh Gupta, one of the Indian secretaries in the smallpox unit. A month before, I had been sitting beside him working as an administrative assistant. Now I was shaking. Forget about any equanimity I had learned through meditation. All I could think about was that I might have endangered the entire program. They had given me a chance to prove I could be an epidemiologist, and I had let it go to my head.

Mahesh Gupta quickly pulled out the file marked "Meerut special campaign" with all my papers: *There was my expense report, and the report I dropped off at the office a couple of days ago, and thank God, thank God, it was all there.* Correspondence, invoices, and official orders between the Delhi Flying Club and the six district magistrates of Meerut district, confirmations from the district magistrate of Saharanpur, Moradabad, and Dehradun, and the commissioner of Meerut district. I was so grateful for the obsessive compulsive filing system Nicole had set up for the smallpox program. Included in the file were signed minutes to a meeting chaired by the Indian minister of health of Uttar Pradesh, agreeing to the elephants and leaflets, as well as my letter to all the magistrates with a calculation of how much each district's share would be for the airplane rental, and their return letters with the roughly 500 rupees each as their share to the Delhi Flying Club.

"Look at this, Dr. Gunaratne." I was out of breath and shaking as I handed him the operational plan. "And here's the map of the approved flight plan and government approval for the leaflet and the reward."

Nicole arched a Gallic eyebrow. She knew I was tap dancing. I was showing that no WHO money had been spent, not that the Government of India had approved the flights. Nothing, nothing, nothing in these papers authorized the dropping of leaflets on the WHO office. That was so far out of bounds. She liked my speech, and my passion, but she and the smallpox program needed Dr. Gunaratne's support—or at least his acquiescence—in every part of the program. I had dropped leaflets on what he considered his house and had embarrassed him, a bellicose but big-hearted man.

"Dr. Gunaratne," she said, "he didn't use WHO money, you see that. Yes, he was out of bounds. Blame it on his youth, if you will, but if we don't hear a complaint from the Indian government, can we let sleeping dogs lie, be charitable, and call this a never-to-be-repeated dumb bit of youthful enthusiasm?"

"It won't happen again, I promise," I added.

Gunaratne moved from the table to his large desk, took out his red pen, circled the names and titles of the government officials, and compared the bill from the Delhi Flying Club with payments from the local governments. He noted that the one letter had only been cc'd to the minister of civil aviation, not actually signed off by his office. There was no proof that he had authorized the flight. At the same time, he saw that the flight had been approved by government officers, albeit minor ones, and that no WHO money had been used in the exercise. And while he also knew that only someone much higher up in the central government should have approved the interstate flight, I could see his wheels spinning: jurisdiction between the local government and the national government was complicated. Better to bury the infraction than to put WHO in the middle of a dispute between local and national governments.

He did not ask for my blue passport again.

It was stupid, but not fatal—this time.

"Rein him in, Madam! Rein him in, Dr. Grasset," he bellowed. "Rein him in," he repeated as we quietly backed out of his office.

Nicole and I walked down the stairs to the smallpox offices. She took me into her office, closed the door behind us, lit up a cigarette, put her back against the door, and inhaled deeply, giving me a look that was somewhere between an angry boss and a loving big sister. She wasn't thrilled with having to use one of her precious chips to get me out of hot water, but she loved having teams in the field trying new things, even pushing the envelope.

"You have no idea how lucky you are. Don't tell anyone, no one, no one," she cautioned. "Do not let anyone in WHO know what just happened. Do not let anyone know you saw Gunaratne soften. He would crack down harder than you can imagine if he thought you were telling people you got away with murder. And you just did. So do not—*do not*—ever do anything like this again."

Nicole and I never spoke of the incident again. But the Indian staff members in the WHO office gossiped about it and chided me. The driver who took me home that night held up one of the leaflets. He waved it at me and sang, "Dum Maro Dum." He thought I must have been smoking something to buzz the WHO building. I had not, and I did not smoke anything that would cloud my judgment from the time I joined WHO, but it was certainly understandable to think I might have because of the movie. The leaflets were important. Dropping them on WHO was dumb. But the use of leaflets, rewards, elephants and parades was important.

I had returned to work two weeks after Maharaji's death, in late September, as the first searches of the hyperendemic areas were being planned, three in all, one each in October, November, and December. Late autumn, just after the monsoon rains had damped down transmission. Peak season usually occurred in March, when the weather warms and migrant workers travel through India. We hoped that by going door-to-door to find hidden cases just after the monsoon rains were over we would find so few outbreaks that we could shut down the remnants with the search-and-containment strategy.

We had reason to be optimistic. More than 150 countries were now free of smallpox—and officials in those countries had employed the much less robust strategy of mass vaccination. South India was almost completely smallpox-free. Even Uttar Pradesh, one of the four hyperendemic states I was assigned to, reported only 345 cases the week before the search. This didn't seem overwhelming. The first search of the hyperendemic areas was scheduled for the middle of October, well within the low-transmission season. But no one could predict what would be found when 27,000 workers searched the 140,102 villages in the state. I was in Meerut district, out in the field with the search teams when the reports started rolling in.

Everyone then working in the smallpox program in SEARO remembers how quiet it was the morning of the first day. Around midday, Mrs. Boyer called up from the reception desk to Nicole to tell her that the first telegram of a report of smallpox had come in. Nicole and Bill raced down to the first floor to see what was happening. The telegram read: "SMALLPOX OUTBREAK IN VILLAGE RAMPUR, DISTRICT LUCKNOW, U.P. SEVEN CASES ONSET FIRST CASE AUGUST 21, LATEST CASE SEPTEMBER 30. CONTAINMENT IN PROGRESS." Seven cases did not seem so bad, but if the first case had been on August 21, and today was October 15, the outbreak had gone undetected for two months. Because the smallpox incubation period was about two weeks (seven to seventeen days), an outbreak that had gone undetected for eight weeks would have gone through four incubation periods, or four generations, growing exponentially. Since one case of smallpox might lead to three or four new cases, an outbreak might be expected to grow in eight weeks from 1 case to 4 to 16 to 64 to 256. And yet only seven new cases had been reported. The numbers didn't add up.

While Nicole puzzled over this discrepancy, she got another call from Mrs. Boyer. A mailroom employee had brought her a tea tray piled with telegrams. A few minutes later, the tea tray became baskets full of telegrams. This deluge was a devastating surprise that persisted over the next two weeks. When I returned to SEARO, Nicole had transformed her office into a control room. The maps on the walls were covered with pieces of thin white paper with numbers on them tracking outbreaks and cases, district by district, state by state. As Nicole tabulated the final numbers, she announced the first big shock.

During the October search in Uttar Pradesh alone, 5,989 cases of smallpox were discovered in 1,525 villages and urban areas. The disease was raging in nearly every district, a tenfold increase over what had been known before the search. This meant that 90 percent of smallpox cases had been unreported or hidden. Elsewhere the pattern was the same. In Bihar, there were 614 new outbreaks with 3,826 cases, and in Madhya Pradesh, 120 new outbreaks with 1,216 cases. Special containment teams had been created at block, district, and state levels, but the number of foci detected was levels of magnitude greater than anticipated.

One week of search had detected forty thousand new cases of smallpox—in the middle of the low season—nearly as many cases as had been reported for India for the first half of the year during the high season. WHO Geneva quickly put out a memo calling for an intensified campaign and declared that India had 90 percent of all the smallpox in the world.

The numbers revealed three troubling trends. First, the disease was being transmitted at a high rate in the poorest areas. Second, a very small percentage of the cases, about 10 percent, were being detected by India's regular surveillance network; the search, however great an improvement over mass vaccination, still wasn't good enough. And third, widespread resistance to reporting cases and vaccination still remained.

It also became clear that the three All-India Searches would never be enough. Nicole and Bill sent a telex to D.A. that we would need to extend the monthly house-to-house searches by at least one year, followed by two years of surveillance after the last case healed. That meant more money and more epidemiologists.

It meant the program would have to continue through the end of 1976.

The truth was out. The huge number of unreported and hidden cases of smallpox was news to everyone, but it had different meanings for different groups. People saw in the number what they wanted to. If China wanted a reason to quarantine India, it could say there was a raging epidemic and appeal to the United Nations; this was the concern at the top levels of government, as an epidemic like this could torpedo India's move onto the world stage as a responsible international player. A junior medical worker would be worried about being accused of having suppressed cases. Health-care division heads dealing with malaria and other diseases realized they were about to be forced to lend staff to smallpox, leaving them shorthanded.

Epidemiologists were pleased to see accurate and complete numbers reported for the first time ever in India. A smallpox epidemiologist could see from the peaks and valleys of the week-by-week reports that the huge increase during the week that a search was conducted, followed by three weeks without any cases reported, meant that they were seeing not an increase in outbreaks but an increase in cases *reported*. The *Times of India* and the *Indian Express,* however, did not make the important distinction between an epidemic of smallpox and a newly revealed epidemic of reports. While we had found ten times more smallpox than was known the week before, the increase was a result of better reporting because of the door-to-door searches. But the papers, which were mostly unfriendly to Prime Minister Indira Gandhi, printed stories that the smallpox epidemic was worsening, which put more pressure on Gandhi's already embattled administration. When the Indian public read the stories, they concluded that the government had failed. Skeptics like Dr. Jankowicz felt smug that the program wasn't working, confusing the increase in successful surveillance with a decrease in the containment of the epidemic.

The smallpox team remained optimistic: we had staffed up reasonably well, search teams had already visited more than 85 percent of the villages around India, and it was clear to us, at least, that the strategy of early detection and rapid containment could work.

We kept working state by state. In the meantime, Nicole and M.I.D. convened a meeting in Lucknow with the minister of health of Uttar Pradesh, as well as cabinet members and health department leaders. Akbar Ali Khan, the state's governor and Maharaji devotee, chaired the review session. The governor had become personally involved in smallpox—he and I had a shared secret: we both believed in Maharaji's prediction that smallpox would be *unmulan*.

This was my first state-level review meeting. All the foreign and national epidemiologists came, most staying at the upscale Clark's Hotel on the Gomti River. I stayed a couple hundred yards away in the Hanuman Temple, not far from Lucknow University. It was soothing to hear the sound of the harmonium and tabla, the singing of "Sri Ram, jai Ram" early in the morning, and to see all the photographs and testimonials to Neem Karoli Baba after his *mahasamadhi*.

The temple has a famous statue of Hanuman, Rama's most ardent devotee, ripping open his chest to reveal that Rama and Sita were inscribed in his heart.

Hanuman's commitment to Rama is a mixture of karma yoga and *bhakti,* service and devotion. When Rama's brother was poisoned during the battle with the demons and Hanuman was sent to retrieve the herbal antidote, he didn't hesitate to tear the mountain out of the ground and bring it to Rama, so that someone wiser could identify the life-saving plant. I thought about this Hanuman story during the meetings and at night in the Hanuman temple. I never believed that Maharaji could manipulate God or the activity of the Variola virus to cause the eradication of smallpox. I was then and am still a scientist; I try to make evidence-based decisions. But I do believe Maharaji keenly observed both human nature and the natural order of things. Maybe he was able to *see* trends, the nonlinear eddies and vortices of timelines that most of us can't see, to predict an end to a ten-thousand-year-old disease. I do not know. Maybe he tapped into a very old belief in Ayurveda, the ancient Indian system of medicine, that God provides a cure for every disease, a solution to every problem if only we have eyes to see. I don't know where he got his confidence that smallpox would be eradicated, but it was quite rare among mystics, priests, and gurus of that time to predict the future of public events, as it was reported that he did when he announced the Chinese would suddenly withdraw after invading India in 1962, and as he did when he proclaimed that smallpox would be *unmulan,* eradicated. I believe he drew on his ability to interpret probability to push things in the right direction. Wherever the information came from, Maharaji saw an opportunity to help, and he jumped on it. Ali Akbar Khan and I were two of his many willing soldiers.

I threw myself into the trenches, organizing searches around Meerut district, my division. Being closest to Delhi and still the rookie, I got lots of extra support from the SEARO office, and I tried to build up a model program that any international visitor could observe in a quick trip and see how successfully the strategy of search and rapid containment was knocking out smallpox.

Meerut district magistrate Ramesh Agrawal—who had first suggested we offer a reward for reporting smallpox and found elephants and airplanes for the program—had been promoted to commissioner overseeing the six districts I was in charge of. He was a true believer. He rounded up donations for the five-rupee (about half a dollar) reward, and the printing of the brochures in Hindi, Urdu, and English from the Rotary Club and other private sector organizations.

With Agrawal's suggestions and encouragement, we began to have smallpox awareness parades in every district. It was like the street theater of the Hog Farm. This time, with official permission, I used WHO funds to buy t-shirts, horns, and balloons to distribute to children as a way to show that vaccinations were nothing to be afraid of, that it was just part of growing up. Agrawal helped us get elephants for the parades, and once or twice I rode atop along with the *mahut* leading the procession, weaving through streets accompanied by musicians. I recruited local luminaries to walk along in the parade with us, respected citizens, and magistrates, Bollywood film stars, Rotary and Lions' Club leaders and especially religious leaders—Hindu gurus, Muslim imams, Jain munis, Sikh holy men, and the local Catholic missionaries. At Girija's suggestion, we continued searches at the sites parents were most likely to bring their smallpox-afflicted children—to Shitala Ma, the goddess of smallpox. As Bill showed me my first day in the field, if kids would come running to see the tallest man in the world, they would surely come running for elephants, t-shirts, balloons, and leaflets promising a reward.

The relationship between the WHO Central Team and the Indian counterparts, who were in effect our hosts in their country, was changing. We had gone well beyond official relationships to deep friendships. Often, Indian officials and their WHO counterparts would conspire to break both Indian and WHO rules. T. Steven Jones, a long-haired American epidemiologist trained at CDC, used his WHO expense account to feed people with smallpox who otherwise would have become beggars roaming the streets looking for food and spreading disease. He also used the money to pay watch guards who kept those afflicted isolated.

Years later, M.I.D. would attribute a lot of the success we had in smallpox to "rules and regulations—and the routine breaking of rules and regulations." My specialty was the routine breaking of rules part of this formula.

I have never in my life worked so hard and been so engaged, been so creative, or accomplished so much as during the smallpox days. Many of the smallpox warriors feel the same way about their time fighting smallpox. As the number of cases rose, as we saw the suffering, the dead and dying, the families consumed with grief, as it hit home over and over that eradication was the only way to prevent such suffering, we all fought together against a common enemy. Soviets and Americans ceased looking at each other as adversaries, and Indians and internationals from dozens of countries briefly merged into a single fighting unit. Boundaries collapsed, normally rigid rules and codes of conduct softened into grounds for improvisation, and collaboration became more creative than ever. We banded together the naysayers, the fearmongers, the luddites, the frightened politicians in government and the United Nations.

"To live is to choose," Nicole liked to quote the French aphorism. I chose smallpox. I lived smallpox, thought smallpox, ate, slept, and drank smallpox. I felt like I was doing God's work, and such intense focus mitigated, for the time being, the pain of Maharaji's death, a salve to heal the feeling of being abandoned. There was nothing I could do to bring Maharaji back, to restore the innocence Girija and I felt before he died. Beyond the pain of loss and confusion, I don't remember much. I thought about what my dad said shortly before he died: "I'm not afraid of dying, son. I'm just worried what will happen to you and your brother." After my father and grandfather died, I threw myself into medical school and the Movement. My brother and mother, less lucky than me, had more difficulty finding their way. Years later, in the hardest moments of my life, when my beloved son Jonathan died of cancer, and my heart was broken in a way I never want anyone else to think about let alone experience, I plunged back into work, badly this time, awkwardly, unconsciously, creating a terrible space for myself, in which I was incapable of helping anyone else. But, in India, I could focus on eradicating smallpox, saving other people's children, just as Maharaji said I would. It was karma yoga and psychotherapy all rolled into one.

I starting taking Girija with me everywhere, no matter that WHO forbade spouses from riding in official jeeps or going to meetings with government officials. Indian doctors liked meeting an American woman named after Shiva's wife, and her Hindi accent was much better than mine. Besides, most of the satsang had left India, and I did not want her to be alone in our tiny apartment after Maharaji had died. Being on the road again together reminded us of our journey east on the Hog Farm buses, but this was hard work, every day. We lived like hippies out of my jeep; we slept there sometimes or we stayed in temples, *dharamshalas,* or government hostels, *dak,* bungalows made of cinder blocks. They looked like prison cells but were many times better than the mud huts scattered across India. They at least usually had electricity and running water.

Most of the time, when I entered a new town I went straight to meet the civil surgeon or medical officer. The minute I started talking about smallpox, the Indian official's eyes would glaze over and he would politely usher me out of the office. I attached a huge picture of Maharaji to the windshield of my jeep, yet another thing I wasn't supposed to do. But when these Indian doctors noticed his picture, they would ask, in that very Indian way, "Who is this guru, and who is he to you?" I would tell them the story of Maharaji's prediction that God, through the hard work of dedicated health workers, would make smallpox disappear. They would then ask some variant of "Is that the same guru who advised the Nehru or Gandhi government that the Chinese invaders would turn around and go back on their own?" "Is that Ram Dass's guru?" "Is that the guru who stopped the train?" After I confirmed that he was, the real work started; I was escorted back inside, where the local medical officer and I could have another cup of chai and an honest conversation, not about gurus and prophecies, but about early detection, early response, reporting, and vaccination.

Once a month, Nicole gathered the staff back from the field for status updates. At heart, Nicole and Bill were world-class idea catchers. They used the monthly meetings to disseminate to teams throughout India the latest innovations. Nicole created a way to get everyone to share their best ideas and most effective methods—what we call "best practices" today. After one meeting, for instance, we heard that an epidemiologist in Bihar had started using a "rumor register," keeping track of clues such as extended absences from school or work. Some teams were inspired by the idea of Steve Jones and hired neighbors as watch guards to enforce quarantines. Still others had added the use of the indelible red clay to record pertinent information on the walls of each house. They also recorded the current amount of the reward offered for reporting cases, knowing that because we periodically increased the cash reward, that information told us when a search worker had last been at that location.

Of all the innovations, the cash reward for reporting a case was the most controversial. It was not unheard of to do such a thing, but many thought it was a slippery slope to pay people to report on each other. Even our most far-fetched worst-case scenarios did not anticipate that years later, Prime Minister Gandhi would authorize the Indian government to issue rewards for bringing people in for sterilization in order to slow population growth. This led to thousands of unnecessary and unethical vasectomies and tubal ligations being performed on India's elderly poor. I rationalized favoring a reward for reporting smallpox by believing that issuing cash rewards was a short-term intervention. Without a reward, I believed, cases would likely remain hidden, which would mean that hundreds of thousands of children would continue to die every year.

The results of the second search of Uttar Pradesh in November proved that we were making a difference. After the dramatic rise of cases in October—40,000 nationally; 6,000 in my state of Uttar Pradesh—the number of cases fell to 1,000 in Uttar Pradesh, and proportionately elsewhere. Sick people were being found more quickly, and ring vaccination, a term we never

Above: Nicole Grasset and Larry at WHO meeting, New Delhi, 1974.

Above: Dr. Halfdan Mahler, WHO director general, honoring smallpox workers, New Delhi, 1976.

Right: Larry with "Papa" (Dr. M. I. D. Sharma), in front of Shitala Ma painting, 1974 or 1975.

Left: Doctors R. N. Basu and M. I. D. Sharma with Saiban Bibi, last case of smallpox in India.

Below: Larry receiving award from SEARO regional director Dr. Gunaratne, New Delhi, 1976. ("It turned out all right," he said. "I forgive you for bombarding the WHO office.")

Above: Larry with D. A. Henderson (second from left), head of the WHO smallpox program, during Henderson's visit to the Chotanagpur headquarters in Ranchi, Bihar, 1974.

Right: Larry with Dr. Dave Sencer, director of CDC, Bihar, 1974.

Above: Tata staff and WHO epidemiologists, Tatanagar, 1974.

Above, right: Shitala Ma, goddess of smallpox.

Right: Larry and Girija with Czech epidemiologist Dr. V. Janout showing smallpox recognition card, Ranchi district, Chotanagpur, Bihar, 1974.

Below: Another view of patient in recognition card—he survived.

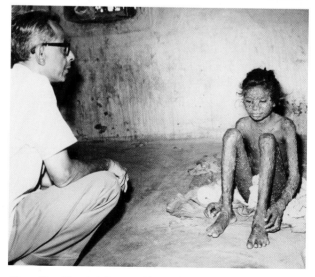

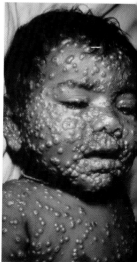

Above: Tata Hospital doctor with smallpox patient, Tatanagar, 1974.

Left: Letter of advice from Maharaji in 1973, when Larry was distressed after seeing his first case of smallpox. Maharaji's advice in Hindi was one word repeated over and over, "God, God, God" (Ram, Ram, Ram).

Below: Larry with smallpox-infected child near Tatanagar, 1974.

Above: Smallpox-blinded beggar, Kainchi, 2005.

Right: Girija (top right) with Maharaji and other devotees, including R. P. Vaish, at the home of the Barman family, New Delhi, 1973.

Above, left: Smallpox workers enforcing ban on travel outside the city without vaccination, Tatanagar, 1974.

Above, right: Larry, Girija, and Paula and Bill Foege, Amman, Jordan, 2012.

Above: Global Commission to Certify Smallpox Eradication statement signed by commission members, 1980.

Right: Rahima Banu, last case of killer smallpox, Bhola Island, Bangladesh, 1975. The photo was taken by Larry; the balloon was printed two years prior in San Francisco.

Left: First days at Google as executive director of Google.org, 2006.

Below: Steve Jones, M.I.D. Sharma, Girija, and Larry in Ann Arbor, 1977.

Left: Wired magazine cover story on the Well.

Below: Larry using an Apple II computer donated to Seva by Steve Jobs, Kathmandu, 1979 or 1980.

Above: Larry giving polio vaccination, Lucknow, 2005.

Right: Larry with His Holiness the Dalai Lama, San Francisco, 2009.

Below: With President Barack Obama, at meeting about Ebola, Roosevelt Room, White House, 2015.

Above, left: With slum dwellers in Allahabad during polio campaign, 2005.

Above, right: With Jeff Skoll at Reagan Presidential Library during meeting of Global Zero campaign to eliminate nuclear weapons.

Left: With Mikhail Gorbachev (right) in San Francisco after discussing the Soviet Union's attempt to weaponize smallpox.

Above: Iris Brilliant, age three, in California.

Below: Maharaji in one of the last photos taken of him, probably in late August 1973, a few weeks before he died, taken by a Western devotee on Larry's Rollei camera.

Above: Joe Brilliant, age one, in India.

Right: Jon Brilliant, age twenty-four, in Beijing in front of President Jiang Jemin poster.

used then but is common now, was containing the outbreaks. Things were, however, still bad in the neighboring state of Bihar—to the west of Uttar Pradesh, where twice as many cases of smallpox had been found. But even in this poorest state, things were headed in the right direction. In December, another 1,000 cases were found. We didn't know if it meant the number of cases was plateauing, or if it meant high transmission season was beginning and the search had become less effective. Were we slowing down smallpox or was the program slowing down? I hoped it was the former and, like everyone else in the program, worried about the latter.

It looked like smooth sailing until the Arab oil embargo hit, causing oil prices to skyrocket 400 percent and immediately taking many government jeeps off the road. We could count on only enough petrol to keep a handful of WHO jeeps moving. Then a strike by Indian airline workers jeopardized the shipments of posters, search forms, and the special bifurcated needles we used to vaccinate people.

We soldiered on, continuing random assessments to double check prior searches. I was on my way to the Himalayan foothills to visit a remote village that had come up in the random draw. Just outside Dehradun, my driver swerved to avoid an oncoming truck going too quickly down the winding, hilly road. Losing control, our jeep went off the side of the hill, rolling, sliding, and tumbling twenty-five feet down. I was thrown from the jeep and knocked out. The driver, even with badly injured legs, walked several miles to summon help.

The next thing I remember is waking up in a small clinic in Dehradun to the sight of several lovely smiling Indians hovering around my bed. They were incredibly kind. Other than a headache and sore neck, I felt okay and was grateful that Girija had not been in the jeep with me that day. The doctor told me I had whiplash, gave me a soft cervical collar and some aspirin, and I went off to a local hotel, which to my great relief had clean sheets and hot running water.

The clinic had no x-ray machine, so I didn't find out then that I had fractured two cervical vertebrae in my neck. I might have gone back to work even if I had known; it seemed everyone was hurt or sick anyway. Zdeno had some kind of pneumonia; Nicole had dysentery; and even our rock, M.I.D., who had never taken a single day of sick leave or vacation in thirty years, was starting to feel the effects of months on the road. We all kept working—the demon of smallpox was a great motivator—until I wasn't allowed to work anymore.

In December 1973, the clock ran out. My tenure as a six-month consultant was over, and so was my Government of India visa. Nicole offered to promote me to a position as an officially sanctioned medical officer, full-time UN staff. But with my visa expired I had no choice but to leave India.

For the first time in five years, if you count the time with the Hog Farm, Girija and I returned to our mothers in Detroit and Cleveland over Christmas. Coming back to America was a more dramatic culture shock than going to India had been. People looked the same as they had before we left, though the clothes had changed a bit—bell-bottoms, beards, beads, and long hair were gone. But even though most of the country and its people were recognizable, Girija and I no longer recognized our home. India was a riot of color, a cacophony of sound; it was disordered, out of control, a giant wild garden with weeds everywhere. In comparison, America looked black and white, two dimensional, like Pleasantville. We couldn't feel the same spiritual depth, or the sense of purpose, in Detroit that we felt in India. It was as if one of the senses were missing.

Barry, my younger brother, did not understand why I would choose my new life in India over being with my family in the States. "Why do you travel so much?" he asked. "What are you looking for that you can't find here?" My mother didn't understand why I wasn't spending time with her. She thought I was chasing after money. If I was, I certainly had a bad sense of direction. My monthly pay as a WHO consultant was $500, less than I had earned as an emergency room doctor in one weekend and just about what was in the bank when Maharaji asked me how much money I had in all the world.

I never wanted anything so badly in my life as to be a full-time medical officer for WHO. But the temporary clearance D.A. got for me to be hired as a clerk wouldn't be sufficient for the more permanent UN appointment. I had to complete the loyalty clearance. Many things I had been involved in could be a problem: *The Body Politic.* The SDS. Martin Luther King.

The big *uh-oh* was Cuba. We never went but we didn't know if our names were still on the passenger list for the trip with the Venceremos Brigade that turned out to have been loaded with informants.

I'd hoped it would be a short trip back to the States because the fight against smallpox was so urgent; Shitala Ma was not going on leave just because I was. It was so important that we remained fully staffed. The feeling of being in the center of the fire of the epidemic had become almost a physical addiction. I quickly learned that I am an adrenaline junkie. I crave these challenges. If I weren't addicted to the rush, I wouldn't do something that makes those little glands atop the kidneys pump like crazy. I can go from zero to catastrophe in a nanosecond. Girija says that over forty years or so, I have accurately predicted ten of the last two disasters. I needed to get back to SEARO but we had to wait for the judgment of the loyalty board. We went to Detroit to visit what was left of our families, visit my dad's grave, and to Cleveland to visit my mother, and Grandma Ida's and Grandpa Abe's graves.

Sometime during that month in exile, I went to the University of Michigan hospital to have them look at my neck. I'd had continuous neck pain and weakness in both arms after the jeep accident. I got bad news when they read the x-rays and discovered that two vertebrae in my neck were fractured and other discs in my neck were compressed. I was diagnosed with brachial plexus palsy, which caused frequent bouts of pain shooting down my arms. Some of the surgeons were alarmed that I wanted to go back to India, to rough, washboard roads and jeeps with lousy suspensions. They worried about permanent injury and even paralysis. They wanted me to consider a spinal fusion, but that would have taken months to heal and I wouldn't be able to go back to the fight against smallpox. Traction in bed was the only other way to treat it, and that too would have taken me out of the game. So they gave me some thoracic outlet exercises and told me to do traction every day for a couple of hours. They handed me a pulley, some string, and a plastic bladder to fill with water that would act as a counterweight to stretch out my neck while I was sitting in a chair. The contraption was portable, so I'd be able to take it back to India. WHO jeeps were always getting into accidents. I'd been in several, so it was likely that I'd be in another; the doctors warned me that some people with fractured cervical vertebrae who have a second bad road accident end up paralyzed. But I was twenty-nine and immortal and on a mission to help make Maharaji's prophecy of the eradication of smallpox come true.

When we got to Cleveland to visit my mom, she told me that an official-looking envelope had arrived at her apartment. The International Organizations Employees Loyalty Board had judged me loyal and I got the clearance to become a UN medical officer. Years later when Girija and I got our file through the Freedom of Information Act, I was surprised to see just how much surveillance had been wasted on me, as well as the fact that although I had been judged "loyal," the vote was not unanimous. If I read it right, there were about ten judges. One or two thought I was of questionable loyalty. The file is hard to read through the blacked-out redacted text that still hasn't been declassified. The votes against me, however, had nothing to do with loyalty or security, nothing to do with marching with Dr. King, nothing to do with building vest pocket playgrounds in slums, helping the Indians on Alcatraz, or being part of the alphabet soup of civil rights and antiwar groups. Instead, the votes against me were based on a kind of provincial foolishness that alarmed me. Apparently, one of the people I had worked with in Tonopah, Nevada, had told the FBI that Girija wore ankle bracelets—the Loyalty Board thought that was strange—and that I carried a Tibetan cotton shoulder bag, which had made someone feel awkward that I was a man carrying a purse. I am very glad the majority declared me loyal and patriotic; I am loyal and patriotic. But I can't help but feel weird that sartorial choices could have caused anybody on that Loyalty Board to vote otherwise.

A few days later a special delivery package arrived from Geneva, along with a bright new UN passport and a long-term visa for India. There were dozens of forms to fill out. I had been promoted from my administrative assistant position to full-fledged medical officer and made a permanent UN staff member, pension and all. Better than that, I was going to be one of the permanent internationals on the Central Team at SEARO.

WHO provided Girija and me with a generous freight allowance to move our household goods. Importing goods into India at the time was heavily restricted, but not for UN officers. We got two large aluminum trunks and filled them with a half dozen sleeping bags; two dozen pairs of Levi's, mostly for friends from behind the Iron Curtain (Zdeno Jezek and his family and several other Russians working with WHO); a portable tape recorder for the administrative secretary Mahesh Gupta, who was also a playwright; Swiss chocolates for the administrative assistants; several bottles of Scotch for the Indian doctors; a zoology dissecting kit for Maharaji's grandson, who wanted to become a doctor; a portable radio for Nedd Willard, the WHO public relations official; several of the new Hewlett-Packard scientific calculators for the epidemiologists; French perfume for Mrs. Boyer; a table tennis paddle for Prem Gambhiri; new color photos of Maharaji that we had printed in Detroit for our friends at the ashram; several hundred balloons I had printed with the words in Hindi "Smallpox can be stopped"; and t-shirts of miscellaneous sizes that said "Smallpox Target Zero." We also had the traction device. We shipped a big Westinghouse air conditioner, with a special fault-resistant compressor to deal with New Delhi's erratic electrical service; it was waiting for us in India.

The young renunciates who years ago had gone to India with only orange-colored backpacks and parkas were returning there loaded with stuff and exploiting their UN shipping allowance. It seemed trivial that my fingers were tingling and the neck pain was constant. I was happy, and so was Girija. We were going back to India to stay until there were zero cases of smallpox, until it was eradicated, pulled out from the roots—*unmulan*.

CHAPTER 13

Tales of the Jungle

We are all faced with a series of opportunities
brilliantly disguised as impossible situations.

—Charles Swindoll

We returned to the capital of India, alive with parades
and pageantry, the celebration of the twenty-fifth anniversary of modern nationhood for this ancient land. It was the
26th of January, 1974, and for Republic Day posters and banners
honoring the accomplishment were tacked to nearly every tree
along the road in New Delhi from the Palam airport to our little
barsatti in Jor Bagh.

There were no celebrations at WHO, however, when I arrived
to work the next morning for a very somber status review. D. A.
Henderson and Isao Arita had flown in from Geneva to meet
with the Central Team. Everyone had been working themselves
ragged; they were all gaunt and sick. The office looked like a
hospital ward: shingles, pneumonia, various tropical infections,
and now I added my damaged neck. Nicole had been suffering
through kidney stones, an occupational hazard for many of the
foreign epidemiologists who faced a Hobbesian choice between

drinking contaminated water or dehydration, which could precipitate kidney stone attacks.

D.A. reported on the global smallpox situation, and said pretty much only the Indian subcontinent stood in the way of eradication, at least for *Variola major,* the form of the disease that was called killer smallpox. Bill brought everyone up to date on India. Three of the four hyperendemic states had undergone three rounds of searches. Madhya Pradesh had started late due to a prolonged monsoon. With each successive search, fewer and fewer new cases were found. Those that we did find were discovered much sooner, preventing spread and limiting the size of outbreaks to a handful of cases. However, each month several previously hidden enclaves of the disease were reported. These new foci of disease were just where we might have expected them: in the poorest and most remote communities, the most vulnerable, the places farthest from the reach of government and the public health staff.

The main topic of concern at the meeting was whether these foci were the last dying embers of the great epidemic or something new to worry about, an unending stream of new disease in a country with more than one thousand dialects and niche cultures and tribes. Our fear was that the cynics would be proved right and the problem of India indeed would be unsolvable, being a perfect storm of complexity, poverty, and bad governance that would wear out the world's patience. One hundred and fifty countries were smallpox-free. Three of every four human beings sick with smallpox now resided in India. Our Indian colleagues bore the weight of these statistics, especially M.I.D. and Mahendra Dutta, who seemed to feel most of the awesome weight of

Key Leadership for the Final Phase

The Central Appraisal Team played a critical role in India in the intensified "final phase" of the program. Using as many as 150,000 workers for special searches and a rapidly evolving set of tactics, they led the effort that stopped smallpox transmission in just twenty-one months.

Indian Government

Dr. Muni Inder Dev Sharma: director of the National Institute of Communicable Diseases (NICD); Dr. Rabinder Nath Basu: assistant director-general of health services; Dr. Mahendra Dutta: director-general for cholera; Dr. Mahendra Singh: deputy assistant director-general for health services (smallpox); Dr. Sachida Nanda Ray: deputy assistant director-general for health services.

WHO

Dr. Nicole Grasset: SEARO principal adviser; Dr. Zdeno Jezek: WHO staff; Dr. William Foege: consultant, on loan from the CDC; Dr. Lawrence Brilliant: SEARO staff.

responsibility for their country while it contained the last dangerous foci of smallpox on earth.

The three phases of the intensified campaign had shown that no corner of India could be assumed to be free of smallpox without monthly house-to-house searches. The four international members of the central team and our Indian counterparts, among them Doctors M. I. D. Sharma, R. N. Basu, Mahendra Dutta, C. K. Rao, and Mahendra Singh, agreed but everyone was a little apprehensive about the scale of operations ahead.

The routine search of half a million villages and visits to more than one hundred million houses would require a massive infrastructure, including workers, jeeps, managers, and epidemiologists. The payroll and expenses would be enormous. D.A.'s mindset was becoming more military: he took to reading books about Generals William Tecumseh Sherman and George S. Patton. The monthly meetings became battle plan updates. I felt in my element, as General Subrahmanyum, despite my own antiwar background.

After the review meeting, Nicole assigned me to create a new state-level program in Madhya Pradesh. Roughly the size of Kentucky, this Indian state sits in the center of the country, and at that time, its population was around thirty million people. The team reasoned that Madhya Pradesh would be the first of the four hyperendemic states to eradicate smallpox, as it had the fewest sick people and the least dense population. Running the program in this large state meant that I would be outside New Delhi for a prolonged period, unable to commute on weekends to one of Maharaji's ashrams and be with the satsang.

WHO made the capital, Bhopal, my official posting, which cleared Government of India hurdles to allow me to take my family, Girija, and set up household. The wonderful coincidence was that Bhopal was where Maharaji's son and grandson lived. Anurag "A.S." Sharma, the eldest son of Maharaji, was the man who had greeted us with shaven head at his brother's house in Agra the day after Maharaji's cremation ceremony. He had invited us to visit him in Bhopal, but I never anticipated being able to take him up on it. It was hard to ignore the feeling of being in sync again as Girija and I packed our suitcases for a long stay in a part of India we knew next to nothing about, except that Maharaji's son lived there.

If Americans think of Bhopal at all, they probably think of the Bhopal disaster, the deadly gas leak at a Union Carbide pesticide plant in 1984, a decade after Girija and I lived there. The disaster killed more than eight thousand, sickened more than half a million, cost hundreds of millions of dollars, and rendered much of the area uninhabitable. The Bhopal we knew in the 1970s, however, was one of India's loveliest and most progressive cities. It was a giant garden with a well-cared-for population, in stark contrast to Delhi's pollution or Calcutta's pavement dwellers. At the center of the city was a beautiful lake, like the reservoir in New York's Central Park. The streets were wide, the avenues filled with flowers, just as Vancouver is when the azaleas and rhododendrons are in bloom.

Madhya Pradesh had less fertile land than the *doab*, the fecund area between the Ganges and Yamuna rivers that defines the agricultural belt of North India. Its undulating landscape and big sky, like that in Wyoming or Montana, provided the state with ample space and water, and in Bhopal, reasonable housing. With competition for resources less desperate compared with much of India, where there was never enough water, food, or space, Bhopal enjoyed a comfortable coexistence of Muslims and Hindus, with a smattering of Jains, Christians, Buddhists, and Adivasi tribes. All the old British infrastructure—trains, Victorian buildings, the courthouse—had been preserved. It was an extraordinarily beautiful place—except for the heartbreaking sight of children dying from smallpox.

A.S. was a member of the Madhya Pradesh state civil service and seemed to know everyone in Bhopal. His family opened their home and their lives to us. We moved into their modern three-bedroom house while arrangements were completed for our own. A.S.'s son Dhananjay bore a striking resemblance to his grandfather, a teenaged version of Maharaji, with teenaged ideas and teenaged interests.

Our first night there was bittersweet as we recalled the circumstances in which we met, the sad day Maharaji died. A.S. told us we would now be his new brother and sister. I asked him whether he had known anything about Maharaji's prophecy that smallpox would be eradicated. "No," he said. "I had heard there was a Doctor America in the Kainchi ashram, but I didn't understand the connection to smallpox. I only learned at the funeral that he sent you to work at WHO. But Maharaji always seemed to be able to see or predict the future, so it doesn't surprise me."

I was curious what it was like growing up with a man who was father to him and guru to so many. "He was Maharaji to you, a guru, a spiritual man," he told me. "To us, his children, he was of course that as well. Though he traveled all over India for his devotees and disciples, he never failed once to fulfill his duties as a father. You noticed his long absences, mysterious trips. Those were the times he came for my wedding, for the birth of my daughter Sashi, my son Dhananjay. For my sister Girija's wedding, he personally negotiated her arranged marriage as any father in India would. You may say he led two lives, but growing up with Maharaji as a father, it seemed we got his best life, a very wise, loving father. I know that many of the longtime Indian devotees wanted to keep his family a secret. But they were never asked to shield his devotees from the fact that Maharaji was a family man. Except when we were small—Maharaji did want to keep away a rush of interest in us, curiosity that might have overwhelmed us as we grew up."

I arrived in Bhopal in time to help with the third search in January 1974. Since the first search of Madhya Pradesh had been delayed because of late rains, we were a month behind the other hyperendemic states. The first search revealed 1,216 cases of smallpox in 192 villages—a huge epidemic anywhere else in the world, but the smallest of the four badly infected Indian states. The second search in December uncovered one-sixth as many cases, only 215 people sick with smallpox in 53 villages.

The state smallpox program apparatus was a bit like Swiss cheese: the solid parts ran smoothly, but the deep holes scattered around the state had become hiding places for hundreds of cases of smallpox. Children were dying in the Adivasi regions, as those peoples lived apart from modernity. The other holes in the smallpox program were in the lawless *dacoit* (bandit) area in the hills near Uttar Pradesh to the north, in the brick kiln work camps, and in the jails.

One of the first people to greet me when I arrived at the Ministry of Health was Zafar Hussein, my new paramedical assistant. He would quickly become one of the most important people in my life in India. He was short, with a noble, if grizzled, face from years working in the sun, first as a sanitary inspector and later as a malaria inspector. His face was coarse and he had a large nose, like the Mughal paintings of commanders and soldiers, black hair, and the blunt calloused fingers of a worker's hands. His smoker's deep, gravelly, quiet voice made people hush and strain to hear him. No one in the organization reported to Zafar, but it seemed like everyone worked for him. He knew so much more about smallpox than any of us; having him with me meant I would make fewer mistakes. We would be together probably fifteen hours a day, most days, for three years.

The smallpox program quickly outgrew the single room we were given in the government building, so we rented an office close to the state health department in Bhopal. It had three rooms, a long white wall perfect for pinning up maps, a typing pool, and a big dusty parking lot, where we parked our twenty-five or so jeeps. A crew kept the jeeps under lock and key—there was always trouble with theft of petrol. Zafar taught me to have the fuel tanks filled twice each day, at six o'clock every evening, and then again, by someone other than the driver, at six o'clock the following morning so we could calculate how much had been stolen overnight. Zafar knew exactly how much gas was in each of our jeeps. If he heard that a driver's father had died or his daughter was to be married, he would expect a gallon or two to disappear; but then he would have a quiet word with the driver and it would not happen again. If a driver stole more than that, he was endangering the mission and would be fired. It was a fine line to walk. Drivers were among the most poorly paid staff. If we didn't allow a little larceny, the team's morale would be destroyed and drivers would quit. If we allowed too much, the jeeps would run out of gas and we would have to fire everyone. Zafar taught me not to let "perfection destroy progress," or as Nicole liked to say, "Don't let 'better' become the enemy of the 'good.'"

Chasing down outbreaks in Madhya Pradesh usually meant eight- or nine-hour drives from Bhopal and at least one "night halt." Typically, upon arrival, the team, including Zafar, would enter the village looking for signs of new cases or facial scars from old outbreaks, checking on the status of previously searched areas. We worked so hard, I had to improvise periods of rest so that I could deal with my neck injury. While Zafar walked the village, I would find a tree with a low horizontal branch to sit under, sling my water-filled plastic bag over the branch and attach the counterweight to my neck brace so that I could put on the traction device, sit under the tree, and get some relief.

It took only a few days for the hot Indian sun to rupture the plastic bag the hospital had given me in Michigan—and it is not fun when a counterweight attached to your neck explodes mid-traction. In one village, the *pradhan,* or headman, saw me struggling with the leaky plastic bag. That night, he brought me a freshly killed goat and in front of me he cut out its bladder, which he helped me fill with water and hook up as a replacement to the burst plastic bag. It smelled just as bad as you think it might, and I had to bury it before moving on the next day. But his kindness led me to a ritual. Each time we arrived at a village, I would find the *pradhan* to ask about smallpox, a place to make a "night halt," and the nearest butcher or goat herder so I could purchase a bladder. Most of the time, I had to purchase the whole animal, and then the person who sold me the animal would cook the rest of it for a small neighborhood gathering with cooked meat for everyone, except me since I was still a vegetarian. Maybe I was a hypocrite since even though I did not eat the animal, it was killed for my needs, but I had to hope it was for a greater good. It was like the killing of cows to make smallpox vaccine. Each time I thought about it, the pockmarked faces of children and their mothers' anguished cries drowned out any hesitation I had.

Being connected to a contraption hanging over a tree turned out to be a splendid way to get to know villagers. Local children gathered around me, talking about smallpox, telling me where the hidden cases were. Sometimes I gave out balloons or sweets. Sometimes the driver would tell the kids about the Bollywood movie I had been in and they would all sing "Dum Maro Dum"; or Zafar would tell them my name was Doctor America and I would get lots of questions about what life was like in the United States. Often, the *pradhan* would know someone who knew someone who had a cousin who was an Indian doctor who had moved to New Jersey. I enjoyed those moments practicing Hindi or Urdu and stretching my neck and my worldview.

I had been in Bhopal only a week or two when we got a telegram from the head of the program in neighboring Uttar Pradesh. It was a "cross-notification" form, reporting what he thought was an exportation of smallpox from our state to his. He was concerned about smallpox spreading from a notorious jail in Gwalior, which is located in Madhya Pradesh right across the border from Uttar Pradesh. The health officers in Bhopal had known for some time that there was an epidemic there and that some of the prison guards and their children had smallpox. But Indian medical officers had refused to go because there was a long-standing myth that whoever entered Gwalior prison never came out alive.

So I agreed to go. I called Nicole in Delhi and told her I was going to the prison; she asked me to stop en route at the ancient fortress city of Jhansi, another area on the border with Uttar Pradesh. Girija came with us on her way to a meditation course near Gwalior.

There was a rumor of smallpox at one of India's large religious gatherings, called a *mela*. Though this *mela* was smaller than a huge *kumbha mela,* like those in Rishikesh and Allahabad that can attract twenty or thirty million people, it did draw a unique group of spiritual seekers, a few hundred *naga babas,* followers of Shiva who wandered around the country naked, living off the generosity of villagers and devotees. They were celibate, covered in dust, and had matted dreadlocks. There was little food in the rocky, sandy canyon, but lots of hashish, and a circuslike atmosphere around a specific type of physical prowess. One *naga baba* climbed a ladder with a bucket of water tied to his penis. Another rolled his penis around a stick and secured the stick to his body with a string. A third appeared, and I am sorry to say I got close enough to see him seem to suck water out of a pond with his penis and spray it like a garden hose.

Zafar reported that few of the thousand *naga babas* there had been vaccinated. I vaccinated the first couple of babas with a bifurcated needle, telling them in Hindi about Neem Karoli Baba's prophecy. I do not know if that moved them as much as seeing a white face like mine speak Hindi. After vaccinating a few, I left one of our vaccinators there with enough needles and vaccine to finish the job, and promised him we would send a jeep back for him later that evening.

Gwalior prison was a couple hour's drive away and as geographically isolated as San Quentin or Alcatraz. Prison guards and other staff lived in the city, which had a kind of company store to buy provisions, but it was far from a thriving metropolis. We met with the medical officer there on February 8 and confirmed the outbreak. A prison guard had contracted smallpox on a visit to Bihar; he and his family spread it when they went to Jhansi in Uttar Pradesh for provisions. In order to put a ring of containment around the case, we needed to vaccinate the prisoners and the rest of the staff. As soon as the inmates heard this, they started rioting. Not one of these big, strong, hairy criminals was willing to get vaccinated; they were terrified of a tiny bifurcated sewing needle pounded flat and split in order to hold exactly one drop of vaccine. The most stubborn inmate was a man named Maan Singh,† the biggest, meanest, scariest criminal in Gwalior. He was afraid of nothing except this little needle. Nobody else would let us vaccinate them unless Maan Singh went first.

The burly six-and-a-half-foot Maan Singh had led murderous rampages from village to village in Madhya Pradesh, seeing himself as a kind of Robin Hood figure, robbing the rich and giving back to the exploited poor, killing everyone in his way. My determination to convince him to take vaccination was a nice idea from outside the prison, before the doors locked and the walls closed in, before I signed the we-don't-negotiate-for-hostages waiver informing us that the guards wouldn't help us if the prisoners got ahold of us.

Maan Singh lived in a wing of the prison dedicated to the most violent criminals. They were usually held in smaller cells off the main corridor, in dark and dank solitary cubes, but Singh had procured a dozen cells and connected them to create his own internal palace. He towered over us from behind bars. At first I pretended I couldn't speak Hindi so I could concentrate. Zafar was with me and he introduced me as a doctor from America who had come to help India free itself of the yoke of this terrible disease that affected police and *dacoits,* prime ministers and prison guards.

"Sir," I said in English, "it's important to get vaccinated. Smallpox can kill you."

"I'm a Rajput," he responded in Hindi after Zafar translated. "We are not afraid of death."

"It's a terrible, extremely painful death, and there is nothing we can do to make a smallpox victim comfortable." I should have been afraid, being near this big man who boasted about the necks he had snapped, the men he had stabbed. Maybe it was the experience with the violent Green Beret on Alcatraz. I'd already been threatened by a big scary guy and lived to tell the tale. I surprised myself at how calm I was.

"A Rajput can handle anything. I'm not afraid of smallpox."

"Guard, please open the door so Maan Singh and I can have a cup of tea," I said in Hindi.

I saw a flicker of pleasure in Maan Singh's face. I wasn't sure whether it was because I could speak Hindi, or because he would get a cup of tea, or if the fragile neck of this clueless American looked too easy to snap.

I entered and we sat down. Maan Singh patted me on the shoulder, pushing me around like a bear playing with a rabbit. But I wasn't afraid. Maharaji had told me smallpox would be eradicated. I would persuade this guy to be vaccinated.

"Look, you are the most famous *dacoit* in the world. Mrs. Gandhi, the WHO chiefs in Delhi sent me here. Everyone is afraid of you. I am afraid of you. I know you killed twenty people."

"Twenty-five," he deadpanned.

"If you don't take the vaccine, no one here will take it, and everyone will die."

"I don't care."

I noticed there was a small Hanuman among his collection of statues in his cell. I hoped there was a way to appeal to a sense of karma, of repairing some of the damage he'd caused by making reparations.

"I see that you honor Hanuman. My guru was a devotee of Hanuman, like you. Hanuman flew to the mountains to bring back medicine to save Rama's brother. You should be like Hanuman and bring this medicine to others in the jail. Perhaps you can save more lives than you took."

He paused and I knew I had him.

"I'll think about it," he said. "Come back tomorrow."

Zafar and I left the jail for our dak bungalow, to sleep. We came back the next day, and Maan Singh and I had another dharma talk. I recited the *shloka* that Maharaji had told me to memorize—Krishna's advice to Arjuna about following your dharma, which is better for you than anyone else's dharma. Maan Singh loved it. It closed the deal.

"Okay," he said, "if a white monkey is going to come to my cell and tell me about Hanuman and recite the *Bhagavad Gita,* the world has turned upside down, so I will be vaccinated."

To show him how simple the process was, I did what all the vaccinators did every day and vaccinated myself.

"That's it?" he said. "If a puny little weakling like you can do it, I can do it. Here." He put out his arm. I asked him to wait and let me do it in the center of the prison courtyard so everyone could see.

"If you will agree to let everyone watch, you can rough me up as much as you want," I told him.

"Ha! You are too small to bother to beat up. Can we build a stage?"

"Sure."

"And you will be the one to vaccinate me," he demanded.

We built a stage the next day. Maan Singh stood in the center, telling the rest of the prisoners that since he was the baddest sister fucker—that is the worst swear word one can use in Hindi—no one could have ever forced him to be vaccinated. He was doing it to show the prisoners that they needed to stick together and save lives by vaccination. "I'm not afraid of the puny white monkey vaccinating me," he told everyone. "You shouldn't be either."

I vaccinated him, and within minutes, lines formed at every vaccination table.

By March, after five monthly searches, smallpox was disappearing from Madhya Pradesh—from 1,216 cases in the first search in November to a single outbreak in only four months, in Shahdol district in the eastern part of the state. It seemed certain we would reach zero in a month or two, and then begin the two-year surveillance phase to make sure there were no new cases.

I hurried to call Nicole to tell her we were down to the last outbreak, and we agreed it was time for me to return to Delhi and rejoin the Central Team. I would visit the last outbreak, follow up on some outstanding rumors, and then WHO would send a Soviet epidemiologist for me to train so he could take over Madhya Pradesh.

"You're Jewish?" Lev Khodakevich asked when he arrived from New Delhi at the office in Bhopal. "I've got a little Jew blood in me too," he declared, at a time when few in the Soviet Union would have volunteered that information.

Lev looked more European than many of the other Russians that had joined WHO. He was tallish, slender, and had a bright inquisitive way about him. He and his wife, Lydia, were going to live full-time in Bhopal the way Girija and I had. Lev and I settled into an old British partner's desk with chairs facing each other across the desktop. It was the first time I had a WHO doctor reporting to me. He was already a polished and experienced epidemiologist who had been all over the world. I thought of him as another teacher, to help me understand the history of epidemiology. He saw me as his boss.

My time in Madhya Pradesh, and the relatively rapid success we had had with smallpox, liberated my sense of humor, but Lev was tough. I remember the first time I saw him laugh. We were in a village looking into an outbreak that hadn't been well contained. Zafar told us it was because the vaccinator was running a scam. Vaccination was supposed to be free for everyone. But this guy was telling people that if they didn't pay anything, he would use the Soviet vaccine, which could cause a bad reaction because it was so highly concentrated. If people paid the guy two rupees, he would give them the Canadian vaccine, which caused no reaction. If they paid five rupees, he'd skip them and record them as vaccinated. We even heard that the guy was telling people that the Soviet vaccine might turn them into communists! Lev exploded at the vaccinator first because of the insult to the Soviet vaccine. Then he started screaming at Zafar and the Indian doctors who had looked the other way. But then he decided that Indians feared the Soviet vaccine because it must have been "stronger." "I can't believe that an American believes that anything made in Russia is ever stronger than you!" He bellowed with wide-mouthed laughter, revealing the not so fine art of Soviet dentistry.

In our dak bungalow Lev and I shared a single room and stayed up talking most of the night. I was concerned about his outburst over the corrupt vaccinator.

"Lev, if you want to make this work, you're going to have to loosen up. If you scream at everyone, the only thing the Indians will see is an angry white guy and you won't get anything done—they'll all start hiding problems. You need them on your side so that when it gets difficult, they won't hide cases or problems from you. Yes, the vaccinator is corrupt. But we have to go back to Bhopal and get the superintendent of police to do something about it. We can never permit ourselves to get righteously indignant."

He'd been tense, unsmiling, and indignant about everything since he had landed in Bhopal. He was offended by the dirt, by Indians shitting in fields. He was so wound up, I thought he was going to get an ulcer.

"But what about the corruption?" he asked. "Do we just ignore it?"

"No, of course not. This culture of petty bribes, the *baksheesh,* will stop India from becoming great," I said. "It is even worse than you think. Indians say there are only two kinds of jobs—wet jobs, with a chance to earn money through bribes, are called *gila,* and dry jobs *suka,* and only a fool would take a dry job without the chance to make extra *baksheesh,* the way you can as a customs officer or a civil surgeon. But our job is not to be Indian revolutionaries and remake the entire system; our job is to eradicate smallpox. Meanwhile, I'm not slowing down for a driver who steals a little petrol, or one vaccinator out of thousands who is an extortionist. We can both hate the crimes but you and I are both guests in India and we are on the same team, fighting the same enemy. We are not fighting the Cold War here in Madhya Pradesh. Capitalism and communism both suck. Yes, there is this corruption, but you won't fix it all in your two years here. But you can get rid of smallpox. After I go you will be in charge and they must not hate you or you will be ineffective. There's no time to get angry."

Lev was smoldering. "Okay, then let me meet this saint of yours, Maharaji. If he is what will make the world change, then I want to see him for myself."

"Maharaji died last year, Lev, but you should meet Mother Teresa. Her approach is offering charity as opposed to going after systemic change; she is a saint."

"Forget it. I hate her," Lev said. "People like her are just putting the masses to sleep, and they are stopping India from going through the necessary revolution to get rid of princes and caste. All religion is just postponing the revolution. Russia and China grew up and got over religion. India will have to as well. Nothing will get better until that happens."

I don't remember who had the last word. I do remember that we agreed to disagree on religion and politics, but we did agree on smallpox.

The month of March, or *chet,* was the time of season change in India and it was bringing to Madhya Pradesh a large scale movement of migrant laborers—the "March people" or *chetwallas.* We received word of an outbreak in Shahdol—the victim came from somewhere in Bihar, and we feared this was the first of many smallpox importations. Zafar took Lev to the north of Madhya Pradesh, near the border of Uttar Pradesh, to check up on progress at the Gwalior jail and surrounding villages, while Girija and I headed south and east to investigate Shahdol. On our way, we sidetracked to look into a rumor of a large outbreak in the village of Kahani in a forest preserve in Seoni district, on the Pench River at the border between Madhya Pradesh and Maharashtra. The report was three dozen ill with pox and fever and five deaths. We did not know if it was smallpox, but I was worried: I had told Nicole that Shahdol was the last outbreak left in the state.

Seoni district, made famous as "Seeonee" by Rudyard Kipling as the setting for the Mowgli stories in *The Jungle Book*, was every bit as magical as Kipling's description of its natural beauty, flora, and vivid wildlife. I was most interested in the monkeys—the notification we received said, "Cases might be either smallpox or monkeypox as so many wild langurs are near the village of Kahani." The Bandar-log or langur monkeys in question are also called Hanuman monkeys.

The forest was filled with huge ancient teak, mahua, and other hardwood trees, whose clusters towered like mountain peaks over the smaller scattered white kulu, or ghost trees. The mahua tree has flowers that are used to make an alcoholic drink like beer that the Adivasi enjoy. Mahua is also eaten by some of the large cats. We heard reports of tigers asleep under mahua trees, in the middle of the day, apparently happily drunk.

The road to Kahani wove in and out of the Seoni tiger preserve. It ended about two miles from the village; our four-wheel-drive jeep continued off-road another mile and a half before we had to leave it in the jungle. After that it was about a mile trek through intense green forest. The gray langurs looked bright white as they leaped through the dark green treetops, their three-foot-long tails—around two or three times longer than their bodies—trailing behind them like hanging question marks. Girija and I were happy to hear their sweet whoops. Suddenly, the langurs became agitated. They danced frenetically on branches, their tails pointing straight up, sweet whoops becoming harsh barks. I looked for signs of a predator—jungle cats were common there. But there was no sign of Kipling's famous Bengal tiger, Shere Khan.

If we had understood langur whoops and barks, we might have known what was coming next: five or six of them launched long, arcing streams of warm monkey pee on us like boys at summer camp having a pissing contest. It happened too quickly for us to avoid getting soaked; Girija's salvar kameez was drenched. A dozen of them chased us through the trees, escalating their artillery to a hail of monkey feces aimed, accurately, at me. Their faces looked a little like those on the statues of Hanuman. It was hard not to wonder whether this meant that Hanuman was shitting on my smallpox mission.

Covered with sweat, humidity, and monkey piss and shit, Girija and I ran to the clearing of the village, a Gond community of a hundred or so huts surrounded by a bamboo fence meant to keep out predators. The first order of business would have been a bucket shower, but the beginning of March is fully three months before the rains, and water was scarce. Our driver scraped most of the monkey feces off me, and a kind village woman gave Girija some privacy to do what she could to dilute her monkey urine–soaked blouse with some water.

About two dozen cases of pox had been reported. I examined each of them, but it was obvious that this was an outbreak of *Varicella*—chickenpox—rather than smallpox or monkeypox. Chickenpox begins with clusters on the torso rather than on the hands, feet, and face. The five deaths reported in the village were of people in their twenties and thirties. It is uncommon in most places for chickenpox to kill, but in this sparsely populated area, isolated villages might go twenty or twenty-five years without a single case of chickenpox. When the inevitable child comes home from a visit to grandma's distant village and brings chickenpox, most of the villagers—babies, teenagers, and young adults whose immune systems have never been exposed to the disease—will get it. While it is mild in children, it is much more serious in young adults and causes death more often than you'd think. In some communities, like the isolated island of Kerala in South India, I found villages with a dozen or more deaths from lab-confirmed chickenpox in young men and women in their twenties. We took scab samples to send back to WHO for confirmation. As darkness fell, we walked about a mile through the forest to a dak bungalow and, we hoped, a bath.

The bungalow had no hot water, but Girija and I managed a cold-water bucket shower. We cleaned off as best we could and went to bed. In the middle of the night, we both woke up itching and scratching. When we turned on the lights, a mass of quivering insects scurried away; the whole mattress was covered in bedbugs. We moved to a straw mat on the floor only to be awakened by an attack of fleas. It was three in the morning and too early to go anywhere, so we went outside to sleep under the stars. It was beautiful until the mosquitoes started biting. We ran back into the bungalow, turned on the lights, swatting and scratching until dawn and the possibility of an escape from the pestilence of the jungle that Rudyard Kipling's editor must have deleted from his stories.

Our driver heard that across the border in the state of Maharashtra there was a Circuit House, one of the more upscale government rest houses that dotted India. It was a higher level of government accommodation, which I was more or less entitled to since I was being driven in a UN vehicle. Circuit Houses were usually mobbed; the rooms were clean and large, included dinner, and, best of all, were free to government workers. It was first-come-first-served for a room, with allocation determined by a loose protocol that the biggest sahib trumps the smallest. We hoped my status would get us a room in which we could wash and sleep overnight.

We crossed the Gomti River, eased into Maharashtra state in the late afternoon, and by dinnertime found the Circuit House. It had one empty room, beautiful gardens, and hot water for bucket baths. Girija and I undressed in our room, scraped the residual monkey feces off, luxuriated in the hot water we poured over each other, and put antibiotic ointment and papaya extract on our various bug bites. We were wrapped in towels, relieved to be clean, about to crawl into bed to take a siesta when there was a knock on the door.

It was the cook. "We are very sorry, *bara-sahib* [big sahib], but there is a *maha-bara-sahib* [much bigger sahib] coming." Really big boss trumps little boss. Girija and I sat down on the bed, still wrapped in our towels, and waited, hoping that there might be room to negotiate with the very, very big sahib.

The double doors to the room burst open, with the kind of energy that reminded me of Maharaji bursting through the doors at Kainchi, depositing a maroon-robed lama in our midst. It was the Dalai Lama. The Dalai Lama stood at the threshold to our room, in the most remote corner of India, in a room we thought God had given us to make up for the worst night of our lives. Somehow it didn't surprise me.

The Dalai Lama was in Maharashtra state serving as a kind of pastor to his flock of Tibetan refugees. He was visiting the Norgyeling Tibetan Settlement nearby. He glanced at the one bed and at us in our towels and immediately understood we were being evicted to make room for him and his entourage. He smiled and said, "We can share."

Girija and I had always wanted to meet the Dalai Lama. Like everyone else, I wanted to ask him about the meaning and purpose of our lives. All of the entourage left except for one attendant. We settled into sharing tea. My Tibetan was nonexistent and His Holiness's English was not yet as good as it is now; it had only been a little more than a decade since his escape from Tibet in 1959, and he hadn't traveled much to the West. We were speaking to each other in Hindi while his attendant sat on the floor.

His Holiness was jovial, trying to make the awkwardness disappear. We were sitting on the edge of the bed, Girija on one side of me and the Dalai Lama on the other. The conversation began to deepen. I was about to ask my question about the meaning of life when I became transfixed by the vaccination marks on his arm. He had four scars from old smallpox vaccinations. I forgot what the verse of the *Gita* had said about getting lost in what you were attached to. Instead of seizing the moment to ask about the meaning of life, my brain was hijacked by the four smallpox vaccination scars.

"Yes," he said, "there was a terrible smallpox epidemic in Lhasa in 1948, and because I was the Dalai Lama, each of the four Buddhist sects wanted to make certain that their vaccine was used to protect me. They vaccinated me with a device that left scars, and they did it four times." The four circular scars were probably made with an old rotary lancet, a brutal procedure that was no longer used. He told us that long ago in Tibet, they had used hollowed-out bones, probably from birds, to blow powdered crusts from actual smallpox into the noses of Tibetans using a process known as variolation, which is all they had to prevent smallpox. As bad as his scars from the rotary lancet were, the elder monks thought it was much safer than either variolation or no vaccination at all.

The Dalai Lama asked about how we had gotten to this Circuit House, and we told him about smallpox, WHO, the monkey shit and piss, the bedbugs, and Maharaji and smallpox eradication. His Holiness said, "Yes, I've heard from Tibetan refugees living near where Buddha achieved enlightenment, in Bihar, Bodh Gaya, that there is quite a bit of smallpox there. And yes, I have heard the name of Neem Karoli Baba, but I did not know he made a prediction about smallpox." At the same time, I knew nothing about this horrific smallpox epidemic in Lhasa and wanted to know more. I figured we had all night so it wouldn't hurt to ask a few more questions.

The Dalai Lama started telling the story of the outbreak of *ladrup*—Tibetan for smallpox—in 1948. He talked about the poor villagers and children who contracted the disease and died in that epidemic. By 1974 Tibet was supposed to be a smallpox-free country. So I started worrying, *Oh, my God, we're going to eradicate smallpox in India but maybe it is still hidden in Tibet and it will come back again.* I hoped the cool climate at twelve thousand feet, the elevation of the capital Lhasa, slowed down the transmission speed of the disease, if it hadn't been eradicated.

That the Dalai Lama was engaged by the subject delighted me. He was so compassionate. He mentioned how the suffering of smallpox was just one of the kinds of suffering Buddha taught about in the Four Noble Truths. For months, I had been visiting various religious leaders, trying to persuade them to advocate the eradication program. Many refused, believing that one should not interfere with God's will. Here, though, was the Dalai Lama, a man who was both holy and practical, mystical, with a deep love of science. He raised his hands, softened his eyes, chanted something in Tibetan, and gave us a blessing on eradicating smallpox.

The night was relaxed and easy. The Dalai Lama had Girija and me, and even his very cautious translator, laughing so loudly that another Tibetan knocked on the door to ask whether everything was okay. They told us it was way past His Holiness's bedtime and that he had to wake up at 5 A.M. to begin his day. The Dalai Lama joked about the one chair and giggled about the sleeping arrangements. We all three lay down on the bed. Girija was on the side farthest from the Dalai Lama out of respect for the fact that he was a monk and the implied intimacy of the room. I lay between them.

We woke up to an abrupt knock on the door; His Holiness's attendant leaped up from his bedroll to answer. Just as I was about to say, "Your Holiness, wait . . . I have one more question about the meaning of life," his troupe came in and said, "Time to go. They are waiting for you at the settlement." His Holiness smiled effervescently, gave an Indian *namaste* salute with folded hands, and, in an improbable combination of a *basso profundo* and a soprano's chirp, said in English, "Okay! Bye-bye!" and glided out the door.

As we packed up our clothes, I was sad. Indians say that motivation distorts perception: "When a pickpocket meets a saint, he will see only his pockets." I shared a night with a saint and only saw his vaccination marks!

I did not have much time to indulge in guilt. As we headed out of the Circuit House, the *chowkidaar* handed me a telegram from Lev Khodakevich: "TEN NEW OUTBREAKS SAME DAY. STRANGE. HUNDREDS OF KILOMETERS APART. EMERGENCY. RETURN BHOPAL IMMEDIATELY. PLEASE."

CHAPTER 14

City of the Tatas

Seek out the way.
Seek the way by retreating within.
Seek the way by advancing boldly without.
Seek it not by any one road. To each temperament
there is one road which seems the most desirable. But
the way is not found by devotion alone, by religious
contemplation alone, by ardent progress, by self-
sacrificing labor, by studious observation of life. None
alone can take (you) more than one step onward.
All steps are necessary to make up the ladder.

—Mabel Collins, *Light on the Path,* 1885

Our driver raced across hilly, curvy, horribly bumpy Indian roads all day so that we could arrive in Bhopal while it was still light. Lev was agitated. He handed me a fistful of telegrams from all over the state, each a notice of a new outbreak of smallpox in areas we thought had been smallpox-free for months. Half a dozen newly infected villages were discovered in a single day. Where the hell had they come from?

We had a hard time getting answers by telephone. We sent a team to every outbreak.

Zafar and I went to investigate a village just outside of Bhopal where a young man hardly out of his teens had arrived home covered with pox and died. He had just been cremated a day or so before we got there. No one would admit to knowing anything about the young man, his job, or his travels. "He went someplace for work in a coal mine," we were told. "We don't know where. He came home very sick and died the same day." Nobody else in the village had come down with smallpox. We made sure the rest of the villagers had been vaccinated and, frustrated, returned to Bhopal to await news from the other teams.

The barrage of telegrams increased, arriving several times a day at Madhya Pradesh headquarters in Bhopal, bringing news of more people sick and dying from smallpox. After a week of plotting the epidemic with pushpins on hand-drawn maps, a pattern emerged. Each outbreak began with a working-age young man who returned home to his village and often died before he could be questioned. We assumed that he'd been somewhere looking for a job. These cases were importations, coming from wherever these young men had gone looking for work.

The few who were well enough to speak admitted they had come from—or traveled through—the bordering state of Bihar. Lev and I mapped the routes of all of India's bus and train schedules, particularly the long-distance trains. No matter where the trains carrying these sick men originated—Bombay, Calcutta, or even Delhi—they all made stops in Bihar.

Two new cases appeared in a Gond village near a Shiva pilgrimage site called Amarkantak. A young father had died from smallpox, and now his four-year-old daughter was infected. Zafar and I drove overnight to investigate. The tiny one-room home had clay floors and fading whitewashed walls painted with auspicious tribal symbols. The young man's widow told us her husband had gone somewhere for work and that he arrived home in a state of confusion and with infected pustules all over his body. He had walked a long way from the bus stop, so she gave him neem tea and applied tulsi leaves, their traditional treatment for smallpox. Everything hurt, he had said, even his clothes. His only smile, a weak one, was when his young daughter clung to his bare leg as he stumbled toward the mat to collapse on the floor. He was dead by morning. That was ten days ago; now the daughter had classic pustules on her hands and face.

The young man couldn't have been infected along the bus route—the timing was wrong. He had been back in Madhya Pradesh only a day or two before he died. He must have come into contact with smallpox between one and three weeks before he became sick. In a heap on the ground outside the open door to the house lay the man's turban wrap and his discarded belongings, saved from the cremation fire so that other villagers could divide his things. Zafar searched the pockets of the dead man's soiled pants. He found crumpled rupee notes and an intact train ticket—by good fortune it hadn't been collected when he passed through the station. The originating station was stamped "Tatanagar."

The thrill of discovery shot through me. We had it: Tatanagar, the steel city, the Pittsburgh of India, was the source. For a moment, I felt like John Snow, the father of epidemiology, who had stopped a London cholera epidemic by tracing its source to a diaper soiled with cholera that had gotten stuck at the bottom of a well, continuously spreading *Vibrio cholerae*. Snow demanded the city council remove the well's pump handle, which stopped that epidemic. We had to stop this one.

Tatanagar, like Detroit in my youth, was a magnet for migrant workers. There were always jobs, legal or illegal, in the steel mills or the nearby coal mines. It didn't matter if you were young or uneducated, dark skinned and low caste, Muslim, Christian, or tribal. It was a mecca for jobseekers.

I phoned the Gwalior district health office and left a message for the Madhya Pradesh team: "Question every survivor in every village about whether they worked in the steel plants or coal mines around Tatanagar or if their train home passed through the Tatanagar train station." Several search workers immediately sent telegrams back confirming they were finding young men sick with smallpox who had arrived by train from Tatanagar.

Some had found work in the coal mines or steel mills. Many others who hadn't found any work had become beggars near the train station, or settled in the *basti,* the slum adjacent to the railway stations. Perhaps someone with smallpox ate next to them or coughed on them. A week or two later came the fever and weakness, and after another few days, the spots. Many failed to find work and returned home feeling punished by Shitala Ma. Dozens of trains left Tatanagar carrying smallpox to Madhya Pradesh every day. If this "pump handle" was not removed, it was only a matter of time before smallpox spread in Madhya Pradesh, across India, and then all over Asia.

Nineteen seventy-four was supposed to have been the year we would end smallpox. April 7, World Health Day, was to be dedicated to celebrating worldwide progress in eradicating the disease. The number of countries infected with *Variola major* had been reduced from three dozen to only four, with India being the worst. To coincide with World Health Day, WHO launched a new phase in the India smallpox campaign and announced an April 1975 target date for complete eradication—in another year. From where I sat, this deluge of new outbreaks made that target seem out of reach.

On April 2, 1974, I sent a telegram to Nicole: "MP [Madhya Pradesh] IS UNDER ATTACK FROM IMPORTATIONS FROM BIHAR. SUSPECT INDUSTRIAL AREA AROUND TATANAGAR RAILWAY STATION. REQUEST APPROVAL TO COME TO DELHI."

Nicole called as soon as she got the telegram and told me yes, to come to Delhi right away.

"We haven't finished the analysis," I told her, "but we have two dozen confirmed outbreaks traced back to Tatanagar and more coming every day."

"Hmm," she finally responded in a somber tone. I expected Nicole to be more animated, but she was quiet. "That may explain some new reports showing up in other odd places." Her voice trailed off. She began again almost wearily, "I'm getting Bill and our Indian counterparts together tomorrow. There are other epidemics being reported as far north as Kashmir, as far south as Tamil Nadu. It is not just Madhya Pradesh that is under attack. Outbreaks are appearing in places we had long thought freed of smallpox. Bring Zafar with you. You will both go to Tatanagar as soon as we come up with a plan. Do you think Lev is ready for the handover of Madhya Pradesh today? If you're right, this city of the Tatas might be the next big battleground."

et's exchange pictures," Lev said to me that afternoon as we were parting.

"You mean take each other's photos? I can ask someone to find a camera."

"No, Larry, I mean a trade: your photo of your guru in exchange for my picture of Lenin. I don't hate your guru now as much as I did when I first met you." My mouth must have dropped open. "Listen, Larry, I was attracted to the notion of communism because Lenin said this was the system that would redistribute wealth so we could feed and clothe the poor. You told me that your guru said, 'Love everyone and feed them,' and that he also said, 'A suffering man is higher than God. Everyone should help him.' That makes your guru like Lenin. Maybe one of them is motivated by a crazy idea called 'God' and the other is motivated by a crazy idea of the perfect socialist. There are enough poor people in India that we need both their ideologies if life is going to be bearable. So maybe your guru was just, well, a different kind of communist."

I laughed and gave Lev my photo of a smiling, bare-chested, *dhoti*-clad Maharaji, and he gave me his photo of a stern Lenin with a fur hat and a pointed goatee. Lev also gave me a Russian bear hug and a gift-wrapped copy of Lenin's writings with a section titled, "What Is to Be Done? Burning Questions." In return, I gave him a book whose title was one answer to that question: *Be Here Now,* written about Neem Karoli Baba by my now guru-brother, Baba Ram Dass. I wondered if there would ever be a reconciliation between the hatred of communism by the religious and the hatred of religion by communists.

Girija and I said a hasty goodbye to Maharaji's family. I still had so many questions to ask his son and especially his grandson, Dhananjay, but there was no more time for leisurely talks and dinner. We flew from Bhopal to Delhi that night.

I had a bad taste in my mouth from the role that corporate America had played in keeping the corridors of power closed to blacks and women, ignoring human rights, aligning themselves with the apartheid South African government, and undermining equal access for blacks to Woolworth lunch counters in the civil rights struggle. Tatanagar was the company town of the corporate behemoth, Tata Companies. I was sure they were no different. Myron Belkind, my cousin from the Cleveland branch of my family, had arrived in New Delhi to become the bureau chief for the Associated Press. I asked for his help; he investigated and gathered news clippings and research on the Tata family industrial empire and came to our *barsatti* in Delhi loaded with information.

Later that night at dinner with Bill Foege we talked about what it would mean to the eradication program if the outbreaks in Madhya Pradesh and elsewhere in India and Nepal were coming from a single, hidden urban epidemic.

"It would be mostly good news," Bill said. "Stopping an epidemic in a city is very hard but is probably easier than trying to stop hundreds of dispersed outbreaks. And if all these new outbreaks are coming from a single source, it would mean we missed one outbreak in a city rather than three hundred separate outbreaks all over the country."

At the same time, if the outbreaks were importations, as we expected, it would also mean that M. I. D. Sharma and the other Indian officials would stop being pressured to scuttle the program every time a state program was successful in uncovering new outbreaks. The Indian government and skeptics like Jankowicz believed that each new outbreak was evidence of hundreds of long-hidden, smoldering outbreaks rather than evidence of the success of our surveillance system.

The next morning I went to the library, got a record of every train passing through Tatanagar, and matched it to the map of new outbreaks in Orissa, West Bengal, and other states. At least three-quarters of those newly sick with smallpox looked like they lived near a train that had come from Tatanagar. I also gathered information on every law I could find related to limiting people's ability to travel in the midst of a dangerous pandemic. Section 269 of the Bengal vaccination act within the Indian Penal Code and several other laws still on the books from the British Raj of the late 1800s made it illegal for anyone to leave an infected area without permission from health authorities. There was no way to make copies of the laws, so I wrote a summary of each one in case I needed the information to persuade local authorities that they had the legal means to quarantine the Tatanagar peninsula.

On April 8, Zafar and I boarded a plane in Delhi bound for Calcutta. We sped down the runway for takeoff. A few seconds after wheels up, the left engine, just outside my window, burst into flames. The plane lurched, followed by a loud pop. Barely one hundred feet off the ground, the plane's nose angled steeply down. Passengers not buckled in went flying, many vomited, most screamed. I hit my head on the seatback in front of me, twisting my poor neck again, even with my seatbelt on. The pilot managed to land the plane at the edge of the runway, clipping a building with the right wing, collapsing part of the landing gear. Evacuation was orderly. The engine was charred from having sucked in a pair of low-flying vultures just at the moment of takeoff. The smell of roasted vulture hovered in the air.

Three or four hours later, we were resettled into another flight to Calcutta. Zafar, who had been on an airplane only a handful of times, was shaken up and quiet during the trip. My neck hurt and my mind raced. The Tatas were Parsis, Persian Zoroastrian fire worshipers who disposed of their dead as the Tibetans do by leaving bodies on high ground for vultures to eat. *Vultures flaming. Vulture capitalists. Vulture plane crash.* Myron's research had shown that the Tatas, the Parsis, were the "good guys" of Indian business, claiming to live by their common expression, "Parsi, thy name is charity." They had built many hospitals and medical research centers. But they were capitalists. They were a huge corporation. I could almost hear Lev saying, "Beware, they will put profit first, and fuck the little people."

Isao Arita met us in Calcutta, and we exchanged notes about Tatanagar. He told me there were now many unexplained importations into West Bengal. Isao arranged for us to take a train part of the way and coordinated with a Bihar district health officer to meet us with a WHO jeep for the ride to the city.

That is how, on April 10, 1974, Zafar and I wound up driving a jeep with a large WHO logo through a wide tree-lined avenue that encircled India's pride, a modern steel city nestled between the Parsi fire temple and the ever-present hot glow of the Tata iron and steel works. We drove directly to the Tatanagar train station, where we saw the apocalyptic vision of a town under siege from smallpox: the young mother stumbling out of the crowd and pushing her dead son into my arms like an offering at a temple, the dead bodies piled up like cords of wood, and the skeleton of a man clutching a train ticket with his pox-covered fingers. My mind raced with a ferocity born of panic. I was the only UN doctor on the scene. Zafar didn't have the answers—he was looking to me. It was the first time I wasn't calm in a storm.

Most of the victories in the eradication campaign had so far been won in rural or less-populated areas. Or in areas with a

large WHO presence. Or with a more seasoned WHO manager. But, oh hell, how would we deal with an out-of-control
epidemic of rapidly spreading smallpox in the middle of an industrial city, where 20 percent of the population was traveling
on public transportation at any given moment, where unvaccinated workers arrived and departed from all over the country,
and where there were rumors of dead bodies clogging rivers and
birds of prey tearing at the pock-ridden body parts of tiny children? What would we do in a city with no centralized government, no public health structure in place, where Tata Companies
had taken over that role and was unaware of, hid, or denied the
epidemic? No one had ever faced a situation like this. Such an
outbreak would require mass quarantine as well as search and
containment on a huge scale, and there was no army or public
health corps or National Guard or centralized entity around to
enforce it. It would require finding every case of smallpox and
engineering a ring of immunity around it, tracing each outbreak
to its source, posting watch guards, and vaccinating nearly every
one of the three-quarters of a million residents of the area.

I was in over my head, filled with self-doubt, far away from
Delhi and out of contact with my mentors. I felt only the full
weight of failure. I trembled.

Zafar and I headed to the Tata infectious disease hospital.
We went bed by bed, counting twenty-two men, women, and
children with smallpox. Another ten patients with pox on their
bodies lay in hallways and on mats on the floor in a makeshift
emergency room. On a bad day in a village in Madhya Pradesh,
I would have seen only two or three cases. The nearby government hospital had just admitted six additional cases. On that
day there were probably more cases in the Tatanagar area than

in any other place in the world. Even Bill, who had seen more smallpox than any of us, hadn't seen an epidemic of this scale before. Maybe nobody had, not in living memory.

Over the years, the horrible things I saw that week have remained vividly burned into my memory. I saw my first case of hemorrhagic smallpox, a rare and particularly gruesome form of the disease. I watched helpless as a frightened older Indian doctor hovered over her pregnant young patient as she was bleeding to death from every part of her body. In sleep, in dreams, in meditations, what I saw that week has been conflated into images of fire and infernos: the Tata steel plants, the Parsi fire temples, the raging inferno of the smallpox outbreak. And the fire that raged inside of me. Watching the pregnant woman bleed to death ignited something in me. Suddenly there was a wind at my back and I knew exactly what to do, without knowing how I knew. Never before, nor since, have I been so singularly focused, so clear in my intentions, so in control of myself and so in command. From a source I cannot explain—but I know began in a moment in Kainchi—I had boundless energy. I was itching for confrontation.

"What the hell are you doing?" I screamed as I burst through the door of the Tatanagar municipal health office, Zafar trying to calm me down.

Dr. Sen,[†] the municipal doctor, the medical officer responsible for this region, stood on his three-step library ladder. "I am organizing my books, as you can see," he said, his face expressionless.

"There is an epidemic of smallpox raging in this city and you're alphabetizing your library? Don't you know what's happening? Don't you know there are dead bodies piled at the train station?" As I became more explosive, Dr. Sen became more placid.

"Of course, I know," he said, not moving from his ladder. "Open the drawer on my desk, the one on the top right." He continued shuffling the books around on the shelves.

The drawer was stuffed full of telegrams from Kerala, Tamil Nadu, Punjab, Rajasthan, Kashmir, Andhra Pradesh, Sikkim, Assam, Nepal, places that were already at zero saying the same thing: smallpox importation traced back to Tatanagar. Zafar and I counted more than three hundred notifications of villages that had been infected. Zafar burst into tears. Years before, Zafar had watched a young child named Zafar die from smallpox, a child with the same name as his own, and had dedicated himself to conquering the disease that killed the younger Zafar. I fell to the floor. I had just seen the person with pocks on his fingers leaving the train station. Two weeks after that, he could have infected others who would die, and they would infect others who would also die. While this was happening, Sen was still on his ladder organizing his books.

"Why aren't you doing anything?" was all I could say.

"What can I do? I'm paid by Tata and the company isn't giving me money for smallpox. I have no resources. I have no staff. How can I respond to any of these notifications if I have no resources?"

"But did you tell them what's happening? Do they know?"

He looked up. His face had the same blank, catatonic stare I'd seen in others helpless in the face of mass suffering, violence, and death. "I don't know if they know," he responded quietly. "I don't know who to tell. I have been here only six months. I work for the government, but I am paid by the corporation. I don't know to whom I report. I have written the state government for help but I have gotten no answer. There is no functioning city government to appeal to." The Tatanagar region consisted of nearly a dozen company towns, basically owned and operated by different divisions of Tata Companies with no functioning central municipal government.

"Who's the biggest boss? Who can change this? Which company is the biggest?" I asked.

"It is TISCO, sir. Tata Iron and Steel Company."

"Who runs TISCO?"

"I don't know. I think his name is Mody."

"What's his first name?"

"I don't know," he answered.

I tore out of the office back to the jeeps. I asked the local drivers the name of the CEO of TISCO. They hedged and finally answered: Russi Mody.

It was about 8 or 9 P.M. by this time, so tracking Russi Mody down at the TISCO offices wasn't an option. I started asking where he lived. No one would tell me. Zafar kept saying we should wait till morning. But I had just held a dead boy in my arms. I wasn't going to wait.

He had to live in the Kaiser Colony, the homes built by Kaiser Steel for company employees before it became part of the Tata empire. As Zafar and I drove through the serene and somewhat surreal neighborhood that had gridded streets lined with cookie-cutter suburban houses, I extrapolated an estimate of all of the smallpox cases in Tatanagar, scribbling numbers in my diary: cases at the railway station, patients in the isolation wards and hospital corridors. Zafar and I passed piles of bodies alongside the road, awaiting cremation or burial. We drove by two men that most Indians called untouchables and Mahatma Gandhi named *Harijans,* or God's children, carrying a corpse to the cremation grounds. Zafar interrupted their singsong chant, *Rama Nama Satya Hai!*—God's name is Truth—and asked them politely to put down a body they were carrying and help us understand the scale of what we were seeing. The *Harijans* cried and told Zafar of the children in their community who had perished from the onslaught and told him of rumors of corpses clogging rivers.

"There must be at least five hundred cases of smallpox among all the company towns, Zafar," I whispered.

"More. Many more," Zafar responded in a defeated tone.

In my mind there were two Indias: the traditional India of the villages, and the modern India, the aspirational India, the rich India of the cities. In modern, rich India, there was no smallpox. The wealthy were vaccinated, unaware, smug. Or so I thought.

We searched Kaiser Colony for two or three hours, knocking on doors until we were told where Russi Mody lived. It looked like any house in suburban America, like my childhood house in Detroit. It looked nothing like the huts in the countless villages I had seen in India, nothing like the slum around the Tatanagar train station.

I sat with Zafar in our jeep trying to screw up the courage to cross the sidewalk to the manicured lawn and make my way to the front door. To psyche myself up, I repeated the following thoughts: *Smallpox is loose in modern India, not just in the villages. If we don't stop this now, we will lose the battle. We can't lose. Maharaji said we would win.* I opened the door of the jeep.

"Larry, you cannot just walk into his house," Zafar pleaded with me. "You have no idea how powerful these people are. Do you really think they don't know what's going on? Of course they do. They are ignoring it. Dr. Sen, their own employee, is even powerless to bring it to their attention. This is not the United States.

You can't just go barge into the house of the head of the largest company in India. You don't know what they can do to you."

As a Muslim in a Hindu world who had grown up in a slum with just enough education to become a sanitation inspector, Zafar feared he could be thrown in jail and disappeared. I never saw anything like that while I was in India, but my white skin, my U.S. citizenship, my UN passport—they, I hoped, would protect me if what Zafar said was true. Maharaji had named me after a general in the battle of good versus evil. General Subrahmanyum could not be afraid.

"I'm going." If I didn't, we might lose the battle. That would make Maharaji's prediction wrong. Maharaji wasn't wrong.

It was now nearly midnight. It was late and I was tentative. A butler answered and I asked for Mr. Mody. "Sir, it is late, he is eating dinner and you may call on him in the morning at his office." The door closed and this time I pounded. When the butler opened it again, I pushed past him into the foyer. I could see Mody and another man sitting at a table in the kitchen at the end of the hall. A Tibetan mastiff grabbed my wrist in his mouth. I could feel its teeth against my skin. I had no doubt that if I moved he'd draw blood or worse. I yelled out to the man in the kitchen, "Are you Mody?"

"Who the hell are you?" Russi Mody demanded as he stomped from his kitchen to the front door. "It's late! What the hell are you doing in my house?"

"Do you know what your company is doing to the world?" I bellowed. "It is ruining the world. You are exporting smallpox to every country. You are exporting nothing but death. And no one is telling you about it. If they tell you everything is fine, you are being lied to!"

"What? What are you talking about? What do you want?"

"I want you to take responsibility for what is happening in your city." He called the dog off but I was now surrounded by male servants, and the dog continued to growl. I rubbed the teeth marks on my wrist. Mody's dinner companion came from the kitchen and held the dog. The butler closed the front door. Zafar remained stubbornly outside with the jeep.

"Exporting death? What are you talking about? Who is exporting death?" Mody demanded.

"Tatanagar!" I was becoming more impatient by the minute.

"Tatanagar? This city? This place?"

"Yes, this city is exporting death all over India."

"I don't understand," Mody was now trying to calm the situation. "Who do your work for?"

"I work for the United Nations. I'm a WHO medical officer."

His body went slack and his face opened in surprise.

"Come in. Come to the kitchen. This is Sujit Gupta, my top lieutenant," he motioned toward his dinner companion. "We are just finishing our meal. Come get something to eat. Slow down and explain what you are talking about. What is this export of death?"

A servant brought a third chair to the table in the hot kitchen. There was no air conditioner. Fans buzzed and a massive dehumidifier rumbled. I couldn't eat. I felt sick.

"Mr. Mody, don't you know the eyes of the world are on your country, and they will be on your city now?"

"It's not my city."

"Yes, but TISCO basically owns it. I just came from Dr. Sen's office, your medical officer, the man you pay to run the municipal health department. He is getting the notices and is not acting on them."

"Who is Dr. Sen? I don't know anything about this. I really don't even know any Dr. Sen."

"Your medical officer. He is catatonic. He is your entire smallpox staff. I was at the Tatanagar train station today and there are dead bodies piled there. I held a dead child in my arms. He was blind. He was covered by smallpox. Can you even think about his mother? There is a rampant epidemic in your town, maybe the worst in the world. Do you even know what smallpox is?"

Sujit said, "Do you mean *basanta?*"—the Bengali name for smallpox, meaning spring sickness.

I pulled out the recognition card and showed it to them.

"Yes, of course we know what smallpox is. But isn't it everywhere? It's all over the world. There's nothing anyone can do about that."

"Oh no, Mr. Mody. No, Mr. Gupta. Smallpox is only here. Only in India. Only in Bihar. Only in your part of Bihar. We have almost eradicated it everywhere else. We have eradicated it from 150 countries. This is the last epidemic in the world. Right here. There is more smallpox in Tatanagar than in all the rest of the world, probably. You are exporting it everywhere. From Kashmir to Kerala, you are sending death all over India. We are on the verge of eradication, and your train station stands between us and our goal. You have one helpless man working on it, and that is Dr. Sen."

"Does our Bombay office know?" Russi Mody was referring to the headquarters from which J. R. D. Tata ran Tata Companies.

"I have no idea. WHO only figured out last week that Tatanagar had caused more than three hundred outbreaks all over India."

"What? Are you telling me that there have been three hundred outbreaks of smallpox in India that came from Tatanagar?" Russi declared more than asked.

"Yes. And most of these entered states and districts that the Government of India and WHO had spent years clearing of smallpox. Also TISCO town has exported at least one or two outbreaks internationally."

"Shit!" Russi said to no one in particular.

"Should we call J.R.D.?" Sujit Gupta asked.

"We have to. And we have to wake him. Okay. I understand. Of course we will help. I had no idea. I did not know. Come to the office in the morning. Excuse me. I will call my chairman to brief him now. We will get this done."

Sujit Gupta walked me to the WHO jeep. I introduced him to Zafar. Sujit and Zafar walked alone together across the street and Sujit asked in Hindi something like, "Is it really as bad as the *Angrezi* says?" Zafar replied, "Worse, sir."

Zafar and I left exhausted to get a few hours of sleep at the dak bungalow that had been arranged for us. Sujit Gupta, a few close aides, Zafar, and I joined Russi in a TISCO conference room the next morning to place another call to Bombay. Russi got J. R. D. Tata and other executives on the line and asked me to repeat what I had told him the night before—that Tatanagar was responsible for one of the worst outbreaks of smallpox in history and had reinfected parts of India and beyond that had been free of the disease.

J. R. D. Tata repeated what Russi Mody had said: "I did not know. I did not know."

By then, Tata staff had brought hospital records to Russi's office. Based on their own accounts, TISCO town had recorded 377 cases of smallpox in the first three months of the year. If that rate held constant for the other fourteen reporting units of the peninsula on which Tatanagar sat in the center of the state of Bihar, it would mean one thousand cases so far this year and as many as four thousand for the full year. With reporting chronically low, it was much more likely that more than two thousand people had gotten sick with smallpox between January and April 1974. Dr. Sen, the Tatanagar city medical officer we had found catatonic in his office alphabetizing his books on that first day in Tatanagar, was coming back to life and started working closely with us. He was still receiving more than one dozen new notices of importations from Tatanagar to other cities in India every day.

Those numbers were staggering. The chairman of India's largest company bellowed at Russi, "Give Brilliant or WHO or whoever is in charge what they need, but stop telling me how bad it is and give me a damn plan." I phoned Nicole from the TISCO office and she was relieved by the response of Tata top executives, but still very much on edge that this huge outbreak was exporting more cases with every day we delayed action.

For the next forty-eight hours Zafar, Sujit, and I worked nonstop. The Government of India sent us a deputy director, Dr. Rao. Dr. A.G. Acharia, the head of the Bihar smallpox program, drove down from Patna. Nicole pulled a Russian epidemiologist, Dr. J. P. "Yuri" Rikushin, from Bengal as well as a Czech epidemiologist, Vladamir Zikmund, from neighboring Orissa. We met each morning to puzzle out how WHO, the Central and Bihar state governments, and a private company like Tata could work together.

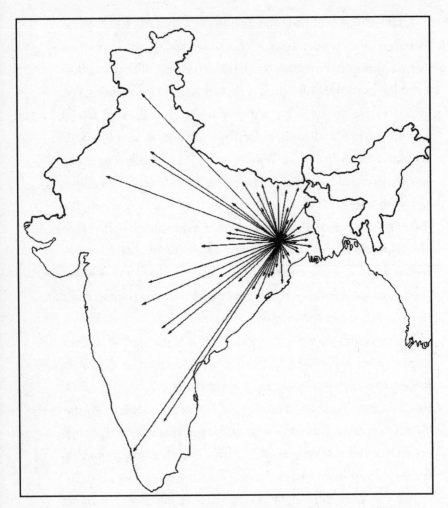

The Spread of Smallpox from Tatanagar (also known as Jamshedpur)

Stopping exportations meant quarantining the city; in fact, it meant quarantining the fifteen diverse company towns and "units" that formed the infected area. Tatanagar was the name of the peninsula formed by the junction of two rivers, the Kharkai and the Subarnarekha. The total population was about eight hundred thousand and was broken down into separately incorporated towns, each owned by a different Tata company. There was nothing like a single controlling county or provincial government. It was painful but less mysterious now to see how thousands of cases of smallpox could have fallen between the cracks.

No one in living memory had tried to quarantine such a large Indian urban area. There would be much resistance from shopkeepers and importers, coal mine operators, and especially railway officials. One by one we had to persuade them of the scope of the emergency and get their cooperation.

Russi called the district magistrate, who agreed to promulgate an official order that the entire peninsula would be closed off to travel. I offered section 269 of the Bengal vaccination act, which the district magistrate cited in his order. All bridges, roads, and railway and bus lines fell under this order and were to be barricaded and staffed by police and vaccinators. Anyone without a vaccination would be prevented from leaving.

Sujit did the same with the general manager of South Eastern Railways, who agreed to put out an order implementing a "no ticket without vaccination" rule. Tata volunteers—along with Rotarians and Lions, who also sent volunteers to be trained—would staff several check points, twenty-four hours a day. They accepted my suggestion that all trains leaving Tatanagar be rerouted to a more remote track, across a bridge that separated the trains from the main platform of the station. From there, no one would be able to sneak onto a train without a vaccination. Trains heading south and east would be stopped and searched at the first station outside of Bihar state.

We concocted a management structure to fill the vacuum between the insular company towns and the government health system and began to implement the plan. We started with weekly meetings, co-chaired by Russi and me. The more he learned about the hidden epidemic, the more he realized, in his words, how much he had "fucked up royally." The spread of killer smallpox had happened on his watch, and he was angry at his failure to know about it. I had a brief moment of bewilderment: *I have never met a CEO or managing director before, and now I am co-chairing a meeting with one of the most powerful CEOs in India—and he's a genuine human being.*

We needed an independent set of evaluators, who were not part of Tata or the Indian government, to report back on spots that were missed, individuals who were not doing their jobs, and so on. I asked the newly arrived Dr. Rikushin to oversee this process. We borrowed sanitary workers from a technical training school in Tamil Nadu. Like many South Indians, they were horrified when they saw the poor conditions of workers in Bihar. Because these students spoke English but not Hindi, we paired them with Tata and Rotary volunteers who spoke Hindi but did not understand public health. Under Dr. Rikushin, those teams became our eyes and ears. They would tell us when cases were being hidden, whether vaccinators were extorting villagers, and whether anyone was trying to sneak out of the containment area without being vaccinated.

The Tata administrators helped us put together the plan in the "Tata way," which included terms I had never heard before: "deliverables," "action items," and "management by objective." Teams of Tata vaccinators trained by WHO staff conducted door-to-door searches for new cases to execute the containment vaccination required by our protocols. The outline, which included an operating plan, a budget, duties, and responsibilities by person and time, was the most comprehensive document I had ever seen. Russi sent one of his own aides to hand-carry a dozen printed and bound copies of this plan to Bombay and duplicates to Nicole, M.I.D. for the Government of India, and Dr. Acharia for the state of Bihar. On the final approval call, J.R.D. announced that Tata would bear full financial responsibility for stopping the outbreak and the exportations. He authorized Russi to chair the emergency smallpox campaign and for TISCO to lead all Tata entities. Sujit would have day-to-day operating control.

Within seventy-two hours, Tata vacated a TISCO building on its main Tatanagar campus and turned it over to the smallpox team. They added fifty doctors from Tata hospitals around the country, two hundred paramedical supervisors, six hundred search workers, and fifty jeeps. Along with that came an army of one thousand Tata managers and volunteers.

We organized into three teams. Dr. Sen was given a team of several hundred volunteers and jeeps to run the search activities. He was turning out to be extremely agile, overseeing weekly searches of the nearly two hundred thousand homes on the peninsula. One search worker could cover one hundred houses a day—five hundred in a week. It would take three hundred full-time workers to search each house in a five-day week. To make sure that sick people stayed put during the period they were contagious, we posted watch guards at the doors of every infected home. To keep the sick from going out for food, we arranged for meals to be sent to infected houses as I had learned from Steve Jones, who began the practice in the area of Bihar just northwest of us near Patna. And unlike WHO, Tata never complained about using company money to pay for food to prevent destitute people with smallpox from becoming beggars. As for containment, a separate team of vaccinators accompanied the search teams; we set up municipal vaccination centers and vaccinated at temples, mosques, local markets, and schools. Tata made sure we were staffed for sufficient searchers and vaccinators and had money to hire on the spot. The company sent dozens of top-flight managers to the field as tactical advisers.

Tatanagar was buttoned up tight. No one could leave by bus or car or train without being vaccinated. No one. No exceptions. Tata teams, operating under the written orders of the district magistrate and accompanied by police from each of the fifteen administrative units, carried out a near perfect quarantine of the entire peninsula. It was tight as a drum.

I devised challenges to test the system, offering a month's wages to some smart young Tata workers if they could sneak through our cordon sanitaire by getting onto a train or bus or even into a taxi to try to get through the barricades without being stopped by our teams. Not a single one made it.

At the train station, our enthusiastic vaccinators stopped a well-dressed party of five who refused to be vaccinated. I did not know this at the time, but when one of the men in the group showed he was a member of parliament, there was a tense jurisdictional standoff. But the Tata vaccinators countered with signed orders from the superintendent of police and the district magistrate. In a rush to catch his departing train, a very angry MP agreed to be vaccinated, muttering, "This is not the end of this," as he boarded his train.

It was time for me to go back to Delhi. It had been less than two weeks since I barged into Russi Mody's house. During that time my image of Tata had gone from thinking of them as an apathetic, amoral entity to seeing them as a fast-moving and efficient partner in the battle against smallpox. Dr. Acharia had gotten permission from the Bihar state health minister to come to Tatanagar to take over. Everything seemed in place to succeed. I had never seen any program erected and put in place so quickly and so well. In my final phone call with J. R. D. Tata before leaving his city, I broached the subject of extending Tata financial and logistical support to the area around Tatanagar, Chotanagpur, and I confided my fear of a ping-ponging of the epidemic between the less-developed area of southern Bihar and the developed industrial area. He understood immediately and said, "We may be willing to help there as well."

"I'll get in touch with my boss, Dr. Grasset, and we'll put together some thoughts."

J.R.D. was willing to meet in Delhi or Bombay, but he wanted to make clear how dubious he was that Prime Minister Gandhi would let Tata participate anywhere except in the area directly within the domain of Tata Companies. There was both personal and professional animosity. Even for the good of the country, even to save lives, J.R.D. doubted that the prime minister would permit the partnership. On top of that, since the Tatas had been culpable in failing to recognize the extent of the epidemic in their own company town, he felt sure that Gandhi would rather score political points against an industry she had her eye on nationalizing than let the Tatas help solve the problem.

I suggested that Nicole could facilitate a meeting between J.R.D. and Dr. Karan Singh, the Government of India health minister. J.R.D. was as abrupt on this point as he had been gracious on the others: "No," he said. "This is between the prime minister and myself. I will have some indication of how it will go when I meet with you and your WHO boss in Bombay or Delhi."

While I moved to another room to report the idea of a public/private partnership with the Tatas to Nicole, Russi and Sujit stayed on a separate line with J.R.D. Nicole was intrigued, but none of us knew how well it would work given the political tensions. WHO was running out of options to fund the increasingly expensive smallpox campaign. D.A. had created a workaround for the limited budget by setting up a "special fund" to receive contributions from countries or foundations willing to support global smallpox eradication. The Soviets had donated a great deal of vaccine through this fund. Canada, USAID, and Scandinavian countries had made donations, as had the United Kingdom. But the Arab oil embargo had raised the cost of petrol severalfold. Some of the poorer states, especially Bihar but also Assam in the east, were cutting down the number of jeep trips according to what they could afford. Nicole was in conversation with the office of the shah of Iran and with some Iranian doctors at WHO. She planned to visit the shah on her next home leave to get a donation to subsidize petrol for jeeps. D.A. had gotten $900,000 from the Chinese government by way of China foregoing its annual payment from the United Nations, which was given as aid to developing countries. China felt it was no longer a developing nation and did not want to be seen accepting charity. The government of Sweden, through the Swedish International Development Cooperation Agency, SIDA, was considering a multimillion-dollar grant, but all of that might take a long time.

Whatever the Tatas' motivation, which included both self-interest and public service, the managerial skills of Tata executives were a revelation to me. Maharaji's confidence that smallpox would be eradicated seemed unmoored from the actual work that was needed to achieve it. But now came help from a place I would have least expected it: a huge capitalist corporation, whose leaders' motivation to make money seemed to be tempered by either an enlightened self-interest or something more profound. And we had gotten luckier than anyone could have imagined: three weeks after the quarantine of Tatanagar was in place, India muddled through their biggest railroad strike in history. If the strike had happened any sooner, or the containment of Tatanagar had been later, we wouldn't have been able to mobilize enough personnel or supplies to get the epidemic under control. No Tata workers could have reached Tatanagar from Bombay, no government support could have reached us from Delhi. During the strike, thousands upon thousands of people overran buses and trucks, and the few trains that did move had hundreds of illegal passengers on their rooftops; even more mobilized and marched to protest the government and the strike. Operating under those conditions would have made containment next to impossible.

Just before leaving Tatanagar, I called Lev. Importations into Madhya Pradesh from Tatanagar had slowed almost to nothing. On the plane back to Delhi, while writing up my report for WHO and the Government of India, I was exhausted but also proud. The worst exporter of smallpox in the world had been shut down. States all over India could mop up fairly easily. But I was also quite aware that the huge area surrounding Tatanagar, full of uncharted jungle and off-the-grid villages, would be really tough. If Tata would fund that part of the program as well and Prime Minister Gandhi would permit it, we could chase smallpox out of the state.

Incidence of Smallpox

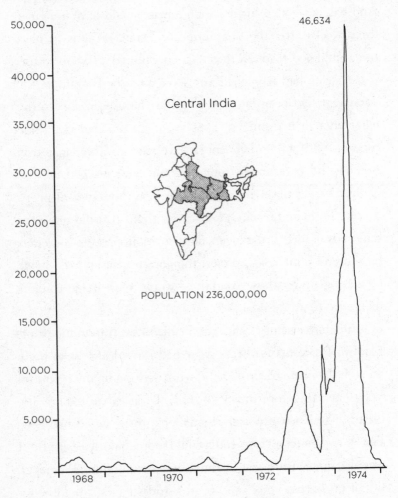

Central India

POPULATION 236,000,000

46,634

CHAPTER 15

Smiling Buddha

Sometimes the light's all shinin' on me,
Other times I can barely see.

—Grateful Dead, "Truckin"

M ay Day in Socialist India was usually a time for workers to celebrate their achievements. It wasn't true on May Day 1974 when the country was simmering with labor protests against Prime Minister Indira Gandhi and her Indian National Congress government. One of the most powerful union leaders, Georges Fernandes, president of the All India Railwaymen's Federation, split with the prime minister and declared a nationwide strike, initially taking nearly 1.7 million railway workers and almost all the trains in India out of commission for a month. More unions threatened to join the work stoppages. India could grind to a halt.

If the trains weren't moving, vaccine, vaccinators, and equipment might not get where they needed to go. If health workers joined the strike, it might kill the smallpox campaign in India. Prime Minister Gandhi jailed Fernandes; in retaliation Jayaprakash Narayan, one of Mahatma Gandhi's most beloved disciples and "the Prophet of people's power," organized marches to replace her government with a "people's government" in Bihar. The chaos was terrible for the smallpox campaign.

The longer the campaign took, the more everything cost. WHO was running out of money. Our leadership team at SEARO in Delhi was also shorthanded: Bill Foege had returned to CDC in Atlanta to try to convince the U.S. government to increase its support; Zdeno was in South India fighting off importations from Tatanagar; Nicole, alone in Delhi and struggling with kidney stone attacks, was strongly advised to be medically evacuated to Switzerland for surgery. Fortunately, the Tatanagar quarantine had stopped the reinfections. This was the first good news after setbacks with the Government of India, the railway strike, and WHO's cash shortfall.

J. R. D. Tata agreed to meet Nicole and me in New Delhi in spite of the fact that Mrs. Gandhi hadn't yet approved the partnership. He was seriously contemplating our request to expand Tata funding from the containment of Tatanagar peninsula to the campaign for most of Bihar, the most troubled state. Nicole and I worked with our Indian colleagues to draft a plan, creating a new and separate entity, the Chotanagpur Smallpox Eradication Program, named for the six districts in the region where the epidemic raged. It would be the first joint venture of its kind, with WHO, the Government of India, the Bihar state government, and the Tata Companies in a partnership to eradicate smallpox.

With thousands of search workers and vaccinators, dozens of junior doctors and highly skilled mid-level Tata managers transferred from their related companies, we felt we could clear smallpox from the southern half of the state in six months. But our counterparts in the Indian government remained skittish; they didn't believe J. R. D. Tata would agree to the huge amount of money needed, or that Prime Minister Gandhi, no friend to private industry, would permit it. No one from the Government of India had come to the Tata meeting because Mrs. Gandhi had yet to give a nod to the arrangement.

We arrived at the Tata House, located on Prithvi Raj road, an area usually reserved for embassies, in a WHO jeep with Nicole's suitcase in the backseat. Having already delayed her surgery beyond reason, she was in a lot of pain, though she tried to hide it. If all went well she would leave directly from J. R. D. Tata's home, pick up what she needed from WHO, and continue on to the airport for a night flight to Geneva for surgery. Sujit brought a two-page plan accompanied by appendices of charts, graphs, and budget projections that we had prepared together.

My cousin Myron Belkind from the Associated Press helped us prepare for the meeting with J. R. D. Tata. He supplied us with articles from the French press reporting that not only had J.R.D. been born in Paris to a Parsi Indian father and a French mother, he had attended French schools and boasted of his "French-ness" when away from India. Nicole could not have been more French, and she never looked more French or more elegant than she did for that meeting. She sauntered toward the entrance to the house like she was strolling along the streets of Paris.

J. R. D. Tata was full of élan and a burning curiosity, the picture of old-world elegance. He had been educated in France, Japan, India, and England, and we learned that day that he had also been a soldier in the French Army. This Persian-Indian-French legend helped develop some of India's largest industries—airlines, railways, steel, tin, and other commodities. He was lean and straight, charismatic and direct. As chai was poured from intricately designed silver teapots into fancy English china, J.R.D. fired off staccato commands in Hindustani to his household staff, spoke in businesslike English with Sujit and me about what he wanted to accomplish in this meeting, and spoke warmly in French with Nicole, from whom he evoked what looked almost like a coquettish smile.

"Dr. Grasset," he started, "I recognize my company's obligation to clean up the mess we caused by our own inattention to the situation in Tatanagar. I am deeply sorry that unemployed youth—unemployed I might add because of the prime minister's policy of nationalization of industry—were caught in the smallpox epidemic in Bihar and spread it through our towns and beyond. I have deployed our employees to help the district magistrates and the police enforce the quarantine, and I want to thank you and WHO and this young Brilliant here for helping us. I am willing to support cleaning up our mess and will fund the containment of smallpox in our towns.

"As far as the rest of the state is concerned, as far as the Chotanagpur area, why should Tata do the work of the Government of India? All the government does is try to stifle us. Besides our industrial grievances with the government, why stop with just this one disease? Your proposal is for Tata to provide jeeps and manpower and forty-two lakh rupees just for a single disease. I don't mean to be unkind, but as long as people are poor, they will keep having more children. Until India has massive economic reform, you will never eradicate smallpox. Even if you do, the population will continue to explode and it will be the end of India. Tell me you will work on family planning, and I will give you lots of money."

Nicole replied, trying to persuade J.R.D. that he and his company could have the chance to play a historic role in the eradication of the first disease in human history. "We four people drinking tea, sitting at this beautiful marble table, you and Sujit Gupta and Larry and I, we are part of the warp and woof of history." She then offered him a chance to step into a key role on the stage of history, joining the Russians and Americans, the Indians and Africans, the doctors and United Nations visionaries.

The French government and French people would love him and regale him, she added, if he, as much a Frenchman as an Indian, helped conquer a disease that Napoleon himself had created sanitary rules against and that Louis Pasteur had battled; the disease that had killed the French monarch Louis XV, Louis the Beloved. She placed J.R.D. into history as an Indian patriot helping to liberate a country from an ancient scourge. Nicole reasoned that only an Indian businessman, not the government alone, could accomplish this. "In the end," she said, "it is not about socialism versus capitalism, government versus industry; it is about what kind of a man you are. You can help to eradicate smallpox forever. You can be part of the greatest public health success in history."

Then she brought her high-minded overview down to concrete examples. She spoke about what D.A. had done organizing a worldwide program, and what Bill had done in Africa. She offered Madhya Pradesh as proof of how an entire Indian state had been cleared of smallpox in six months. When J.R.D. countered with the bad press over sky-high levels of smallpox, Nicole brushed it off, reminding him that these new reports of smallpox were the result of a well-organized house-to-house search that broke open decades of case suppression. It was good news, not bad.

"I appeal to your brain and your sense of duty," Nicole finished in French, "but I also shall appeal to your heart on behalf of your French mother to do this."

Sujit Gupta stared at me with horror. Nobody talked to The Chairman that way!

J. R. D. Tata started to laugh. It was as if the Frenchness of Nicole's request had hit his funny bone. It lowered his defenses and settled the question. "Well," he chuckled, "I have been in many negotiations, but never one like this. I can see I can't stop you or change your mind. And I accept your analysis of the need to eradicate smallpox, although I do not rationally see how you can do it." He looked at me and said, "Let me see the plan." I handed him the two-page document. He read every word, but it was obvious that he had already made his decision.

"Madame, I'll do it if Mrs. Gandhi will write a letter saying that her government will accept Tata help. She must sign it personally, and it must be public. If she doesn't, our participation will not be taken seriously, and we will have no authority over the process. Sujit must be able to attend meetings, and he tells me that he and your young fellow with the Brilliant name—how can you live up to a name like Brilliant?—can run the thing if the government either joins us or gets out of the way. The prime minister is in a lot of political trouble these days. I certainly do not want to rescue her, but I am willing to help with smallpox if she is also willing to meet us halfway." Tata promised to put up forty-two "lakh of rupees"—the equivalent of $500,000 then, millions of dollars in today's valuation.

On the drive to the WHO office, Nicole could hardly catch her breath or contain her pain. I thought I could see some fear in her face. If Tata did not follow through or Prime Minister Gandhi did not agree, we couldn't contain the five hundred outbreaks in Bihar on our own. If Prime Minister Gandhi would not permit Tata vaccinators to stop travelers and detain them at train and bus stations until they were vaccinated, we might not be able to even keep a lid on exportations from Tatanagar.

"Larry, to get this started, D.A. will need to get the director-general to personally intervene with Mrs. Gandhi." That meant Dr. Halfdan Mahler, the director general of WHO. He was a Danish doctor who had worked on tuberculosis in India and was very well regarded by a generation of Indian doctors and politicians. "I will try to see D.A. in Geneva after my surgery. You need to keep the planning going with Sujit Gupta and see what you can learn from M.I.D. or Basu about the politics."

We got to WHO and went up to the smallpox unit. Nicole packed papers and went over last-minute details. She rattled off a dozen ideas and instructions. "Larry, you're on your own here in SEARO for a while. We need Zdeno to make sure none of the importations catches fire in the south. When Bill gets back from CDC, he is going to go right into meetings in Patna in Bihar. He will have to beat back the skeptics in WHO and the Government of India. I know I can count on you to represent us all in Delhi for the next few weeks."

Then, as she rushed out of the office for her ride to the airport, she said, "You did a great job with Tatanagar and the Tatas. I will work with D.A. to figure out how we are going to get Mrs. Gandhi to write that letter. J.R.D. is quite a man, isn't he?

Very smart. J-R-D—find out what those letters stand for and let me know. But vain, I think it is vain, to demand she sign something. But I think she will have to do it, won't she?

"Let's be optimistic. You and Sujit go figure out how we are going to best spend the rest of J. R. D. Tata's money when we get it. We will need more. I still plan to stop in Iran before I come back and try to get the shah to give us money for petrol. Don't tell Gunaratne that I am planning to go to Tehran and meet the shah. And do not tell a soul that I'm rushing to Geneva for kidney stone surgery.

"I know I can count on you to keep things going while I am gone," she repeated.

A few days after Nicole left, May 6, 1974, was a full moon—the "Buddha moon" or "Buddha Purnima," dedicated to Buddha. By tradition, it was during the full moon in May close to twenty-six hundred years ago that Buddha was born. Years later, also during a full moon in May, he reached enlightenment, and again, years later, on the full moon in May he passed into *parinirvana* on his death. The full moon in May is an important time for Buddhists all over the world, and Kainchi, though nominally a Hindu temple, celebrated Buddha as an emanation of Vishnu.

The day before the full moon was my thirtieth birthday, and Girija and I celebrated with a quick trip to the ashram. Quite a few Indian families and Western devotees were staying there: Ravi Das, one of our closest friends, Mike Jeffery, a Yale-educated U.S. lawyer who would later become a judge in Alaska, was there. Kainchi was beautiful in the light of the bright moon. There was no better place to celebrate my birthday, almost a year into working for smallpox eradication, no better thing to do than to sit in front of the tucket Maharaji had sat on when he told me, time and time again, "You will get this job with WHO and smallpox will be eradicated."

During the next two weeks I was the only international WHO medical officer in SEARO, so technically I was the acting program head. I did my best not to break things. All the reports from the countries in the region, from Sri Lanka to Mongolia, Indonesia to Burma, had to be read and answered. A large number of expense accounts had to be approved.

Most of all I oversaw the analysis of the April smallpox reports from Nepal, Bangladesh, and India. We processed the search results from all the endemic Indian states up to the end of April, and while the numbers of new cases from the searches had increased, the early reports in the first two weeks of May began to show a decrease, as we had hoped. The incidence of smallpox was decreasing across India. Exportations from Tatanagar had stopped completely.

The whole office was engaged in helping our Indian counterparts with planning for the next search in May and June. Bill Foege had been successful in getting CDC to send more young, energetic epidemic intelligence service officers. Both D.A. and M.I.D. sent word that it looked like Prime Minister Gandhi was probably going to sign the agreement. I confirmed with Sujit Gupta, and we made tentative plans to open a new office in southern Bihar for the joint venture. The Tatas rented a large complex in Ranchi, a small town located a couple of hours' drive northwest of Tatanagar. Sujit went there to open it up, and I readied myself to join him after Nicole returned. Sujit purchased a dedicated telex terminal so we could stay in touch from this remote area. I asked him to buy the telex address "Zeropox."

Two weeks later, on May 18, 1974, amidst the monthlong celebrations for Buddha, the teacher of peace, India exploded its first nuclear device, thus becoming the first country outside the five members of the UN Security Council to do so. The newspapers said, "India has become the world's sixth nuclear power." The name given to the underground test was "Smiling Buddha."

That same week, WHO published the official results of the April All-India Search. It was old news to me, but not for the general public. Our latest internal numbers for May showed declines in smallpox, but the data that was published for the April search hit the all-time peak—8,664 infected villages with "pending outbreaks," a new term Bill Foege had introduced to reflect the burden of smallpox on health-care resources. Altogether, 11,000 men, women, and children were reported sick with smallpox in a single week.

WHO and the government did a terrible job explaining to the press the counterintuitive truth that finding a higher percentage of smallpox cases was a success, not a failure. It was an outbreak of better reporting, not an outbreak of new cases. Some reporters for the *Times of India* and the *Indian Express* wrote front-page stories that the smallpox epidemic was raging out of control. The truth was that even though smallpox was indeed raging, it was not out of control. But some of our internal WHO reports, including my confidential report on how bad the exportations were from Tatanagar, had been stolen from the Patna state government office and leaked to reporters who used them to add "color" to the numbers.

Smallpox Eradication in India: Number of Cases per Week

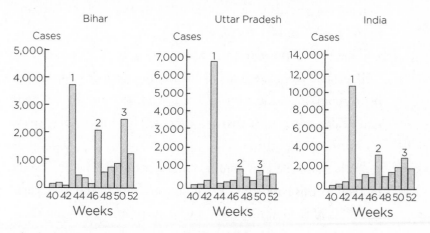

The shock: impact of active searches on reporting of smallpox cases, India, 1973.
1 = first active search; 2 = second active search; 3 = third active search.

As news broke of the Smiling Buddha nuclear explosion, reporters from all over the world streamed into India to cover the test and report on what it meant for nuclear nonproliferation and the balance of power around the world. The United States threatened sanctions. Pakistan vowed to follow suit with its own bomb. Journalists also saw the Indian headlines that the smallpox epidemic in India was history's worst; Myron told me that several had contacted him for background material. Everyone was looking to write a variation of the following story: "As India takes one step forward into the nuclear age, the worst smallpox epidemic in history takes the country two steps back." Having already interviewed the scientists responsible for creating India's nuclear device, international reporters next wanted to meet the idiot who was head of what the newspapers called a failed smallpox program.

That idiot, on that day, was me.

One morning, as I walked past Mrs. Boyer's desk in the reception area of SEARO, she stopped me. "Some people are waiting in the boardroom for you, Larry."

That was all the warning I had.

Reporters from every major international paper jammed the boardroom, the same room where I had first heard the Mongolian health minister discuss death rates. There was barely space for me to squeeze through.

"When are the cars coming to take us to the field?" "Why did you let this happen?" "What do you think of India's nuclear test?" "Is Mrs. Gandhi's government corrupt?" "How did these outbreaks get past WHO?" "Why is smallpox getting worse when so many millions of dollars have been spent on eradication?" "How is it possible that WHO has failed again?"

The questions came at a staccato pace. I had been interviewed by the press only once before—the day after the baby Wovoka had been born on Alcatraz. I tried to explain that the search-and-containment strategy was working, that to epidemiologists it was good news that we were finding a higher percentage of hidden outbreaks. I wasn't worried about the shower of reports—we expected them. I was more worried about the Indian rail strike, which would keep vaccine from getting to the field.

I was thirty years old and had no skill in untangling the conflation of the epidemic of reports and the declining numbers of suppressed cases for the press. I wished Nedd Willard, the WHO PR man, was with me, but he was out of the country. I wished D.A. or Bill or Nicole were there. I fumbled through the press ambush, leaving the journalists with one new concern: what the hell was WHO doing appointing an inexperienced kid to run the smallpox eradication program for eleven countries? Their articles reflected that: reading the papers the next week stung.

I called D.A. to warn him. He thought I was overreacting—until he read the first article: "Smallpox Outbreak Catches WHO Epidemiologists Unprepared." Over a crackly phone line, he was very mellow and simply asked, "You need a little help, son?" With Nicole recuperating in Geneva, both D.A. and Isao Arita flew to New Delhi to my rescue. It was not just the international press we needed to mollify; it was also the Indian government, which was deciding between ramping up the smallpox program, with outside funding provided by CDC, the Swedish government, and the Tatas, or giving up on eradication altogether and resuming mass vaccination.

When Gunaratne, the same regional director who had torn me apart for leaflet bombing WHO, read the papers, he was furious. He had been alarmed by the huge increase in cases revealed by the house-to-house searches, but Nicole had convinced him that we needed to suffer the pain of uncovering a higher percentage of cases in order to avoid outbreaks smoldering undetected and erupting out of nowhere later. After the negative press coverage, Gunaratne berated me every day. "Where is Nicole! How could she leave you in charge? Where is Foege? Zdeno Jezek? This is no time for on-the-job training, Dr. Brilliant. This is not a good time for Madame Grasset to go home to Geneva for a holiday! She is being incredibly irresponsible."

My youth continued to be a huge affront to Gunaratne, and I was willing to accept that, but Nicole was my hero and I wouldn't let him blame her for this mess.

"It's not her fault, sir," I tried. "She is not on holiday, she is on sick leave. Please."

"What kind of sick leave requires her to be out of the country, back at home, at the peak of an epidemic she is in charge of?"

So I told him, "She's in Geneva having emergency surgery for a kidney stone."

He didn't take my word for it until D.A. arrived. D.A. went straight from the airport to give Gunaratne his assurance—personally and professionally—that the smallpox peak was because of our effective search and was not the sign of an epidemic out of control. I will never forget that he went to bat for me. D.A. must have told Gunaratne that the same kid that he had worried "appears to have gone native" had done important work in clearing smallpox out of Madhya Pradesh and ending the nightmare of Tatanagar. He asked Gunaratne to back off and not be angry with me for the press making the obvious comparison between India becoming a nuclear power while still the world's major source of smallpox. It was sobering, D.A. told Gunaratne, that this number of cases—or more—had persisted, hidden, in India for years, maybe even decades. Gunaratne, D.A. said, would be a hero if he held firm. He could be at the helm when we reached zero smallpox in a year. However, knowing D.A., he might have hinted to Gunaratne that he could also be a goat if the press learned that there had always been this number of cases in India year in and year out for every year that Gunaratne had been the regional director. D.A. offered Gunaratne the choice to be hero or goat. Gunaratne chose wisely.

D.A. gave me my first press relations lesson and, later, asked Nedd Willard to spend a couple of days guiding me. I worried that I had let everyone down; however, in D.A.'s mind this was all simply part of the rookie learning curve.

Bullet dodged. Another about to hit.

L arry, M.I.D. needs to see you at the Health Ministry as soon as you can get there." All the internationals, myself included, loved the charismatic M. I. D. Sharma, but after the press ambush and Gunaratne yelling at me again, I expected the worst.

In addition to being the head of the National Institute of Communicable Diseases, M.I.D. was now becoming the commissioner of health for the Government of India. The Health Ministry was in the old, imposing British government buildings. His office was in Nirman Bhavan, or the Health Palace. I greeted his personal assistant with the usual *namaste* and received in return the salute of palms together. M.I.D.'s office was in a large wood-paneled room with a huge circular desk that had the capacity to seat six. M.I.D. was a head taller than most of the Indian doctors. Charismatic and well-respected, he was a big, warm teddy bear of a man. It was always good to see him, and I was happy as long as there was not another bad surprise.

"Larry," he said, "perhaps from now on I should call you 'Sonny' and you should call me 'Papa.' "

"That would be wonderful, M.I.D. Is there some special reason?"

"I was in a meeting with Mrs. Gandhi a few days ago about the quarantine of Tatanagar. Do you remember hearing anything about a politician at the train station being vaccinated by force?"

I vaguely remembered hearing about an unhappy member of parliament. "I don't know, M.I.D. Maybe. It wouldn't surprise me if there hadn't been a few like this. The Tata volunteers had to be aggressive about getting proof of vaccination and not letting anyone on trains. You know we had to button up the city, vaccinate everyone, no exceptions."

"Your volunteers were enthusiastic, to say the least. But this particular politician turned out to be a member of parliament. He was so humiliated he launched an investigation into how Tatanagar came to be quarantined, and your name came up."

In response to the look of panic on my face, M.I.D. raised his hand to stop me from interrupting.

"Wait," he said. "It gets worse, Larry. This MP called his cousin. Do you know who his cousin is?"

I had no idea.

"His cousin is the chief minister of Bihar. He called his cousin to complain that WHO had flouted Indian sovereignty by forcing a member of parliament to be vaccinated against his will. The chief minister wanted the entire organization to be kicked out of India."

My mind went blank. My ears started to ring.

"The chief minister of Bihar heads the Muslim coalition that Mrs. Gandhi relies on to keep her base of power. Especially in Bihar, where Jayaprakash Narayan's movement to create a parallel government is so strong. This MP who was forced to be vaccinated has considerable power."

Oh shit.

The airplanes, the leaflets, the reward, Gunaratne yelling at me over the press, my leaked report on Tatanagar—I could see a long list piling up. Maybe I was too conspicuous, too loud—too

American. Maybe it was my ego again, exactly what Maharaji had warned me against.

My stomach tightened and I braced for the final blow. "Most of the others did not agree with kicking WHO out of India, or stopping the smallpox program, because of the international implications. But Mrs. Gandhi had to do something. So she compromised and she decided she would not evict WHO. But you do know she would have to do something, don't you? She decided that you should be deported. She asked that a Quit India notice be made up immediately for you."

M.I.D. paused for dramatic effect.

"Oh?" I said when I couldn't stand the silence any longer.

"And that's why I think you should call me Papa."

I didn't understand.

He smiled. A huge smile. A chuckle began to break through. And then more laughter. I was beyond confused.

It turns out that M.I.D. made a last-minute plea to the prime minister and he related the rest of the conversation: "Madame, a request." He was already an Indian public health hero. He was a notoriously hard worker; it was widely reported that he hadn't taken a day off in thirty years. Additionally, he had run the malaria eradication program and was one of the top doctors in modern India. People listened when he spoke.

The prime minister stopped for a moment. "What is it, Dr. Sharma?"

"Madame, will you delay the Quit India notice for Dr. Brilliant if I request it?"

"Why?"

"I need seventy-two hours."

"Very well, Dr. Sharma, but please tell me why?"

"Because you are prime minister and may do anything you wish."

I do not remember exactly what he said to me because I think I had stopped breathing. But since he told the story several times again to his wife, my wife, and some of our friends when he visited us later in Ann Arbor, I can summarize what this good man told Prime Minister Indira Gandhi of India on my behalf.

"If you give me seventy-two hours I will adopt Larry, and then you cannot deport him. I will make him an Indian citizen; this is already his adopted country. And, Madame Prime Minister, we need him, and we need all these young, strange, aggressive smallpox workers. We need the Russian scientists, the Czech fieldworkers, and we need these bearded, energetic, creative Americans. We need them. And we also will need the money from Tata and the Swedes. I have not worked to improve public health in India for thirty years to see us become the laughingstock of the world. Smallpox is a global priority. India may be the last place on earth with smallpox. Pakistan has already eradicated smallpox. Pakistan! Pakistan! This is embarrassing. Please do not use this as a time to malign the foreigners.

"And by the way, his guru, Neem Karoli Baba, who, you remember, when the Chinese invaded, predicted they would leave without provoking war, has predicted that we would eradicate smallpox. We have had two hundred thousand cases of smallpox in the last twelve months. India has nearly 90 percent of all the smallpox in the world, but the Baba said that we would eradicate smallpox. So I am willing to adopt Larry to keep him here."

M.I.D. finished telling me what had happened and then chuckled as if at a private joke and said, "For both of our sakes, I hope I did the right thing, Sonny."

From that day until the day he died, this brave, wonderful man called me "Sonny," and I called him "Papa."

The bad press did lead to some good things. The articles lampooning India's attempts to enter the nuclear age amidst a huge outbreak of smallpox finally spurred Prime Minister Gandhi into action. She agreed to swallow her pride, gave support to the surveillance-containment strategy, and put her signature on the public-private partnership with Tata Companies.

The summer was full of amazing advances and heartbreaking setbacks. The Tatas continued to pour in manpower, money, and managerial skills. J.R.D. became more personally involved. Over the next year he would write Nicole and me separate letters on the first day of every month. His typewritten letters always began with a warm, flowing, handwritten salutation, "My dear Larry," in turquoise-colored ink, asking about case counts, jeep deployments, and progress in other countries. Nicole never did show me what J.R.D. wrote to her.

Even as the actual case count declined, the cumulative effect of skepticism and innuendo, however, began turning more WHO officials in Geneva against the search-and-containment strategy. They felt the smallpox campaign was sucking up all the oxygen, diverting staff from malaria and family planning and sanitation and even other immunization programs. It was taking too long. Jankowicz, the WHO communicable disease director who said he'd eat a Land Rover tire if smallpox was eradicated in India, began throwing up roadblocks. His support for reverting to mass vaccination was tantamount to giving up on eradication and settling for a Band-Aid of routine vaccination.

To keep up the house-to-house searches, we needed more health workers. We needed millions of vials of vaccine and hundreds of millions of bifurcated needles to administer the shots. After surgery, on her way back to Delhi from Geneva, Nicole stopped over in Iran. She knocked on the door of the shah's palace and persuaded him, charmed him perhaps, as she had J. R. D. Tata, to contribute oil to keep the smallpox jeeps moving. The oil never materialized because of Indian government pride, but other support did. The British charity Oxfam managed to buy nearly one hundred jeeps for the Chotanagpur program. Nicole found the money for five more epidemiologists from the Swedish Development Agency, which would eventually donate millions of dollars. J.R.D. added to the original sum with several more grants, including one specifically intended to bring more international epidemiologists to help India along the border with Bangladesh.

I was still alone in Delhi, still nominally acting in place of Nicole, when I was called to brief the Indian secretary of health, a Mr. Karmachandran,† on what I assumed would be about the importance of holding fast to the search-and-containment strategy. Bill was in Bihar attending a critical strategy meeting on the same subject.

Mr. Karmachandran was a tall, thin man in his sixties, dressed in a white shirt and Indian khadi vest and trousers, with an elaborate sandalwood *tilaka* on his forehead. Two trails of red powder began on both sides of his forehead and ran below the hairline, joining at the bridge of his nose, where it dipped into an elongated U shape. This mark symbolized the foot of Vishnu, indicating Karmachandran was a Vaishnavite and so also devoted to Ram and Krishna. Finding this connection made me feel like I was meeting a spiritual cousin.

As I told Karmachandran about our plans, he was most curious to learn we were about to order two hundred Mahindra and Mahindra jeeps for the campaign in the jungles of Chotanagpur, sourcing them for the first time in India instead of using Land Rovers and Toyotas.

"Oh, very good that WHO is buying Indian-made jeeps this time," he replied. "But you will like my cousin's jeeps better. They are called Indian Standard jeeps. They are much better than Mahindra's."

"I wish we could order them, sir, but the Standard company makes only two-wheel-drive jeeps. They won't work in the jungle and remote villages. I'm sorry."

"Oh, that's too bad. Especially when things are going well and you have Indira Gandhi back on your side," Karmachandran continued. "It would be disappointing to see things go badly for the smallpox program now when you are so close to finishing the job, Dr. Brilliant. I think you should cancel the order for Mahindra and buy the Standard brand instead. And you'll need to place that order within forty-eight hours."

"But the two-wheel-drive jeeps will mean that we won't be effective in the remote villages," I repeated, near panic. "We can't risk not getting to every corner and making sure we have gone after every case of smallpox."

"You have to choose, my young friend," Karmachandran responded coolly, "between more effective jeeps or a more effective relationship with me."

I thought the floor had dropped out from underneath me. I was being extorted by a man who advertised his spiritual beliefs on his forehead. As with my first press conference, I wasn't equipped to deal with this.

"I am just an underling at the WHO offices," I stalled. "I don't know what I can manage."

That same week, Lama Govinda's wife, Li Gotami, contacted me. She was worried that he was having mini-strokes again. Girija and I agreed to make a weekend visit. When we arrived at their house in Almora, near the Kainchi ashram after about a ten-hour drive from Delhi, Lama Govinda was in a lighthearted spirit. He had indeed been experiencing transient ischemic attacks, but as far as I could tell, there was no long-term damage. So far. He and Li were thinking about accepting an offer from some American Buddhists to go to the United States for an extended visit and medical treatment. Meanwhile, I couldn't do much except make sure he was limiting his salt intake to avoid dangerous spikes in blood pressure. As usual, Lama Govinda asked how he could pay me, and as usual I demurred.

"Is there anything I can help you with, Larry?"

In fact he could. This business of the jeeps was deeply troubling. I did not want to give into a bribe.

I shared my dilemma about the health secretary, who I thought had me in a bind. I conjured up an image of thousands of dead children if I angered Mr. Karmachandran. I couldn't get that image out of my head. I presented the story like someone debating whether or not to sell their soul to the devil to keep all those children from dying.

"Are you sure you are correctly placing yourself in the story?" Lama Govinda asked me. "Don't overly dramatize your role. Be very clear what is asked of you and the likely outcome of your behavior. Then be sure that your actions are for the benefit of the children you are trying to save. If they are, decide only on the basis of the children, not whether or not your hands are getting dirty by giving in to extortion. When compared to the lives of children, your hands getting dirty is not as significant as you are making it out to be. Do not make the problem and your role in it into grand theater nor bigger than it actually is."

Given the tenuous relationship between the Government of India and WHO, I did think that the smallpox program could fail, and more children would die, without a good relationship with this strange and powerful bureaucrat.

I decided. I would sign a purchase order for two hundred two-wheel-drive jeeps if it meant that the Government of India— and Karmachandran—would keep supporting the program. I rationalized the purchase by thinking we could allocate those jeeps to the big cities.

On Monday morning, back in Delhi, I walked into the Health Ministry and approached the desk of Karmachandran's personal assistant.

"Mr. Karmachandran wants to see me," I announced.

"That's impossible," he replied.

Oh, no. I didn't act quickly enough. "But I have to see him today. He gave me a deadline. He's waiting for this."

"It will be impossible for you to see Secretary Karmachandran today because he was transferred out of the central government and sent back to the South India office," the clerk replied. "Would you like to see the interim secretary who is here now?"

Relieved, I told him that that would not be necessary.

Karmachandran knew he was being transferred when he insisted I buy his cousin's jeeps—he was hoping for one last perk from his high position and I was an easy target. In the end, WHO bought only four-wheel-drive jeeps, no one was offered or took a bribe, and Nicole was happy that I had steered the order through WHO and the Government of India, although she was surprised that it had happened so fast.

The entire jeep drama was an illusion in which my righteous indignation was revealed to be just another trick of the ego. Lama Govinda was right: act on behalf of the kids; the results take care of themselves. I also learned a very big lesson: I should have called D.A. in Geneva or Bill in Bihar, but, in my own confused mind, I thought I had to be the hero.

Nicole finally returned in July, free of kidney stones. I worried about how she would react to learning from D.A. about my being overwhelmed by the press. She not only forgave me, she even apologized for putting me in that position.

"You did a very good job while we were gone," she told me in her office. "I was so relieved that Tatanagar was contained and J.R.D. was willing to put up more funds; I was right to hire you as a clerk." She laughed. "Do not worry about the thing with the reporters. We didn't equip you for the news media. But everything is working. The states are making progress. You should make a career in global health. You should stay on with WHO in India after we eradicate smallpox. I thought about some of the things you have done while I was in Europe. The reward leaflets, the elephants—we won't discuss the leaflet drop over the WHO building, will we? Madhya Pradesh is now smallpox free. Tatanagar has stopped spreading its poison. Zdeno and Bill will be back soon and we'll be at full strength again. You won't have to worry about being left alone with a pack of reporters. D.A. gives me credit for sweet-talking J. R. D. Tata, but I could not have done it without you. Tata told me himself that you created quite a favorable impression with your midnight raid on the home of Russi Mody. The corporate officers like your missionary zeal. And you have a real supporter in M.I.D. It is not easy for an American to be so accepted by so many different parts of Indian society."

We walked together through an adjoining door to Zdeno's office. Then she turned to face me.

"By the way, Larry, how did Gunaratne find out I was having surgery for kidney stones?" she asked.

"I told him, Nicole. He thought you were taking a vacation, not a medical leave. He was screaming that you had been irresponsible leaving me in charge to go on vacation. I had to tell him you were having kidney stone surgery so he wouldn't think you used your medical leave for something else."

Thwap! I never saw it coming. Perfectly coiffed, in a new French outfit, red lipstick, and nail polish, the Hurricane on High Heels hauled off and smacked me across the face. My cheek burned. Her fingerprints on my skin bore witness.

"Nicole! What was that for?"

"For telling people I was sick!"

"But, Nicole, I didn't tell anyone who didn't already know. Gunaratne is your boss. You signed a request for sick leave. He knew you were sick but wanted to know why you left so quickly and left me in charge without his knowing. He demanded to know what you had that made you leave so abruptly. I thought he would understand if he knew you had something that required urgent surgery, and he did. He dropped the matter when he found out it was a kidney stone."

"I told you not to tell anyone I was sick and I trusted you with my secret! You'll see," she continued. "One day you will be old and the last thing you will want is other people gossiping about your infirmities. But it's done. You have done more good than bad. Now let's get back to work."

In retrospect, that was the first annual review I had ever received as a UN employee. I was embarrassed and my cheek stung, but I never had nicer things said about me. The French twist at the end was a little bit of a surprise. It came suddenly, like the deluge of the monsoon rains, hitting all at once, and then moving on, nothing lingering behind.

CHAPTER 16

The Goddess of Smallpox Fights Back

they ask me to remember
but they want me to
remember their memories
and I keep remembering
mine

—Lucille Clifton, "why some people be mad at
me sometimes," from *Blessing the Boats*

I spent the rest of that summer in the villages of Bihar, battling Shitala Ma, far away from the politics of New Delhi—the continuing protests against Mrs. Gandhi, the transportation strikes that left our supplies baking on the tarmacs of Indian airports. I was unaware, unconcerned with the news coming out of America. A grand jury had indicted Gordon Liddy and his fellow Watergate criminals, implicating the president of the United States in a criminal scheme to destroy democracy. At the same time, the *Times of India* covered the U.S.-backed coups toppling democratically elected leaders in Latin America, while the war in Vietnam, which had galvanized my generation into political action, came to an ignominious end. Our Russian and Indian friends, tired of the holier-than-thou manner in which our diplomats deified American democracy, had a field day with U.S. expats. Lots of new arrivals to Kainchi and some old friends came to WHO for lunch while we were in limbo waiting for Prime Minister Gandhi and J. R. D. Tata to agree on a way forward. The café had good clean food and it was air-conditioned, a treat if you had been living on an ashram like an ascetic sadhu. Two years before, I had done the same; Girija and I met an American USAID worker and would come down from the hills for a good meal and a blast of cold, breathable, air.

One day, Mrs. Edna Boyer, the cheerful face at the WHO front desk, gave me a message about a visitor. "He just arrived in Delhi from your ashram. You don't know him," Mrs. Boyer said. "He's a young man who came to India looking for your guru, but your guru had already passed. He's intense, a little anti-social I think, and well, may I say he does not smell like a Parisian perfumery. He shaved his head and he didn't want to wear shoes. I sent him out to get clean clothes and shoes or I can't let him into the WHO dining room."

The nineteen-year-old in front of me for lunch that day was Steve Jobs, although I did not know his name then. He had come to India to meet Neem Karoli Baba. Like many young Westerners arriving in India, Steve was scrawny, hungry, and poor. The only remarkable thing about him, in retrospect, was how he managed to get to India. He scraped together the money for his trip by assembling and selling illegal electronic devices known as blue boxes, which, at a time when long distance was outrageously expensive, allowed you to hack into payphones and place all the calls you wanted to anywhere in the world for free.

I don't remember much about the encounter, but Steve reminded me twenty years later that our first conversation was a disagreement about my diet. Steve inhaled his first fresh salad since coming to India, while I ate buffalo liver. I had been a vegetarian for nearly a decade but had begun to feel I was not able to work as hard fighting smallpox because of my vegetarian diet. My French, American, and Russian colleagues who ate meat had more protein in their diet and, I thought, had more energy because of it. Nicole, being French, recommended liver: "Think of it as medicine," she said, "not food."

I lied to myself that I was still a vegetarian because I hated what I was eating. Steve flat out busted my chops. "You're still contributing to killing," he practically shouted while consuming an orgy of fresh vegetables in a room packed with serious diplomats from a dozen countries eating lunch.

He was right; I was a hypocrite. "And how do you justify ending the existence of this form of life, smallpox?" he asked, piling on. "Who are you and your colleagues to take life into your own hands? The Jains wear special sandals so they won't step on insects. So aren't you, in effect, stepping on a really tiny life-form by killing off the smallpox virus?" I was too tired to get angry. Part of me wanted to drag him off to an infected village in Bihar to watch children suffer and die from smallpox and see if he still felt that way about buffalo liver and the smallpox virus. He might have been right about the liver, but he was wrong about the virus.

Five years later we would meet again and begin a friendship that lasted four decades.

The standoff between J. R. D. Tata and the Government of India ended when Prime Minister Gandhi acquiesced, writing a letter. She insisted that she would only write a personal, not an official, letter thanking J. R. D. Tata and accepting his help. J.R.D. must have agreed because everyone else said they had struck a deal. With the partnership finally begun, Girija and I left for Bihar to finish the setup of the Chotanagpur program at its new headquarters in Ranchi, a few hours' drive northwest of Tatanagar.

The Tatanagar train station had by now been turned into a museum, a shrine to the smallpox eradication program. Artists covered the walls with murals depicting the history of smallpox. The names of the victims who died at the station were memorialized. Mourners brought flowers and small religious statues. The sign that signaled to oncoming trains that they had reached Tatanagar was replaced by one that said, "You have reached the Temple of Anti–Shitala Ma land." Tata Companies continued to export a lot of steel and coal, but Tatanagar never again exported smallpox anywhere.

An ebullient Sujit Gupta greeted us at the station and took us to the TISCO guest house. The executives of the Tata Companies and the hospital doctors used the occasion of our return to throw a celebratory dinner with traditional Indian cuisine. There were many toasts. They drank to everything they'd accomplished. They toasted J. R. D. Tata and WHO. They drank to the efforts of Tata employees—assembly-line workers, clerks, drivers, executives, managers—who left their posts to volunteer in the containment effort. And most of all they drank to the fact that the Tata name had been, if not cleared, given a chance for redemption.

During the several weeks of quarantine, commerce in Tatanagar had ground to a halt. The lines to get out of the city—at train stations and on the roads—were huge, and Tata exports had slowed to a trickle. It was clearly bad for business, but not once did these executives talk about how much money they were losing because nearly one thousand of their employees had been diverted to smallpox work. They were most excited about shutting down the exportation of smallpox, about doing the right thing. I was moved by how the three men I had worked with most, J. R. D. Tata, Russi Mody, and Sujit Gupta, had prioritized getting rid of smallpox over making money. Nothing is ever all good or all bad, but sometimes the better nature of the individuals even in the most financially driven company can still trump the bottom line.

Our first Chotanagpur strategy meeting was convened by Sujit Gupta. Dr. Rikushin, the Soviet epidemiologist from the Pasteur Institute in Leningrad, returned from the villages to brief us. A wizened professor who had worked on cholera in Africa, Rikushin was recruited by WHO to be a consultant in tribal Bihar. Besides his clipboards, pens, and folders, he had with him his ubiquitous basket of mangos. He'd never had a mango before coming to India and became so obsessed with the fruit that his mouth was always red and swollen from eating the last of the meat too near the skin. "I love mangos," he joked, "and I will never go back to Russia unless I can have shipments airmailed to me."

Many of the villages inhabited by the Adivasi peoples were located deep in Bihar state, far off the grid, embedded in the jungles of Chotanagpur. Professor Vishwakarma, whom I'd found when I put out a call to anthropologists around the world for help, brought the maps he'd made for his Ph.D. dissertation on the tribes of Chotanagpur. No one, not even the government, had known these maps existed. Vishwakarma had coded them by language and tribe, so as soon as we learned the surname of an Adivasi smallpox victim, we could trace outbreaks back to at least the region from which a person came. Lots of villagers worked in Tatanagar, bringing home extra money and food for their families; if a villager was infected with smallpox, the virus could bounce back and forth between Tatanagar and the tribal villages for as long as people went unvaccinated.

The Ho tribe suffered the worst outbreak. Eradication in their community was up against a major challenge. While they were ethnically Adivasi, several splinter Ho tribes had adopted an orthodox and strict Hinduism, unlike their Santhal and Gond counterparts, so members of this tribe were vehemently against killing cows, and therefore vehemently anti-vaccination.

Rikushin was telling me about his investigation into a source of infection near the Tatanagar steel mills. He traced it back to a remote jungle village, only to discover those villagers, the Munda, were relatives of the Ho tribe. They lived almost as hunter-gatherers in the remote jungles. Rikushin and his team drove several dusty, bumpy hours into the Munda territory where they discovered village after village decimated by smallpox. Rikushin tried to communicate why he was there and tried to vaccinate people, but no one would cooperate. He asked to be taken to the *mukhia,* the village leader.

"No," the *mukhia* replied through a translator. "I will not be vaccinated. Smallpox is sent by Singbonga, Big Friend in the Sky. We will resist your vaccination so that we don't offend Singbonga. Now get out." Rikushin and his team were escorted to their jeeps by Munda members holding drawn bows, arrows pointed at the smallpox team. The tribe was chanting, "We have changed the name of our tribe. We are not Ho. We are not Munda. Now we are *takka nai,* our tribe's name is 'no vaccination.'"

Rikushin had an idea for cooperating with Munda cosmology. Since the Munda saw Singbonga as being in the sky, Rikushin asked the Tatas if they would underwrite hiring a small plane from which to drop leaflets telling villagers it was permitted to get vaccinated. Vishwakarma helped get the leaflet written by hand in the Khmer-like script of the Munda language. Along with the captain of the Tatanagar flight club, Rikushin coordinated an ad hoc mission from the gods.

On Rikushin's next trip to the village, the *mukhia* greeted Rikushin's battalion of WHO jeeps with a warning, "Singbonga would not approve vaccination. You are endangering yourself by returning. Get out now!"

"Wait," Rikushin said through one of the Ho translators. "I am sure Singbonga would approve of vaccination. Just wait a moment." Rikushin listened for the sound of the plane. When he heard it coming near, he repeated, "Singbonga will approve vaccination. You will see." At that moment, the leaflets fell from the sky. A literate tribal member picked one up and read it to everyone. The *mukhia* reversed himself, and the villagers lined up for vaccinations.

To repeat this process all over Chotanagpur would take two hundred sorties, and we didn't have enough personnel. Someone needed to be on the ground communicating with the villagers, and someone other than the pilot needed to drop the leaflets. "I bet our wives would enjoy flying over the villages and dropping leaflets," Sujit said. And they did. Girija went first. She did dozens of leaflet-dropping sorties over Chotanagpur. At the end of the meeting I picked up one of the leaflets that Tata had printed to read it myself. I was most impressed by what was *not* in them: not a single mention of Tata Companies or their sponsorship.

Dr. Vishwakarma enhanced our search teams to double check on the effectiveness of the leaflets by adding transitional leaders from the various villages as supervisors—people who had been to modern schools but lived in the villages and could translate to the rest of the team the language of their ancestors. We created more than four hundred search teams to work in the villages. They all reported into the new Chotanagpur smallpox headquarters in Ranchi, each team had a driver, an Indian medical officer from the government, a WHO medical officer, a transitional leader from the tribe the team would be visiting, vaccinators, a representative from Tata, and a paramedical assistant assigned to each foreign WHO medical officer.

Waves of foreign doctors came to the Ranchi headquarters. The program attracted volunteers from Oxfam. A young couple drove almost straight from Oxford University to Ranchi and volunteered to help in the program. Canadians Alan Morinis and his wife, Bev Spring, arrived in their VW camper. She was studying yoga; he had completed a Rhodes Scholarship. They were the first to be hired officially as a couple for WHO. Bev ran one of the most difficult programs of all, stopping smallpox among homeless pavement dwellers in Calcutta. Around that time, Justin Bhakla showed up in Ranchi. Unusually tall and handsome, he shared the confident posture of the many young tribal men who had gone to Christian schools, where he probably had gotten his Christian name. He was joyful and enthusiastic, and even though he was far less educated than the doctors, he spoke better English because he was educated in "English-medium," while the doctors were educated in "Hindi-medium" and learned English as a second or third language. Though Justin was from the Santhal tribe, he seemed comfortable in every setting, from tribal village to stately Kaiser Colony home.

Justin's family and friends had greeted us with suspicion at first. They didn't trust the Indian government or Europeans— all of whom had lied to them over the redistribution of land, pushing them ever deeper into remote terrain as the Raj and the Indian government grabbed as much land as they could take. But as we demonstrated the vaccine—I vaccinated myself again and again to show it was safe—we began to gain their trust. Justin had his whole family vaccinated, and none of them got sick or got smallpox. We hired Justin to be a watch guard, paying him to make sure those who were infected stayed at home and, as we had learned from Steve Jones, to buy food to keep the quarantined from going out to beg.

Just as Tatanagar had become an exporter of smallpox to the rest of India, there was one more foci that was exporting back to Tatanagar and elsewhere in Bihar, located deep in the forest. I was eager to head out with Zafar, Sujit, and Justin to this village deep in Ho territory, where a resistant chief, let's call him Mohan Singh,† was keeping his village from being vaccinated. Our teams had been to see him many times, begging, cajoling, and even bribing him to accept vaccination. If we didn't vaccinate their leader, no one in the village would allow us to vaccinate them. In charge of the trip was Dr. Lakshmi Kant, one of the many retired epidemiologists whom M.I.D. had brought back into the field. He was a cholera expert and a well-known public health guru. Also in the jeeps were Tata managers dressed in crisp white shirts, black pants, and ties.

We drove through the remote jungle area for hours until we admitted we were lost. We needed to find a place to settle before the sun went down and predators came out looking for food. We found a huge, flat, round clearing and decided to make camp. We pitched tents to protect the vaccine from spoiling in the morning sun and curled up in the jeeps to catch some sleep.

At 2 A.M., the sound of deafening, terrifying wails snapped all twenty of us out of sleep. Lakshmi Kant approached me and said quietly, "Sir, you have parked the vehicles in a place that perhaps was not wise."

"Why wasn't it wise?" I asked him.

"It was not wise, sir, because the elephants are coming," he told me.

"Elephants?"

"Sir, these are the elephant mating grounds. The sound they are making means they are coming to use them."

"How do you know these are mating grounds?"

"Why do you think there is a flattened circle in the middle of the jungle?"

"I don't know. I've never been in this jungle! Why didn't you say something before?" I couldn't believe he was telling me this now.

"Sir, you did not ask my opinion."

There was nowhere to go in the dark. We were encased by dense jungle that was hard enough to navigate during the day. And we were directly in the path of twenty tons of a horny animal stampede. But Lakshmi Kant knew what to do. Following his directions, we moved the jeeps into a circle facing outward and left the headlights on all night to keep the elephants away. We kept one jeep in the middle of the circle with the lights off.

Because the headlights drained the batteries, we would need the jeep in the middle to jumpstart the others in the morning. If we hadn't done that, I wouldn't be here to tell the story.

Daylight came. We packed up camp and started the jeeps one by one. Several of the old epidemiologists took out machetes to clear a path large enough for the jeeps. Everyone, especially the young Tata managers, took turns at cutting through the jungle. With each hour, they shed their office garb, their jackets, ties, and crisp white shirts, until they were as bare chested in the hot and humid jungle as the local guides.

We arrived on the outskirts of the village in the middle of the afternoon, where we met with the deputy superintendent of police, the assistant district magistrate, and the chief medical officer of the district to debate how to break Mohan Singh's resistance so that we could do proper containment vaccination around this outbreak. I was exhausted and on edge. Rikushin had already dropped his leaflets on this part of Bihar. There were no parades to stage, no Hog Farm tricks to play. The reward hadn't worked in this village. We were facing the real possibility that forcible vaccination of Mohan Singh might be our only option to keep smallpox from coming back to the tribal areas. As a card-carrying member of the ACLU, this was not something I wanted to be a part of. But if this remote foci of infection wasn't stopped, the virus would continue going back and forth between the Adivasi region and Tatanagar. Our fear was that smallpox would reignite and explode through the subcontinent. No one was comfortable with forcible vaccination but we didn't see another way. We knew from our experience at the Tatanagar railway that we had the legal authority, but this peaceful Adivasi community deserved better than a full-on clash with police. We had to plan how many rifles to show, how visible the foreigners would be, and figure out who spoke which languages so that our interpreters could be in the front lines.

We settled on a strategy and waited until most of the villagers had gone to bed. In the early hours after midnight, we took up our positions around Mohan Singh's house—policemen and vaccinators to either side of the front door, vaccinators ready to push the door down. I stood outside the inner circle, watching from the sidelines.

Mohan Singh leaped out of bed when the government vaccinators burst through the bamboo door of his simple adobe hut. His wife, Laxmi,[†] awoke screaming and scrambled to cover herself with a thin sari. Singh grabbed an ax and chased the intruders into the courtyard. As he rushed through the door, a squad of doctors and policemen overpowered and pinned him while a second vaccinator jabbed smallpox vaccine into his arm, more frequently and more forcefully than needed. The wiry forty-year-old leader of the village squirmed away from the needle, causing the vaccination site to bleed. The government team held him until they had delivered enough fluid to vaccinate him a dozen times over.

They then seized his wife. Pausing to suck out the hated medicine, Laxmi Singh pulled a bamboo pole from the roof and swung at the strangers restraining her. She bit deeply into a doctor's hand. While two policemen held Mohan Singh back, the rest of the team subdued the entire family and vaccinated each in turn. When it was all over, our vaccination team gathered in the small courtyard outside the house. Mohan Singh and his exhausted family members stood by the broken door of their home. We faced each other silently across a cultural chasm, neither side knowing what to do next.

By now, the whole village was awake. People gathered in the courtyard as the dawn illuminated our unfolding drama. Mohan Singh surveyed his disordered household. After a moment's hesitation, he strode to his small vegetable plot and stooped to pluck the single ripe cucumber left on the vine. He walked over to the puzzled young Indian doctor whom his wife had bitten and handed him the cucumber. Justin translated for Zafar and me.

"My religious duty, my dharma," Mohan Singh said, "is to surrender to God's will. Only God can decide who gets sickness and who does not. It is my duty to resist your interference with his will. We must resist your needles. We would die resisting if that is necessary. My family and I have not yielded. We have done our duty. We can be proud of being firm in our faith. It is not a sin to be overpowered by so many strangers in the middle of the night.

"Daily you have come and told me it is your dharma to prevent this disease with your needles. We have sent you away. Tonight you have broken my door and used force. You say you act in accordance with your duty. I have acted in accordance with mine. It is over. God will decide.

"Now I find that you are guests in my house. It is my duty to feed guests. I have little to offer at this time. Except this cucumber."

The morality play lasted a moment, the mere "blink of an eye," what the Germans call an *Augenblick*, but it felt to me like a postgraduate course in cultural relativity. I felt numb and torn and wondered whether I was on the wrong side. Mohan Singh was so firm in his faith, yet there was not a trace of anger in his words. I scanned my teammates' faces, looking for someone to respond to Mohan Singh's challenge. Everyone stared at the ground.

At length, Zafar stepped forward, bowed slightly, and crouched in deference to Mohan Singh. He addressed the tribal leader humbly. "You are a good man. You live by God's will. I, too, have surrendered to God's will—that is what the word 'Islam' means, one who has surrendered to God's will. These vaccinators are of your tribe; they also share your faith. But what is God's will? Is it God's will that you go hungry, or is it his will that you plant rice and eat? Is it God's will that you walk naked, or his will that you make cloth and cover yourself? Look around you at your children. How many are absent today, dead from smallpox? How many are scarred? That boy over there is blind forever. This girl with her scarred face will never marry now. Three hundred Ho have died suffering from this terrible disease.

"You are strong. You fight this needle, but its medicine will prevent smallpox. There are so many diseases we cannot prevent, but smallpox can be stopped with this vaccine. Could we bring the needle if it were not God's will? Could we make the vaccine? Could this *Angrezi* doctor come ten thousand miles to your village if it were not God's will?

"The *Angrezi* also shares faith in God's will. He came to India to study Hindu dharma. His guru sent him out of the ashram of learning into the villages to give vaccinations. His guru was a great yogi, a great saint who said that it is God's will that smallpox shall be eradicated. He said the end of this disease is God's gift to humankind. No more children dead from smallpox. You think it is God's will that this disease will always kill your children. I think it is God's will that our people don't have to suffer like this anymore. I think it is God's will that we take this vaccination."

Zafar arose from his respectful crouch to his full five feet three inches, though he seemed to be a six-foot-tall hero of Indian mythology. His whisper became a bellow: "It is God's will, and my dharma is to protect your children from smallpox."

Zafar walked over to Justin, who was still translating what Zafar had just said. Reaching into a jute bag marked "National Smallpox Eradication Campaign," Zafar took out another ampule of vaccine and several needles. Sensing that the crowd was now wavering, he broke open the vaccine and vaccinated Justin, then took my arm and vaccinated me. "It is my dharma to fight smallpox!" he declared. An elderly man slowly came forward. Zafar brought his palms together respectfully, and then quickly and expertly vaccinated the old Ho tribesman. One by one the villagers came forward. Soon it was over. Five hundred were vaccinated. No one else resisted. The tension evaporated in the morning sun. My anguish did not.

CHAPTER 17

The Final Inch

The realm of the Final Inch! . . . The work has been almost completed, the goal almost attained, everything completely right and the difficulties overcome. . . . Finishing touches are needed, maybe still more research. In that moment of fatigue and self-satisfaction it is especially tempting to leave the work without having attained the apex of quality. . . . Not to postpone it, for the thoughts of the person performing the task will then stray from the realm of the Final Inch. And not to mind the time spent on it, knowing that one's purpose lies not in completing things faster but in the attainment of perfection.

—Alexsandr I. Solzhenitsyn, *In the First Circle*

Shitala Ma was on the run. The previous year at this time there had been 8,600 smallpox-infected villages in India; now there were only 25, and those paltry few were all well contained. Two-thirds of these outbreaks were importations from neighboring Bangladesh, which was the last of the heavily infected countries in the world. During the All-India Search in April 1975, almost 150,000 health workers searched 100 million homes door-to-door and discovered not a single new case, not one. Zero. For the first time during the campaign, probably for the first time in India's history, a week went by when there were no new cases of smallpox. As our coach, commander, and cheerleader-in-chief, D.A. wrote a global summary, a memo called "The Final Inch," reporting that Bihar was the last remaining state with smallpox in all of India, urging us to complete the task, to get to the magical zero pox number, to summon all our remaining reservoirs of energy and goodwill; to never let up even for a second. "Maybe," he said "we are nearing the final inch." And with that, Nicole sent me to Patna, the capital, to try to take to the rest of Bihar what we had learned in Tatanagar and Chotanagpur.

Girija and I closed up our *barsatti* in Delhi and left for Patna right away. With a long stretch of living there ahead of us, we set up a cozy communelike house we called the Zero Pox Guest House, with plenty of rooms for expat epidemiologists, Government of India visitors, and WHO officials to stay with us when they needed to. Living in a commune like the Hog Farm buses had taught us that nothing builds community like a shared kitchen and good food, so I hired the top Bihari cook from an old English estate to make whatever anyone wanted after difficult days in the field—English puddings, Russian borscht, or Indian *masala dosa* or *laddus*. I moved the telex into the house that Tata had set up for us in Tatanagar, with the callback code Zeropox, and our dining room quickly became the program's nerve center.

For the next half year I traveled by jeep to every corner of Bihar, trying to imitate D.A. and urge each of our nearly four dozen smallpox epidemiologists to redouble their efforts now that we were in the "realm of the final inch." I had a lot of time driving in jeeps over bumpy roads to think about it. The raging fires of Tatanagar and Chotanagpur had calmed enough to give me more time to contemplate the India that Girija and I had traveled from the United States to live in. It had been five years since a burst of idealism deposited me on Alcatraz Island with the American Indian occupation to deliver the baby Wovoka. It had been five years since Girija and I had run away with the circus and I had joined the Medicine Ball Caravan movie crew as their hippie doctor to live on psychedelic buses traveling across the United States, Europe, and Asia. I had spent half of those five years studying compassion, religion, and love with Maharaji, living in the ashram in the Himalayas; I had spent the other half becoming a WHO medical officer fighting smallpox. We had experienced moments of transcendental love and clarity in the ashram and had made pilgrimages that lifted us spiritually. I had also grown and matured as a leader and manager through working with Nicole and Bill. Girija and I were smitten by the intensity, riot of color, crash of sound, crush of humanity that was India.

Our love for each other was wrapped in the shared experience of India. But there was a gathering darkness in my soul from the relentless suffering and death that I had seen, and from decisions I felt forced to make that made me queasy. The faces of the children who suffered from smallpox, the young adults killed in the flower of their lives by a demon goddess, the parents whose bodies wracked with sobs of helplessness watching their children die. I had seen the faces of hundreds or maybe thousands of children with smallpox. I struggled to absorb the humanity of the staggering statistics: more than a quarter of a million Indians had gotten sick or died from smallpox since the day I left the ashram and entered the WHO office.

While I honestly believed it was the final inch, that we were close to the final case of smallpox, still there was an internal accounting. The cumulative toll was crushing. Girija and I both had a hard time sleeping. I questioned many of the things I had done—the force used with Mohan Singh, my rage at the nearly catatonic Dr. Sen as he alphabetized his books, barging into Russi Mody's house. I wasn't second-guessing the need to do these things for the program, but I was concerned about their impact on my heart—the growing darkness, anger, and depression overtaking me. I was beginning to turn the anger toward God.

On the Hog Farm buses, we often referred to God as "The Management." While I had gained a new appreciation for the effect of very different styles of management by watching D.A., Nicole, and Bill, and especially the Tatas, I was starting to think of God as one hell of a lousy manager. For a supreme being who was supposed to be omniscient, omnipotent, and benevolent, there was way too much cruelty and suffering in the world. To my mind, no sin, in this life or a previous life, committed by the child, his father or grandfather, could justify the extreme suffering of hundreds of thousands of children in India and millions, perhaps billions, of human beings throughout history because of smallpox.

The images of dead bodies piled on the railway platform, the memory of dead children thrust into my arms, the rumors of vultures pulling at the pock-ridden arms of dead children played in my head day and night.

There was a missionary hospital nearby—the Jesuit Holy Family Hospital—at which I would sometimes sleep during "night halt" trips away. The priest was from the upper Midwest in the States. We joked about growing up in the same part of the country and me and my friends being chased off the baseball diamond at the University of Detroit by a bat-wielding Jesuit in a cassock. We talked about our gurus—his bishop and my Maharaji—and the motivation of love behind everything Jesus did or said. "It's the problem of reconciling suffering with a loving God," he said when I told him of all the death and suffering I had seen. "Most of us living in India, seeing children die needlessly, come up against this contradiction."

One morning he saw me meditating in the hospital chapel. He sat behind me for a few moments before asking, "Would you like to pray with me?"

He kneeled and I followed suit. I had long since lost my aversion to bowing down. We meditated silently, and then he asked me whether I would like to take communion.

"Father, did you miss the part about my being Jewish?" I asked.

"No, Larry, I didn't miss that part." He laughed. "But it's not important. Communion," he continued, "is for people who are seeking a state of grace, in the presence of the living God, in communion with the Lord. I sense that you are, although you struggle. I cannot imagine that the God I serve and love would be displeased if you were to enter into deeper communion with him."

This was a different kind of Catholic than my memory of what I had thought were Jew-hating Jesuits chasing us with a baseball bat in Detroit. These Jesuits in India felt like brothers in this dance with God. I accepted.

The ritual, the sip of wine, the incense, the scratchy old record playing music that lifted me, a sudden easing of the burden of suffering. I felt a surge that wasn't Buddhist or Hindu; it wasn't Christian or Jewish. It was all of them, comforting, and healing. The smallpox warriors seemed part of a mystical army of the good ones, the righteous ones working to reduce suffering through the ages. I was grateful for feeling like a small part of that history, yet it was not enough to heal my doubt about why all that suffering was necessary.

Just as I got back to Patna I received a telegram that Justin Bhakla had somehow contracted smallpox. I felt sure the diagnosis was wrong, that he might have contracted chickenpox. I rushed to see him. He had modified, or discrete, smallpox, which didn't cover the whole skin. It presented as a mild case. We took lots of pictures and I reassured him, but I was troubled. I had been certain of his safety and told his family there was no risk. With the number of times Zafar, Justin, and I had vaccinated ourselves to demonstrate its safety, he shouldn't have been able to contract the disease.

Dr. Kitamura, a friend of Isao Arita and a world-class immunologist from the National Institute of Health in Japan, was in Bihar testing smallpox specimens. He brought a mobile lab with him, collecting samples of smallpox scabs to take back to Japan in an attempt to develop a smallpox antiviral. I asked him to bring his lab to the Tata Main Hospital where Justin was hospitalized to draw blood, take scab samples, and help us understand what had happened. Kitamura took samples from Justin and returned to Japan, where he and his colleagues would test them.

Eventually, Justin recovered, but immediately he came down with another shower of smallpox lesions. And then another after we thought he was over it. He kept getting sick, and no one knew why. It was as though all his systems were collapsing. Justin's family and friends now shunned me in his village. Everyone blamed me for ruining his life, and a deep suspicion grew that the protection we were offering through vaccination wasn't real. A lot of tribal vaccinators quit. Vaccination resistance in villages increased. Many of my Indian colleagues began to doubt everything.

Just at that moment, more strange smallpox cases appeared. There was an outbreak in a village called Pawapuri, a Jain pilgrimage site near Bodh Gaya, that continued to confound us. Instead of the usual pattern of spreading from one case to three or four others, the epidemic "tree" widening as it grew, the outbreak in Pawapuri spread slowly, one case sprouting up about every two weeks. The outbreak had been hidden for six months by the time we discovered it. Because it had taken so long to find the first cases, the naysayers postulated that there remained in India hidden cases, perhaps a new strain of smallpox with no telltale symptoms. If that were the case, and an asymptomatic person could spread the disease the way Typhoid Mary had spread typhus, then eradication might, as Jankowicz had insisted, be impossible.

The Jain celebration marking the twenty-five hundredth anniversary of the birth of their founder, Mahavir, took place around the time Justin got sick. A contemporary of Buddha, Mahavir also embraced non-harm, *ahimsa,* as it is called by Buddhists and Jains—the principle that also motivated Mahatma Gandhi and then Martin Luther King Jr. The holiest sites in the Jain tradition were in Bihar, near Pawapuri, about an hour-and-a-half drive southeast of Patna. Jain priests, *munis,* and devotees were coming from all over the world to the exquisite marble temple called Jal Mandir. At our Patna headquarters, we had received well over a thousand notifications warning people in ten different countries that they had been exposed to smallpox at the temple.

The Jains refused to be vaccinated because vaccine could not be produced without killing cows. Their logic bothered me. They did everything to avoid hurting even an insect, yet they seemed unwilling to lift a foot to stop a preventable disease that killed millions of children.

I set up a meeting with one of the *munis* from the Jain Lal Mundir Temple in Delhi. I showed him the postcard with Maharaji's picture and told him about his prediction that it was God's will that, through the hard work of dedicated health workers, smallpox would be eradicated. This *muni* knew of Maharaji. He knew, too, that Maharaji rarely made public predictions. Convinced, the *muni* wrote letters to all the other Jain *munis* on our behalf explaining why the Jain community had to get behind WHO's smallpox eradication program. While acknowledging in the letter that animal lives were in fact taken to create the vaccine, he further explained what the vow of *ahimsa* actually means. One must do his or her best not to kill insects or any other tiny creatures, he argued persuasively, but one must also make sure to do as little harm to people as possible. If we can end a disease that has killed so many millions—and would continue to kill many millions more—then vaccination is a small price to pay for a very great good. His words, which WHO printed on flyers distributed throughout Jain communities, stated that sacrificing a cow to create smallpox vaccine is, as Neem Karoli Baba had said, part of lifting this one form of suffering from humanity.

At the Jal Mandir, Girija noticed a flyer saying that our old meditation teacher Goenka, who had taught us both our first lessons in meditation, was hosting a ten-day silent Buddhist meditation retreat in a nearby Jain monastery. It wasn't easy to find the time for a retreat in the middle of the campaign, but Girija insisted. I was stressed and becoming more irritable and angry; she knew better than I that if we didn't take time to refresh ourselves spiritually, we would drown emotionally.

In the hills of Rajpur, the Jain temple was carved of white marble with delicate soaring arches. The grounds were exquisitely landscaped, alive with animals, and lush with flowers and hedges. Birds darted in and out of the courtyard. Every morning, Girija and I woke to their chattering and singing for the first meditation session at four o'clock.

Goenka began and ended every one-hour silent meditation session with the same *metta* (loving kindness) chant, which translates from the Pali as, *May all beings be peaceful. May all beings be happy. May all beings be free.*

When he finished the opening chant on the first day, I was neither happy nor at peace. My mind darted from face to disfigured face of infected children, their fragile arms and legs covered with pustules, their mothers wailing. Even as my brain knew we were near the end of the battle with Shitala Ma, my heart was flooded with memories of pain and death. There in the retreat, surrounded by the peace and calm of my companions, I started to sob. I could not talk to Girija because we were supposed to keep silent for the full ten days; I could not explain my pain over being devoted to a God who seemed to be a sadist. Sitting in meditation, I kept trying to find evidence of the compassionate and loving God Maharaji had shown me. But over and over I was stuck in one recursive thought: *What kind of crime would have to be committed for a merciful, omniscient, omnipotent God to deal this kind of suffering on a baby, or on all of humanity?* With each session, I became more agitated, more uneasy. I was spiraling silently into depression and anger.

Five or six days into the retreat, an hour into a session, there was a rustling at the back door, followed by the stomping of heavy boots. A deep American voice yelled out, "Goenka, what makes you think you're so fucking pure?"

Goenka was silent. No one moved or turned around.

"Goenka, who gave you the right to judge everybody?"

Silence.

"Goenka, I know you're a fucking fraud."

The tirade became relentless, over and over: "Goenka, I know you are a fucking fraud!"

I wanted to hide under my meditation cushion; I suspected we all did. But just as suddenly as he appeared, the American left. The eyes of the meditators remained closed, I noticed as I peeked at the stoic, white-robed rows of Jain monks. Goenka's *metta* chant closed the session. We left the hall as usual.

The next morning everyone was restless. Goenka began again with the *metta* chant, but the room felt like a worm squirming to avoid being pulled out of a bucket and stuck on a hook. Goenka ended the session with the same *metta* chant: *May all beings be peaceful. May all beings be happy. May all beings be free.* Another day went by in silence.

The morning after that, following the opening chant, Goenka finally addressed the group. "My friends," he said, "two days ago we had an unexpected visitor. He disturbed our search for equanimity. I thought I would tell you how I view this. If you were here in order to take a course on driving a car, but you had none to drive and your friend said, 'Please, borrow my automobile,' you would say, 'Thank you for providing the vehicle on which to practice.' If you were trying to become a chef and didn't have a kitchen, and a friend offered his kitchen, you would say thank you. In every instance when someone loaned you something for you to learn with, you would be grateful. This unexpected guest came and he lent us his anger. He had more than he needed, so he lent some of his anger to us. What are we here to learn? It is to never be angry but to try to be equanimous. We are here to learn to convert the anger others feel or even hurl at us into peace and equanimity. We should send that young intruder our thanks and our love."

In Tatanagar, I was angry at what I thought was a huge, uncaring corporation in a company town undoing all the good the smallpox team had done elsewhere in India. I was angry at the bureaucrats. In Delhi, I was angry at the secretary of health who tried to extort me. Everywhere I was angry at the bureaucrats. I was angry because a woman handed me her dead son and there was nothing I could do.

The American intruder was a jolt to the quiet of the retreat. I had been trying to use the peace and quiet of meditation like a tranquilizer—his raw emotion forced me to face the anger I carried with me. I was angry because I couldn't square the circle of a supposedly loving God and the horrific suffering that I saw day after day, body after body. My mind went back in time and space, back to Kainchi, reeling and sobbing while Maharaji stood on my hand, later saying, "It is better to see God in everyone than to try to figure it all out." Oh, I wish that's the way I felt.

A month into our time at Patna, on May 17, 1975, came smallpox's final gasp in India, an echo from the dying embers of an ancient scourge. An unvaccinated eight-year-old boy in Bihar named Manjho developed fever and rash. He would be the last domestic case of smallpox in the history of India.

M.I.D. called the Central Team back to Delhi for a small, wary celebration to mark the moment. He asked everyone to predict whether there would be any more cases of smallpox, any importations or hidden foci that would turn up later. Most of us thought there would be many importations from Bangladesh. The votes were written, sealed, and pinned to the wall of Nicole's office.

A week later, a thirty-year-old homeless woman named Saiban Bibi from the village of Thauri in the Sylhet district of Bangladesh developed symptoms of smallpox. An ancient place, Sylhet is a finger of Bangladesh thrust into three states of India—Meghalaya, Tripura, and Assam, where Saiban was discovered by smallpox workers. No one ever found out why she traveled the short distance by train to beg for food at the Karimganj railway platform, which is located just across the border from India, but she was poor, alone, most likely hungry, perhaps dazed by her disease. Smallpox workers scouring the area found her within three days of the onset of her rash and immediately reported the new case to Zdeno, who, having worked in Mongolia for five years and at home in hilly terrain, was now in charge of the Assam district. He flew there from Delhi that same day. Although she brought smallpox with her from Bangladesh, the Indians, after some back and forth, counted her as one of their own and recorded her illness as India's last case of killer smallpox.

The speed with which Saiban Bibi's case had been detected was an exclamation point on the self-sacrificing work of almost 150,000 Indian search workers who had made by then nearly a billion door-to-door house calls. One woman infected with smallpox had entered the country of half a billion people and had been detected almost immediately, in a few hours. The area where she'd been found, between Assam and the village of Thauri in Bangladesh, was contained and a ring of vaccination miles in diameter was completed within a few days of Saiban's first setting foot in India. There were zero additional cases of the disease. In 2016 terms, this remarkable achievement would be comparable to epidemiologists discovering the first case of Zika in Brazil, not the millionth, or quarantining the first case of Ebola in West Africa within twenty-four hours instead of the six months it actually took.

The national surveillance system was so good it was almost impossible to believe. To make sure we weren't drinking our own whisky, we hired an outside assessment firm, which asked more than one million Indians several questions, most notably, "Who is Indira Gandhi?" and "What is the reward for reporting a case of smallpox?" The survey revealed that more Indians knew how much the reward for reporting smallpox was than knew who the prime minister was, which made us even more confident that we had gotten our message to every corner of the country.

Immediately after the last case, India entered its obligatory two-year period of surveillance. As for M. I. D. Sharma's game of predicting when the last case in India would occur, both he and Nicole made the best guess, sharing the victory as one, just as they shared leading roles in the conquest of smallpox. I was thrilled with our external progress. I wasn't so sure about my internal progress.

By August 15, 1975—India's Independence Day—less than two dozen people in the world, all in Bangladesh, harbored *Variola major,* killer smallpox. The team could taste victory. Not a single new case of smallpox had been reported in India in three months, since the sad case in May of Saiban Bibi, who had come already quite ill from neighboring Bangladesh into Assam to beg for food. We had no illusions that smallpox could not be re-exported to India from Bangladesh—it was now the only country in the world with *Variola major*—but it was progressing toward eradication: at last report, officials there announced a tremendous, almost unbelievable drop in reported cases in five months, from nearly two thousand to only sixteen active cases of *Variola major.* Dozens of epidemiologists were dispatched to the borders to prevent the spread of smallpox back into India. Though India would only remain free of smallpox if Bangladesh succeeded in finishing off the disease, Prime Minister Gandhi and her government were ready to declare to the world India's independence from the shackles of the world's most ancient plague.

For India's annual freedom celebration, WHO and the government planned a global telecast from New Delhi, the first of its kind. Several reporters came for the event, including Lawrence K. Altman, a physician and writer for the *New York Times* who had also trained under D.A. Henderson as an epidemiologist at CDC. The idea was to play off India's dual independence: from the domination of hundreds of years of colonial rule and from thousands of years of *Variola major.*

D.A. flew in from Geneva with WHO director general Halfdan Mahler. They congratulated Prime Minister Gandhi for India's success in smallpox. They planned to fly from Delhi to Dacca after the telecast to meet with Sheikh Mujibur Rahman, the prime minister of Bangladesh. Director-General Mahler had planned to have an urgent meeting with the Bangladeshi prime minister about how to handle what might be the last remaining cases of smallpox in Bangladesh and the only cases of *Variola major* in the world. The United Nations feared that the Bangladesh government's clumsy attempts to subdue civil unrest by razing slums around the capital of Dacca would make everything worse: slum dwellers might be moved out of the epidemic-ridden capital city and relocated to the countryside, carrying with them incubating smallpox.

The very day of the planned telecast, celebration, and meeting, however, Sheikh Mujibur Rahman was assassinated by a group of conspiring generals. The new regime, convinced there was a military threat from Pakistan, quickly sealed off the Bangladesh borders. But sealed borders did not work to keep torrents of frightened Bangladeshis, afraid of another war, from rushing into India. We feared a repeat of the massive and bloody migration of Hindu refugees from Muslim Bangladesh that had occurred during the war in 1971. Pakistan's generals were in the process of being charged with war crimes for the atrocities committed at that time. Prime Minister Gandhi declared martial law. And now, if refugees came again, they would bring smallpox into disease-free India.

The *New York Times* probably had hoped Larry Altman would go to see the last cases of smallpox in Bangladesh, but with the borders closed, we arranged for him to go to Patna instead; Bihar was the last program in India still running full throttle. Altman was interviewing recent smallpox survivors and epidemiologists in the field when he became trapped by record floods following the annual monsoon season. The city of Patna was swallowed by the water. Altman was stranded on the roof of the apartment building in which we housed team members and guests.

Many other smallpox workers were trapped on housetops and hills in the areas near the Ganges River. Health Minister Karan Singh, M.I.D., Mahendra Dutta, and our new friends from Tata helped coordinate daring search-and-rescue operations. I hitched a ride on an Indian Air Force jet from Delhi to a makeshift runway outside of the flooded area of Patna. After switching to a helicopter, the air marshal took me to tour the devastation. It was surreal to view Patna from the helicopter, the city's few multistory buildings barely poking their pastel-colored heads up over the high waters. The landscape, which a week before had been a network of roads connecting farms and traveled by bullock carts, was now a mass of waterways dotted by makeshift rowboats and life rafts, transporting goods, food, and people from wet to dry land. From the air, I thought we spotted Altman's roof, but our helicopter could not land. We dropped some cooked food and water on the nearby rooftops and mapped his location, but Altman would have to endure another five days of vomiting, dehydration, and watching countless snakes swim past before he was able to get out by cobbling together bamboo poles and air mattresses into a raft. In the report he cabled to the

Times, he wrote, "The life of the half million people of Patna seems to have shifted to the roofs."

If there had been any smallpox left in Bihar, the rapid exodus of people fleeing those floods might have reignited another epidemic. But there were to be no more cases in India. Though we had gone three months without a new case of smallpox in India, we still had twenty-one months of the surveillance period before we could declare the country finally free of Shitala Ma. Once the Indian Army had set up stations for the worst-hit victims of the flood, I drove around Patna in a jeep caravan to make sure the team was as dry and well fed as possible. We used the system we had set up for vaccine and needle distribution to now distribute food and dry clothing, got provisions to those who were in a safe place, and helped rescue those who needed evacuation. Team members in Tatanagar and South Bihar who were less affected by the floods continued their search-and-surveillance system. Finding no smallpox, they turned their focus to tracking down diseases that might be mistaken for smallpox, most notably chickenpox, scabies, and impetigo.

When the waters receded from Patna, the smallpox surveillance system was put into place to make sure Bihar state remained at zeropox. Girija and I flew back to Delhi to our little *barsatti* with the big air conditioner to find out where Nicole would be sending me next. Yom Kippur was coming up, and I felt in need of atonement. Altman's moving accounts of the smallpox campaign and the Bihar flood triggered a surprise call. A cousin I hadn't seen since childhood, Gen. Robert Solomon, was touring Pakistan with the U.S. Army War College and wanted to pop over to Delhi for a family reunion with our other cousin, Myron Belkin at the Associated Press. Although I had been vocally against the Vietnam war, and Bob Solomon had been one of the faces of that war, most of my family had been army in one way or another. All three of my mother's brothers had served, and my dad was in the Michigan National Guard cavalry. Bob Solomon had become a lifer in the military, rising to be a rare Jewish general.

Three American cousins—a peripatetic journalist, a general in civilian clothes, and a radical hippie-turned-UN-medical-officer—met in India to celebrate the holiest of Jewish holidays among the last of the Jews in India.

I had not been to Yom Kippur services in years, and this was my first visit to a Sephardic synagogue. Starting off the Yom Kippur sundown-to-sundown fast, the Kol Nidre service was attended by two handfuls of men, barely enough for a minyan. There was no rabbi, no one seemed to know the right prayers, and the volunteer cantor, an Eastern European diplomat, was lousy. In the midst of the confusion, my cousin the general stood up, walked to the front of the prayer room, and out of his mouth came beautiful, melodic Hebrew chant. None of us knew that the warrior had studied in rabbinical school to be a cantor. He pushed me to lead prayers and told the small gathering that I was a *kohain,* born of the Jewish priestly caste, but I was useless; maybe I could have chanted something in Sanskrit rather than Hebrew.

My dad's birthday, in September, often fell on Yom Kippur. He would have been seventy years old that year. I recited the Kaddish, the mourners' prayer, for my dad, for the thousands of kids who had died of smallpox. I was troubled by the news I'd just gotten from Kitamura—the results of Justin Bhakla's tests. The mystery of his illness was finally solved. Justin had a previously undiagnosed genetic anomaly, a near total absence of the most important part of the immune system, immune globulin IgM. Because of his condition, Justin could have died from any infection—a cold, the flu—but he didn't. He would, two years later, succumb to complications of his disease, and I couldn't escape the feeling that I had put him in harm's way. Often I thought that if we had finished smallpox a couple of months earlier or if Justin had evaded contact with a smallpox case for just a little while, there would have been no smallpox left in India for him to catch. I visited his home, spent time trying to explain his illness to his family. After his death I would tell his parents of all the good Justin had done. I did not know then that my words were meaningless. Three decades later, when my own beloved son, Jonathan, who was about Justin's age, died from lung cancer, everything sounded hollow deep inside the black hole of my grief and I plunged into darkness for years. Physicists like Stephen Hawking say that a black hole is so dense that light can't get out. The black hole of grief is the opposite; light can't get in. Justin trusted me, his family trusted me, just as I trusted the vaccine; but we did not know he had been born without an immune system.

I was missing having a guide. Lama Govinda had decided to take up his students' offer to bring him to Mill Valley, California, for medical treatment. I missed Maharaji with everything in my soul. I felt as bewildered and alone as I'd felt that day at the Tatanagar train station.

Going to the northeast of India, to the foothills of the Himalayas, along the extensive border between India and Bangladesh, where some of the last cases of smallpox had been, was a welcome respite. It was the time of year when the white peaks of the Himalayas set off the brilliance of the red poinsettias, which grew dozens of feet high, clinging to the branches of tall trees— the white, red, and green framed wide-open spaces of the Himalayan valleys. Nicole sent me to oversee the repeat searches in the Himalayan foothills in the eastern part of India—Darjeeling and Assam—and then Sikkim. It was a comfort that Girija was able to get the internal Indian visa so that we could travel together. We flew to Calcutta and drove for a day up to Darjeeling, the tea-growing area dotted by Tibetan Buddhist temples. Its name, Thunderbolt Land, comes from the Tibetan words "dorje" (thunderbolt) and "ling" (place). From Darjeeling we crossed into neighboring Sikkim, the small Himalayan kingdom about to be annexed by India. There, the facial scar survey showed that the last big smallpox outbreak was before the beginning of the WHO program. Convinced we could take Darjeeling and Sikkim off our list of regions to worry about, I sent off my report to Nicole, and Girija and I went off on our own.

We visited the Tibetan-style gompas, monasteries, and temples, but mostly we wanted to visit the Sixteenth Karmapa, the Tibetan Buddhist master of destiny, of karma, whom we had seen several times over the past two years.

The first time Girija and I had heard the name was when we were on our Himalayan trek with Wavy and Bonnie Jean. She was pregnant, and I was weak from dysentery. But much more dangerous, Wavy and Girija had hepatitis; the whites of their eyes were yellow as lemons. If I had been a more persuasive doctor, I might have been able to convince them to stay put and wait out the rainy season in the mountains before attempting the dangerous return. But I was afraid Girija and Wavy wouldn't survive if we were stranded in the mountains by the monsoons.

The trek down the mountains was terrifying—early rains made for slippery terrain and we tired easily, even without our packs, which our two Tibetan sherpas, Dawa Thondrup and Sonam Mundo, carried. Several times we got to the edge of the Kali Gandaki River to find that the only way to cross the gorge one thousand feet above the roiling, rocky river was on tree branches, sometimes not much wider than a fist, that had been laid across it. Dawa Thondrup and Sonam Mundo danced across the trunks over the raging river carrying seventy-pound baskets of Wavy's toys and my medical supplies. They were chanting a prayer I had never heard before—"Karmapa Khyenno," Karmapa knows—like saying, Karmapa knows, the Master of Karma knows how hard your life is; God knows the struggles you have, and God is the Karmapa. I was frightened, but Girija was frozen. I went in front, coaxing her as she scooted on her belly, hugging the trunk. The Tibetans returned to help us, always humming, "Karmapa Khyenno." As Hog Farm guru commissioner I asked who this Karmapa was, a god or a lama, but the answer was vague: to the sherpas, he was both.

Girija and I later went from Vrindavan to our first Goenka retreat in Bodh Gaya, where Buddha had achieved enlightenment. When it was finished, one of the attendees, a French Canadian named Daserat, told us that the Karmapa was nearby in Sarnath, where Buddha had given his first teaching. Girija and I had seen the Karmapa's photo on hippie buses and at meditation centers. His name was fresh in our minds from the trek in Nepal. He seemed to be if not divine, certainly ubiquitous.

The Karmapa was staying at an Indian government Circuit House in Sarnath like the one we had shared with the Dalai Lama. A handful of Westerners from the meditation course were curious, so we went to see him as a group. We gathered in a sitting room; the Karmapa came out, sat down with us, and we all talked with him, casually, just like in darshan with Maharaji. Accompanying the Karmapa was Jamgon Kongtrul, a twenty-year-old, highly ranked incarnate lama. Daserat, who had just returned from Canada with the hottest new Polaroid camera, asked the Karmapa if he could take his picture. "This is brand-new technology," he explained to the lama. "You don't have to wait for the picture to be developed by someone else. I can take the picture and then in ninety seconds it will be ready."

The Karmapa smiled, admired the camera when Daserat showed it to him, and readily agreed; he and Jamgon Kongtrul posed. As soon as Daserat pulled the paper from the camera, the Karmapa looked at his wristwatch and started counting off the seconds. Maharaji never had a watch and never let us take pictures; somehow it felt too materialistic for a spiritual teacher. "Okay, ninety," the Karmapa said. "Ready?" Daserat ripped off the paper, and the Karmapa admired the photo.

Then he said something in Tibetan to an attendant, who disappeared into the back and returned with a box. "Now let me take your picture," the Karmapa said. "We can do it with my new Polaroid camera, which only takes *sixty* seconds." I bellowed involuntarily with laughter. In this remote part of India, there were no other instant cameras within a hundred miles. We were all swept up in the Karmapa's organic, embracing, effervescent laugh. The room felt like a glass of champagne, and we floated upward with the bubbles.

Friends in the government arranged a car to drive Girija and me the fifteen or twenty steep winding miles from the Sikkim capital, Gangtok, up to the mountaintop on which the Karmapa's monastery, Rumtek, was situated. We had written ahead that we were coming but never got a response; we didn't even know if he was in residence.

Situated high in the Himalayan foothills, Rumtek looked like it had been transplanted from Lhasa. The square structure was only two or three stories high, but it was imposing nonetheless, its roof dotted with pagodas painted in brilliant oranges, greens, blues, and maroons. The original monastery, built in Tibet by the Twelfth Karmapa in the mid-1700s, had been destroyed during the Chinese invasion of Tibet in 1959. The structure in Sikkim was then only a decade old, built as a replica of the original after the Sixteenth Karmapa had fled Tibet.

We lucked out. When we arrived at Rumtek, the Karmapa was there; monks took us to a waiting room and served us butter tea. Girija and I had both felt orphaned when Maharaji died, and in the Karmapa, we saw the potential for a new spiritual friend.

The sun was setting and it was getting late. The Karmapa interrupted a prayer session and came to welcome us briefly and introduce us to his translator, Achee, who spoke excellent English. Achee showed us around Rumtek before making arrangements for our meals and taking us to the guest house. We wanted to retire early as Girija had not been feeling well since we arrived in Sikkim.

Near daybreak, Girija woke up feeling like her skin was on fire. She had hives all over her body and was having difficulty breathing. Thank God I had my medical kit with me, which included antihistamines for what was likely an allergic reaction to something in Gangtok. For the next twenty-four hours we did not leave the guest house; Girija slept off and on, but I did not. I stood over her all night, making sure she was breathing, worrying about what would happen if I ran out of antihistamines; she was brave but she kept getting worse. I kept increasing the dose of antihistamines and giving her lots of fluids. Karmapa sent his doctor, a Bhutanese physician with additional training in Tibetan and Ayurvedic medicine. He agreed on the diagnosis, sent someone to Gangtok to replenish my supply of antihistamines, and brought some calming herbs and teas. Every day the Karmapa sent several lamas to check on us. It was three days before Girija was back to near normal.

When Karmapa asked us how we had ended up at Sikkim, Girija and I went through the history with Maharaji and his prediction that smallpox would be eradicated. Karmapa spoke about the Buddha's approach to the inevitability of human suffering. He was excited about the idea of eliminating the terrible form of suffering he remembered witnessing in Tibet as a boy. He laughed at our story of sleeping with the Dalai Lama.

"How will you know when your smallpox work is finished?" Karmapa asked.

I explained the facial scar surveys; the house-to-house searches; the reward, which by that time was 1,000 rupees; the near-absence of any cases of *Variola major* in the world. Of the last fifty cases of smallpox in India, perhaps half had been importations from Bangladesh to the Indian states near Bhutan and Sikkim.

"Have you searched Bhutan?" he asked.

"No," I answered, "but there is a team on the way there now."

I asked whether Karmapa could bless us for our future work. "Do you have a picture of Neem Karoli Baba?" he asked. I did and handed it to him.

After studying the picture, Karmapa said, "Neem Karoli Baba was a great being, one who knows the truth, who is capable of extraordinary feats. I can never replace Maharaji, but I will do my best to help you. Before you leave I will give you the most precious gift. We call it the Triple Gem. I can give you refuge in the Buddha, the dharma [teachings], and the sangha [community]. These two lamas can witness the ceremony." We didn't know exactly what that meant or whether we were supposed to convert to Buddhism, but as Maharaji often said, "Sub ek," "All one." We were up for anything.

Over the next week, we attended ceremonies and mugged for photos with Karmapa, Jamgon Kongtrul, and another prominent young lama, Sharmapa. We sat for meditation with dozens of monks. Karmapa often returned to the question of the eradication of suffering. A single disease could be cured, he argued, but suffering itself is part of the human condition as long as we remain trapped by ignorance, hatred, and obsession, even in their mildest forms. It was up to individuals to eradicate their own personal suffering through insight and the extinction of negative emotions. But he told us it was a blessing to be part of eliminating any kind of suffering.

Karmapa set up the refuge ceremony on the roof of the monastery for our final day. When we climbed to the top of the building, we found the entire community of monks gathered there. Karmapa's brightly painted and brocaded throne was adorned with flowers and white silk scarves. Elaborate offerings of food, flowers, and saffron water in delicately patterned silver bowls were set before an altar full of golden Buddha images. Large trumpets made of human thighbone, and twenty-foot-long curved brass horns, echoed throughout the valley like alpine horns. Above the baritone blast hovered the nasal tones of some kind of Tibetan oboe. Cymbals crashed in a slow and unpredictable rhythm. Some of the most important of the Karma Kagyu and Nyingma lamas alive at that time—Lama Ganga, Khenpo-la, Bardor Tulku, Drupon Rinpoche, Dzogchen Ponlop Rinpoche, Sharmapa, and Jamgon Kongtrul, all in brocaded robes, formed the initial procession. There was a rainbow floating improbably in the cloudless sky; it was one of the most magical settings in the world. I assumed others were coming for the refuge ceremony, but Karmapa was doing this all for Girija and me. We stood by our cushions on the roof in front of Karmapa's throne.

The Karmapa took his seat, and it was as if the final pieces of the universe's puzzle fell into place. Though the rooftop was open, the area felt suddenly contained. We took our seats.

And then I got cold feet.

"Rinpoche," I said as Karmapa picked up his *dorje,* the ritual scepter representing the Buddha's compassion, and began to ring his bell.

"Yes, Larry?" He stopped.

"I really want to do this, but I don't want to be disloyal to Neem Karoli Baba. He's my guru, and I'm not sure how taking refuge in Buddha, dharma, and sangha affects my commitment to him and what he has taught me."

"Don't worry about that," Karmapa said as he laughed warmly. "There is no difference just because the rituals and traditions are different. Taking refuge doesn't mean you will become a Buddhist unless you want to. Your teacher was a bodhisattva—a great being who worked to benefit all. The teachings emanate from the Buddha of Compassion, who is also a bodhisattva.

"During the ceremony, when I say, 'Do you take refuge in the Buddha?' you think of taking refuge in Neem Karoli Baba. The same when I ask, 'Do you take refuge in the sangha?' then you think of your satsang. Dharma is the spiritual path, so when I ask, 'Do you take refuge in the dharma?' think of the dharma your guru gave you, your karma yoga. So you take refuge in those things. It is the same." Sub ek, all one. Perfect.

The ritual resumed; we repeated the vows in Tibetan after Karmapa. He gave Girija a soft and loving smile and a Tibetan name, Karma Sonam Chotsu. I became Karma Sonam Wangchuk.

Later that day, while we were sitting with him in his quarters, Karmapa said, "Rumtek is your home. Just like the home of your father and mother. If you have trouble getting back here, I will help you."

I was so moved I couldn't look up at him; I was afraid I would start sobbing. I spotted a small *dorje* on the carpet. I picked it up and handed it to Karmapa, who tied it to my *mala,* my prayer beads. I sat back to meditate and, just like Maharaji had done so many times before, Karmapa threw an apple in my lap.

CHAPTER 18

The Case for Optimism

May the longtime Sun shine upon you
All love surround you
And the pure light within you
Guide your way home.

—Celtic farewell and communal song
  on Hog Farm bus trip to Asia

As soon as Bangladesh reopened its borders after the coup had stabilized in autumn 1975, I went with a team from SEARO to Dacca to get a status report. Communications between the smallpox team in Bangladesh and Nicole in SEARO had been strained in the aftermath of the assassination of Sheikh Mujibur Rahman. I returned to Delhi with a positive report. Shortly after, a Bangladesh doctor wrote, "We have controlled the epidemic in the northern part of Bangladesh. We are worried about the south, especially the Barisal district in the Ganges Delta. We are very worried about one area: Bhola Island. The 1971 cyclone left our health services there in disarray." Nicole sent me back to investigate.

Located on the southern part of the Barisal district, Bhola Island was where Girija and I had been headed with the Hog Farm buses in 1971 to feed the victims of the cyclone—victims we couldn't get to because of the war with Pakistan.

Bangladeshis thought that Asia's last case of *Variola major* might have already occurred on Bhola. The victim was a three-year-old girl named Rahima Banu. To confirm this report, they wanted one final painstaking search of the islands, the swamps, and the pirates' nests in the area where the cyclone had occurred. Nicole wanted me to join as an extra pair of eyes from outside the program.

After a briefing in Dacca from Stan Foster, a dedicated CDC epidemiologist who had turned his life inside out to fight smallpox, I took an overnight trip to Barisal, packed like a sardine with Bengali families on a slow paddleboat Foster called the *Rocket*. There was barely enough room on the deck to squeeze my sleeping bag into the cramped space. The Hog Farm buses, old as they had been, were commodious in comparison. Nostalgia swept over me as I finally fell asleep. When I reached Barisal, I went to see the area's civil surgeon, a Dr. Chaudhari,[†] who had been feuding with WHO.

Rumor had it that cases of smallpox were hidden in his district, a poor water-soaked area of islands and bays at the very southern tip of the country—cases that Chaudhari refused to report because he wanted to prevent the Dacca government and WHO from interfering in local affairs. I arrived amidst preparations for one of the holiest Muslim holidays, Eid ul-Azha. It is the celebration of the willingness of Abraham (Ibrahim to Muslims) to sacrifice his son Isaac (or Ishmael, according to Muslims) to God. During the holiday, Bengali Muslims bring a young calf into their homes and then, after many days of growing fond of it as a family member, they slaughter it. Much of the meat is given to the poor, but some is eaten at home in an important religious ceremony.

I have always felt uncomfortable—as have many—about the story of Abraham being willing to kill his own son as a sign of submission to God's commands. What kind of God would make such a demand? The fact that God withdrew his demand, providing a ram to replace Isaac, never really mollified me. Loving an animal of any kind, in your home, telling your children that the animal is a "brother" or a "sister," and then slaughtering it brings back all my memories of the same God who allowed so many to die horrible deaths from smallpox. I wanted a God who does not demand death in order to make our lives sacred.

My first meeting with Chaudhari was contentious. "Why does my government trust you, a foreigner, over me?" he demanded to know. "Why is smallpox—something important for the English—more important than cholera, which kills more of our children?"

I could understand his resistance to diverting his time from other diseases to yet one more search for smallpox. Crossing the water to Bhola Island was sometimes dangerous and the village was remote. The cyclone's devastation was still apparent. It was a poor, hard place. Over tea and with time, though, and my little bit of Urdu, we warmed to each other.

"It is true that I have fought with WHO in the past," Chaudhari said. "But now things will be different. We can be friends. You understand my world here a little bit. I will work with you to make sure there is no more hidden smallpox. To show my friendship, I want you to come into my home. This morning we have killed the sacrificial calf. Please eat this meal with us. Abraham was grandfather to both Muslims and Jewish people, so tonight we will eat as cousins." I needed to join this celebration or I wouldn't be able to conduct that final, confirmatory search. The act of friendship, the meal with his family, needed to be reciprocated or Chaudhari wouldn't come to Bhola with me.

I was still lying to myself that I was a vegetarian—only eating buffalo liver when I ran out of energy. It was hard to think of eating beef. I thought of the line in the New Testament, "It is not what goes into the mouth that defiles a person, but it is what comes out of the mouth that defiles," and also about what Lama Govinda had said about taking myself and what I thought would happen to me out of the picture. I focused on what was at stake. I might never determine whether more cases of smallpox still were out there if I refused to take part in this ceremony merely to stick to a rigid belief, a judgment I was holding. So I accepted Chaudhari's warm invitation into his home and ate the roasted calf with his family.

Over the next ten days, Chaudhari and I jointly organized a meticulous search of the entire district. We uncovered thousands of cases of chickenpox and measles, but no smallpox. It seemed that Rahima Banu might indeed be the last case of *Variola major* in the world, and I wanted to see her with my own eyes.

On Christmas Eve 1975, Chaudhari and I left the coastal town of Barisal with our team divided between two speedboats. There had been several boat accidents already; more than one Bangladeshi medical officer had lost his life in the dangerous waterways, the powerful and unpredictable currents of the tidal straits impinging from the Bay of Bengal. As we crossed the rough sea, one of our engines died suddenly; we limped into Bhola Island, pulled by the other boat.

At the dock, we climbed onto small Honda motorcycles to journey to the interior of the island, to the village of Kuralia, where the last outbreak had occurred. We threaded our motorcycles along dirt roads crowded with bicycle rickshaws, sad-faced villagers, and children darting in front of our path until the flat land of Bhola Island merged at the horizon with the open sea. We stopped our motorcycles at the edge of a canal and started on foot. The island's medical officers led our small crew, while Chaudhari and I chatted amiably.

Bangladesh is one of the poorest countries in the world. The average person then earned fewer than twenty-five cents a day, seventy-five dollars a year. But the countryside was dramatic. Large rivers flowed around the island, which itself was ringed with lifeless sandbars. There was nothing between the sea and Bhola Island. The few survivors of the tidal wave that came with the 1971 cyclone had used all their strength to hang onto the twenty-foot-high palms, clinging for their lives for more than thirty hours. The interior of Bhola Island was filled with rice paddies, the intense green of the crop shimmering against the swamp. The rice fields, in turn, embraced clusters of houses. A single length of bamboo stretched between paddy embankments served as bridges between villages, the only thing separating us from the rivulets below as we navigated from village to village.

The first bridge wasn't bad at all, about eight feet long and not that high off the ground, but it was only two inches wide and I froze. Behind me, Chaudhari gently urged me on, and the medical officer in front offered his walking stick, which I grabbed with one hand. I should have been ashamed of myself because compared with other bridges that came later, this one was child's play.

"In Bengali," Chaudhari said when he caught up to me, "we call bridges like these *pul*. The tradition of Islam that came to us from the Sufi mystics and the Arabs teaches about a spiritual bridge. There is a man here we call the Sufi of Bhola Island. He teaches that our bamboo bridges are some kind of reminder of *pul-e-sirat*, the last bridge that extends over hell itself, from this world to heaven.

"This is a world of suffering; beyond it there is either heaven or hell. From this world, there stretches a long, narrow bridge, just like these bamboo poles that link our villages. It is thinner than a hair, sharper than a sword, hotter than fire, and filled with thorns made up of your sins. This narrow bridge arches high over a deep chasm. At the end of the bridge is paradise, but deep down in the chasm burn the fires of hell.

"The soul makes its final pilgrimage from this world to the next across this bridge. At first the pilgrim tries to walk erect and proud, but soon the sins of this lifetime weigh down the soul as the pilgrim teeters, about to fall into the fires of hell.

"Then the soul recalls the commandments he kept and the good deeds he did for others during his lifetime. They buoy up the soul, preventing it from falling. But only he who has clean hands and a pure heart can successfully cross this final bridge—*pul-e-sirat*—to heaven."

Although I fell from bamboo poles many times during my stay in Bangladesh, I did not fall that day. The thought that I would be seeing the last human being sickened with killer smallpox made my otherwise clumsy feet nimble.

As soon as our team entered the village and three-year-old Rahima Banu saw my white face, she began to cry uncontrollably. Clutching her mother, she tried to hide from yet another group of doctors coming to examine her. She looked just like the picture WHO had distributed. As she squirmed and turned to avoid our stares, it was easy to see how badly smallpox had scarred her light-brown face.

The day he took me to see my first case in the field, Bill Foege told me that the day must come when I would see each patient not only for themselves, but also as part of a larger pattern. What I saw in Rahima Banu was thousands of years of history, the perennial battle of good and evil, light and dark, health and disease. She was the last little girl with *Variola major*. When her pox scabs fell to the ground, when she coughed and the last of the virus in her landed on the sunbaked ground, it had nowhere to go, no one else to infect, no more children to kill; finally, after ten thousand years, here in the tiny village of poor Kuralia, the chain was broken in the end by this little girl.

Traditional medical ethics were violated in telling the world this patient's name in the first place. Everywhere, however, a hungry press demanded to know the name of the last case of Asian smallpox. But for Rahima Banu and her family, there was no way to explain the parade of foreigners who came to stare. What does it mean to have the last case of smallpox? How could anyone explain that to a poor Bengali villager? Her father, a day laborer on a fishing boat who earned sixty-five cents a day, had never seen a foreigner before. How could we explain to her family the special meaning that this little girl's health had for all of us who had struggled to cross so many bridges to see this child? Every smallpox warrior who visited Rahima Banu and saw her tears must have swallowed hard and shyly handed her bewildered mother, hardly more than a teenager herself, a few coins or notes, just as I did. I gave Rahima a red balloon on which was printed "Smallpox can be stopped," and took a picture that remains to this day one of the great inspirations of my life.

Rahima Banu was in my head, and to be honest, in my heart. No one could look at her scarred face and not think about sacrifice, about the long and painful trail etched by smallpox through history and of the massive good done by ending this awful disease. I thought about the brief time I had spent fighting smallpox compared with others, like Zafar, who had worked for decades. I thought about D. A. Henderson, whose one-pointed leadership had led hundreds of thousands of smallpox workers to and through the final inch. And I thought about Nicole and Bill and M. I. D. Sharma and the blessing of being part of this smallpox community. As I thought about the dozens of visitors seeing Rahima Banu's poverty, I felt that the eradication of smallpox had to be only the start of a genuine worldwide commitment to lift other burdens from the poor and sick across the globe.

In some ways the burden has gotten worse. If I wanted to go back to Bhola Island to pay homage at the site of the last case of *Variola major,* I probably could not. The melting of polar ice and rising sea levels from climate change have claimed more than half the landmass of Bhola. Half a million were left homeless on Bhola alone. Millions of Bangladeshis from the coast have become climate refugees, fleeing to the north of their country or for Burma and India.

It was late at night on Christmas Eve when we left Bhola Island. Under normal circumstances, we never would have attempted to cross the dangerous waters near the Bay of Bengal after sundown, but the moon was nearly full and the memory of Rahima Banu filled us with courage. We cast off from the island with our one remaining working engine. Midway across the channel, that single engine also failed.

Marooned on the water, we drifted out to the Bay of Bengal on Christmas Eve, the night the three wise men headed toward Bethlehem to witness a miraculous birth.

I started to wonder what my own journey across the razor-sharp *pul-e-sirat* would be at the time of death. Did only my own good and bad deeds count or was there also collective guilt and collective gain? I was confident that if there was a final bridge, that the hundreds of thousands who had worked together from so many countries to conquer smallpox might find their good deeds would tip the balance in any final accounting, getting a lift for everyone who fought smallpox. I remembered something Ray Davis, an African American doctor I partnered with during civil rights inspections of hospitals in the South, said: "Things aren't as bad as they could be, they aren't as good as they should be, but oh, thank God, they aren't as bad as they were." I wondered how humankind would be measured, and I thought about the conversation between God and Noah, of how many good people, how many good deeds, were needed to keep God from again destroying the world. And I wondered about myself, if I would be able to keep doing enough good in the world to complete the journey myself.

As we drifted helplessly toward open water, the words of Maharaji, that smallpox, this terrible epidemic, this *mahamari,* would be *unmulan,* eradicated, came back to me, filling the boat with love, light, and peace. The currents eventually carried us to a sandbar, stopping the boat from drifting farther out to sea. At the end of the night, the tides changed, along with a shift in the winds, slowly moving us back toward the mainland. The sun was rising in the east when we washed peacefully onto the shore, this stage of the journey finished, the deep truth of history moving inevitably, perpetually, in the direction of love.

Epilogue

When I was a boy, my dad sometimes took my brother, Barry, and me out to the Detroit River to watch the hydroplane boat races. More airplane than river craft, these immensely powerful boats flew over the water, their hulls hardly touching it as they reached unthinkable speeds. During World War I, Gar Wood, an inventor and boat maker, set speed records on the Detroit River, not far from the Ambassador Bridge where I first kissed Girija. He won races with a boat called *Miss Detroit*, en route to becoming the first man to exceed 100 miles per hour on water. When these hydroplane boats skim the river, a high plume of water arcs behind them. Locals call its distinctive curl a rooster tail.

We don't usually see our own rooster tails as we zoom through life at high speeds. It's rare to see the effect we have on others, the ripples of karma's wake. The course of our lives, the arc of our rooster tails, is a mystery except in retrospect. In medical school, students joked that the only accurate instrument for diagnosing disease was the very rare retrospect-o-scope. The passage of time has provided me one of those rare scopes. After forty years of an improbable journey, the trajectory of my life begins to make sense.

The 1960s and 1970s brought with it a lot of turmoil and change that became important to the history of America and to the entire world. It was an important time for me as well. These years—of travel, exploration, growth, and action—zoomed by like the hydroplane boats on the river.

In 1962, I met Martin Luther King Jr.; by the mid-1960s, I was a political radical marching against discrimination and protesting the Vietnam war; in 1970, I was on Alcatraz and then met Wavy and the Hog Farm. In 1971, we pitched a teepee and planted the Whole Earth flag by the Bosporus Strait. In 1972, Girija and I were together in Maharaji's ashram in a mystical corner of the Himalayas. By the autumn of 1973, Maharaji was gone and I was a United Nations medical officer dropping leaflets from a plane on WHO headquarters. By 1977, smallpox was gone, I was a professor at the University of Michigan and consulting for UN agencies, and Girija was getting her Ph.D. in public health. In 1980, WHO sent me back to Delhi to close down the smallpox office and retrieve the files documenting every move every smallpox warrior made. There I happened upon D. A. Henderson's note in WHO records, that on interviewing me for the first time, I seemed like a good kid but he worried that I was too Indian, that I had "gone native." He still allowed Nicole to hire me, and he teased me about my counterculture roots right up until our last conversations, weeks before he died as I was finishing this book.

San Francisco, civil rights, the Hog Farm, Ram Dass, the bus ride to the East—my experiences had all turned me into a creature of the sixties. But now that I've got more miles on my odometer, I am aware that I am also a creature of the spiritual revolution that followed, as well as a beneficiary of the public health revolution that fueled the eradication of smallpox, and the technological revolution of Silicon Valley. And I am one of many who wander the path of the eternal quest for meaning, for answers to questions about why we are born, what a purposeful life looks like.

The counterculture transformed many into more deeply spiritual, noble, and generous people. But others died falling down elevator shafts with heroin needles stuck in their arms. Many thrived in stable relationships that lasted decades; two longtime married couples, Wavy and Jahanara (Bonnie Jean), and Girija and I, have been friends for more than forty-five years. Pretty amazing. Yet others have ended up alone, living on the streets or in psych wards. Some people prospered materially; others lost everything to bad drugs, bad luck, or bad decisions.

The best of those days were pure magic, the worst a hell. It was a complicated blend. It was neither all political revolution nor all spaced-out hippies singing and dancing in the streets. It was neither all Martin Luther King nor all Charles Manson. We came of age sexually in the golden era between the advent of birth control pills and the epidemic of HIV/AIDs. Spiritually, it was like a greenhouse in which the most beautiful flowers blossomed alongside the most vicious weeds—sometimes even in the same person at different times. Personally, I like the hothouse. I want to see the flowers grow fast like the forest springing to life after the monsoon in India. I will take my chances with new flowers and remain vigilant for weeds. That's the risk taker in me, the adventurer, the adrenaline junkie. I will bet on the new technologies that arise from Silicon Valley, knowing full well the risk of their potential dark side. Progress demands that humans try to create better conditions for everyone, and change requires risk. What I have learned is just this: leave room for God, leave room for love, and never, ever lose your sense of humor.

Embracing the history of the counterculture is so important for the survival of America, for the restoration of hope, idealism, and optimism. I wish we could have back one specific part of the counterculture, that feeling that the revolution of goodness, mercy, and kindness was right around the corner. I also wish we could do things differently—smarter and more pragmatically. My generation squandered a lot of our moment. The universe opened up, and an instant of possibility appeared, like when the Enlightenment shattered the superstitious hold of the Middle Ages. "Never doubt that a small group of thoughtful, committed citizens can change the world," Margaret Mead said. "Indeed, it is the only thing that ever has." Clusters of people, empowered by the times, set off to change the world—and some groups accomplished just that. Change starts with ordinary people doing extraordinary things. The path to the extraordinary is open to anybody at any time.

With the last case of killer smallpox, Rahima Banu, Girija and I felt that this part of Maharaji's task was complete. In gratitude, we made a pilgrimage, the *adu padu vedu,* to six temples sacred to the Hindu god Subrahmanyum (also called Murugan and Skanda) in South India, as we had promised our teacher before he died.

Saying goodbye in Delhi wasn't easy. The WHO headquarters, the people, the building, the neighborhood, had been the place where I grew up and where I learned to bring all of me—the spiritual and the practical—together in one mission. It was hard realizing I wouldn't see Mrs. Boyer, Nicole, or M.I.D.— Papa—every day anymore. The team was dispersing to the four corners of the world. Nicole wanted an adventure. "I've heard no woman ever drove alone from New Delhi to Paris," she said, so she set off in her old banged-up Toyota with a suitcase, a starter pistol that looked like a handgun, and, being French, a dog. She spent time with J.R.D. before leaving. She said she had to fire the starter pistol to fend off unwanted sexual advances in half the countries she drove through. Typical Nicole.

Girija and I both wanted a formal public health education. We spent time in New York with the satsang and helped Karmapa with his temple. We thought we'd go to Columbia University, but University of Michigan made us an offer we couldn't refuse.

The School of Public Health dean Myron Wegman had been head of the WHO regional office in the Americas and knew about my work in smallpox. He got us retroactive status as Michigan residents so that we could pay a lower tuition and get scholarships. We entered programs in epidemiology, public health, and management. I eventually became associate professor of epidemiology, and Girija got her doctorate.

Though there had been no more cases of killer smallpox, the global commission was visiting every country to confirm the absence of disease. Still there were a few countries like Iran and South Africa over which there was concern about smallpox being stored illegally. In October 1978, WHO asked me to go to Iran to conduct a "special program to confirm Iran's status as free of smallpox." In 1971, the shah had held celebrations of the 2,500th anniversary of the founding of the Persian Empire in

Persepolis, near the tomb of Cyrus the Great, and he suppressed reporting of smallpox cases in Iran. Dozens of kings and queens, presidents and prime ministers, even Ethiopian emperor Haile Selassie, attended. Some of the heads of state were unvaccinated; none was informed that there were active cases of smallpox in the area—men, women, and children begging along the parade route could have had infectious smallpox. It was also known that living smallpox viruses had been widely used in Iran in benign medical laboratory tests. The Islamic Revolution was gaining momentum in 1978. WHO worried about whether or not smallpox still existed in the country, and, if there were live samples in labs, whether *Variola major* might accidently fall into the wrong hands and be used as a biological weapon. We did not have the label "weapons inspector" then, but that was part of what WHO wanted.

Tehran was tense when I arrived. Ayatollah Khomeini was rumored to be returning from exile in Paris—which he would do three months later in February 1979, overthrowing the shah less than two weeks after his return. D.A. asked me to set up camp at the Hilton in Tehran. Every day at 4 A.M., the surging mujahedeen morality police knocked on my hotel room door. "You have British Airways hostesses in here? You are fornicating with them?" they asked. It had become a comedy routine in which they searched every nook and cranny for invisible stewardesses.

Facial scar surveys confirmed that smallpox had indeed been epidemic in Iran but was now gone. I did find vials labeled "smallpox" in medical school labs containing material that looked like very old smallpox scabs. Samples were sent back to WHO, which confirmed that, at least in the samples we took, there was no infectious smallpox found. Eventually only two authorized laboratories, in the United States and in Russia, were allowed to keep the virus stored deep in liquid nitrogen.

One of the darkest chapters in the history of smallpox was during the Cold War. The Soviet Union created a secret plan to weaponize smallpox and even combine it with Ebola—creating an apocalyptic virus that would spread like smallpox and kill like Ebola. D.A., by then the dean of Johns Hopkins School of Public Health, brought this to light through former Soviet bioweapons experts who revealed the Soviet Biopreparat "Vector" program to Congress. Through his testimony we learned that some of the bioweapon program's smallpox seed stock might have been carried from India by Russian epidemiologists who had worked in the WHO eradication program. I cannot imagine which, if any, of my friends—Russian colleagues I worked happily alongside—would take scabs from a child with smallpox in India, bundle them up as if they were mementos from a holiday trip, and deliver the samples to be weaponized and possibly used against the United States. How could anyone who has seen a child writhe in agony and die from smallpox help build smallpox into a weapon? It is unthinkable, madness, more horrible than any other act of terror, because after the first attack, smallpox could reestablish itself as a new pandemic for a new millennium.

The Biopreparat program was said to have been authorized by Mikhail Gorbachev, but no one really knew the whole story.

I got a call in 2006 to attend a lunch with President Gorbachev, who came to San Francisco to meet with environmentalists at Madeleine Albright's suggestion to help Gorbachev develop a political afterlife in philanthropy. I was invited to sit with Gorbachev to talk about establishing a foundation. I was surprised by how much I liked Gorbachev and how comfortable it was to interact with our former antagonist. After most everyone left the room, I whipped up the courage to ask him the question that had been burning inside me for years—and I imagine inside everyone else who had battled smallpox. I wanted to know if it was true that he had signed that five-year plan to spend $1 billion to create that half-smallpox-half-Ebola monster weapon that some Russians threatened could kill 100 million Americans.

"Why did you do it?" I asked.

The former Soviet president heaved a deep and weary sigh, as if centuries of intrigue were being shed from his Russian soul. He took off his glasses, tossed them onto the table, and sat down on a chair with a heavy thud, forehead cradled in his hand.

"It was the worst decision of my life," Gorbachev said, looking up after a long silence. Like a defendant pleading his case, he asked for understanding. "Your president Reagan told me that your economy could allow America to both build nuclear weapons and feed its people, and that he did not need to bomb us into the Stone Age when he could spend us into the Stone Age. We kept pace with nuclear weapons for a while, but our economy wasn't strong enough to keep up. There was dissatisfaction among the Soviet people with the price of bread and the lack of basic goods. As the economy weakened I started moving money away from weapons systems and into food production. One day several generals came to my office in the Kremlin, closed the door behind them, and announced coldly, 'Mr. President, we cannot lose the arms race. If we cannot have nuclear weapons, we need something else for our back pocket. You must authorize biological weapons, or else, Mr. President, we will be forced to get a new Mr. President.'

"So, *da,* I signed the five-year plan. I deeply regret it. It is part of the reason I want to try to give back to the world, to make amends."

When President Clinton turned over the White House to George W. Bush, he singled out known biological weapons programs, like this one, as a priority for the new president. That fear was one of the reasons President Bush in October 2007 issued a presidential directive (HSPD-21) establishing the National Biosurveillance Advisory Subcommittee. I was appointed the first chairman on this subcommittee and served on it for two years. During this time, I learned that a team of some remarkable men and women from CDC and other agencies were permitted to inspect the Soviet biological weapons facilities to help remove any materials that could be used in bio warfare. But removing old weapons is one thing; proving that the world is safe is a more complicated issue. Although we think that the Soviets never succeeded in creating their superbug, the old saying "Eternal vigilance is the price of liberty" remains more true than perhaps most people know.

While the United States has the other lab authorized to keep smallpox, we have been sloppy about minding risks from old smallpox stores here. As late as 2014, live smallpox was found in the United States in an abandoned FDA lab in an NIH facility in Bethesda, Maryland. Until this discovery, I did not favor destroying the remaining legally kept smallpox samples. I felt we might one day need them to create better remedies. But the careless way live smallpox was forgotten in the heart of the United States made me change my mind. WHO should vote to destroy all the smallpox virus in the world and carry this out without delay. Rapid advances in synthetic biology—which means science can now synthesize the Variola virus—render my previous concerns outdated.

Smallpox has been used as a biological weapon even in early U.S. history. The first smallpox bioterrorist was a British officer, Lord Jeffrey Amherst. During Pontiac's War, with Native American tribes over the Ohio Valley and the Alleghenies, Amherst proposed mixing smallpox scabs with blankets being distributed in order to kill some of the "disaffected tribes of Indians." History has preserved his writing, expressing his clear intentions to use germ warfare in an attempted genocide. Amherst left hundreds of Indians killed by smallpox, buried in "pox acres" not all that far from the eponymous Amherst, Massachusetts, and the eponymous Amherst College, which I visited when my son Jon was thinking of attending. So many great minds have emerged from this institution. But the city and college are named after a smallpox bioterrorist. For someone who held a little boy in his arms who was killed by smallpox in Tatanagar, Amherst is a name of shame.

The smallpox warriors stayed in touch. Nicole, in particular, went to Beirut during war and unrest in Lebanon to volunteer with the International Red Cross not long after the smallpox eradication campaign ended. She helped build factories for artificial limbs for amputees who had lost legs during the violence in the region. She and I began writing to each other about working together on something else. We wanted to scale the mountain again, and do something as meaningful as smallpox eradication. This time I wanted to bring in people who had less formal training but huge hearts, like Ram Dass and Wavy, to see what their spiritual common sense could bring to a public health initiative. "Oh," Nicole said when I told her, "you are starting the hippie Red Cross." We didn't know which problem we would end up solving—I wanted to raise money to stop diarrhea, which still kills too many children every year. Wavy suggested we raise money for it by putting on a massive concert with the Grateful Dead and call it "No Shit." When we couldn't get that off the ground, we kicked around other ideas until, as usual, a serendipitous event determined our direction. Nicole, during a WHO conference in New Delhi, discovered a huge and solvable problem—blindness in Nepal—along with funding for it. "We have the money to do a blindness survey," she cabled me, "if the Hippie Red Cross is willing to work on it."

Around the same time, Girija and I wrote an article, "Death for a Killer Disease," about our time in India during smallpox eradication, urging that more be done for global health. Many readers of that article sent us envelopes with small amounts of cash in them, adding up to nearly $20,000. Determined to find a good social use for that money, we invited all the people we had written about in the article to come to Ann Arbor to figure it out. The founders of what would become Seva gathered in Michigan in 1979, representing all the threads of our lives coming together in one room: the Hog Farm, smallpox warriors, Maharaji's devotees, CDC and WHO epidemiologists, and eye specialists from America and India. While we came to a consensus that blindness in Nepal would be our first project, in a short time we were relitigating Trungpa and Wavy's argument over meditation and action, but this time the fight was between Ram Dass and Nicole.

"Don't be in such a rush to cure blindness that you do violence to morality," Ram Dass said, "or we will lose our souls."

"Who cares if I burn in hell for a thousand years?" Nicole countered. "If we slow down, that's one more person who will die blind."

Back and forth it went, the argument over being and doing. Wavy and others chanted, "Do be do be do be do." I had learned by then—from Maharaji, from smallpox, from working with the Tatas—that it had to be both. We had to be good and do good, or we would be of little use to the blind.

We named the organization Seva, which means "service" in Sanskrit. The office was established in our garage in Chelsea, Michigan, just outside of Ann Arbor. I raised the initial $100,000 through a grant to research and write a peer-reviewed academic book, *The Management of Smallpox Eradication in India*, published by University of Michigan Press. Nicole became the WHO blindness program manager in Kathmandu, and I would be the survey director. After the birth of our first son, Joseph Seva Brilliant, I got a leave of absence from Michigan for the six months it would take to do the survey. Girija and I took baby Joe to Kainchi and then to Nepal; his first words were in Nepali. Since its founding in 1979, Seva's programs, grantees, and partners have restored sight to more than four million people in two dozen countries. Most of these surgeries were done for free. So much of Seva's success was due to Dr. Venkataswamy, "Dr. V.," who founded the Aravind Eye Hospital in honor of his teachers, Sri Aurobindo and the Mother of Pondicherry.

Steve Jobs, who had just taken Apple public, read about the smallpox success and remembered our lunch at WHO. He periodically phoned me and offered to help if we ever set out to do something like that again. When he heard that a group of small-pox veterans was going to start a new organization to conquer blindness, he and his former roommate from Reed College, Sita Ram Das, sent $5,000 apiece, our largest individual gifts up to that point. Steve helped a lot with Seva, sending us computers, software, and a dial-up modem so that we could stay connected from Kathmandu.

Evergreen Helicopters donated a much-needed helicopter to fly doctors to remote villages—some of which were as high as 12,000 feet. Wavy got Jerry Garcia and the Grateful Dead to do a concert just to raise the money to transport the helicopter to Kathmandu. The aircraft performed flawlessly, ferrying eye doctors and epidemiologists to 108 villages, where we treated more than 40,000 villagers for eye and other disease. On the last day of the survey, Nicole and several eye doctors were finishing up in a remote area in the flat part of Nepal. On their way back to Kathmandu, they stopped to pick someone up in the country's second-largest city, Biratnagar. As they left Biratnagar, the helicopter engine let out a loud shriek at about 300 feet in the air. The engine had digested itself, and the helicopter began to fall "like an oak leaf fluttering from the tree in the fall," the pilot, Darryl Ward, later said. He would be awarded helicopter pilot of the year for white-knuckling the craft to a safe landing. No one was hurt.

The logistics of getting a new engine installed in the heli-copter and lifting the old engine out of the area were unprec-edented. Other aircraft that had crashed in Nepal years earlier were still there. Because Steve had given us that acoustic modem, and a local UN satellite expert was sitting in the next room in the Kathmandu office, I was able to connect over satellite to the

University of Michigan computer system and set up what was called a computer conferencing meeting. From Seva's offices in California and Michigan, we connected the UN office in New York, Evergreen's headquarters in Oregon, and the Paris office of Aérospatiale, where the helicopter had been built, as well as WHO in Geneva. Using a software system called Confer, we were able to get everyone to agree on who would pay for transporting the new engine to the crash site and how the old engine would be helicoptered out to Singapore. Within seventy-two hours, the problem was solved. I had never seen WHO work so fast. I became intrigued with this new technology.

The communication thread from the computer conference call looked just like the transcript of a telephone conference call, and nearly exactly like Gmail threads look today. When I returned to Ann Arbor from Nepal, I used a variant of that system to hook up Seva offices around the world via computer conferencing.

Steve Jobs came to Ann Arbor in 1982 or 1983, after we got back from Nepal, to give a talk about his growing company, Apple computers. When he came over to our house, I showed him how the system we called "SevaTalk" worked. Later that day, I awkwardly asked him for more money for Seva. He laughed hard and said, "You have your own fucking technology now. Build your own fucking company and fund your own fucking nonprofit. I will help you and show you how." And he did. He eventually joined Seva's advisory board, and the SevaTalk platform became the foundation for what would become the Well, one of the first digital social networks. After I co-founded the Well with Stewart Brand in 1985, *Wired* magazine called it "the world's most influential online community." I had taken the company public years earlier, made some money, and, over the course of the next twenty years, worked part-time in technology to earn enough money to feed my public health habit—my need to work in the field directly addressing blindness as well as polio eradication.

It was the tsunami that hit the day after Christmas in 2004, killing hundreds of thousands in Asia, that turned me back toward thinking about pandemics. There was a historic out-pouring of generosity, especially for Indonesia. But Sri Lanka, where the passenger train had rolled over, tossed like a toy in the waves, had not received as much attention, so many victims were hurting. Cash donations of more than $100,000 rushed into Seva. The money was needed quickly in Sri Lanka, so I decided to avoid the UN bureaucracy and carry it myself to Colombo to put it into the right hands.

I stayed at various Tata-owned hotels in Sri Lanka and lingered in the country looking for a way to help. I headed to Hikkaduwa, the village where the train had been forced off its tracks. Just as happened in Bhola Island after the cyclone, saris and shirts were stuck thirty feet high in trees. Under the canopy of clothes was a tent city of aid organizations from all over the world. They were short on doctors, so I volunteered to stay and treat wounded Sri Lankans for a couple of weeks, dispensing medicines, rebandag-ing wounds, and addressing psychological trauma. In the ref-ugee camp I met several WHO doctors, including the director general, who were very worried about refugees getting the newly spreading H5N1 virus, a pathogenic bird flu, and infecting the volunteers, who could then spread it to every part of the world, as smallpox had spread from Tatanagar, setting off a brand-new pandemic. After a couple of weeks in the refugee camps, I got sick myself with dysentery and had to come home.

While recovering at home in Marin County, California, where I'd moved in 1989, I had a lot of time to think about how we could better prepare for pandemics. I convened a new organization I started in November 2005 called PanDefense 1.0 to talk about it. A few months later, my phone rang. Chris Anderson, the curator of TED, told me I won the TED Prize. The prize was $100,000, but more important, Chris told me I was supposed to think of a wish to change the world, and the TED community would rally behind it and might provide more resources. It was a turning point in my life. My wish was to create an early-warning system for pandemics. Chris sent me to talk about the TED Prize and my wish at technology companies, such as Google, which was about seven years old at the time. I gave a talk about how we eradicated smallpox and how we could use that experience to plan a warning system for pandemics. Larry Page and Sergey Brin were in the back of the lecture room. Two days later, then–vice president Sheryl Sandberg called and asked me if I wanted to join Google as the first executive director of Google.org. Sergey and Larry had written that they planned to give away a billion dollars to address things like poverty reduction, pandemics, and climate change around the world. I called Steve Jobs about the idea—Apple and Google were friendly then. He was very excited by what Google was doing and was "super in favor" of me working with them. "Mark my words," he added, "one day Larry Page will become CEO of Google. He is a really smart guy."

Google announced my appointment the day before I gave my TED Prize talk. The rush of publicity for these dual events was heady. Fortunately, my friend Bill Foege was one of the first to call and congratulate me and, as always, found a way to help me stay balanced. Whenever something big happened, my smallpox mentors—M.I.D. "Papa," Bill, D.A., and Nicole—still helped me find direction; with Maharaji gone and Karmapa having passed in November 1981, these extraordinary human beings were who I turned to for support. That the world sometimes gets things right was demonstrated when M.I.D., Nicole, Isao Arita, D.A., and Bill were all awarded the highest honors in their respective countries in recognition for their contributions to public health: the Padma Shri in India, the Legion of Honor in France, the Japan Prize, and the Presidential Medal of Freedom in the United States. In characteristic style, Nicole delayed receiving her award for several years because French custom required the medal recipient to kiss the French president on each cheek. Nicole hated President Mitterrand and initially refused to kiss his cheeks. They finally worked something out, and she was awarded the honor in a beautiful ceremony.

We all visited one another many times over the ensuing years. "Papa" played in the snow with us in Michigan. I saw Bill and D.A. continue their extraordinary leadership in public health. One of the most difficult reunions with the group was in 2010, when Zdeno, Lev and Lydia, D.A., Girija and I, and others gathered in Geneva to recognize two anniversaries: thirty years since the eradication of smallpox, and one year since Nicole, the godmother of our son Joe, died of lung cancer. She was buried walking distance from WHO headquarters, as she requested in her will. In her wake, she left many wealthy and powerful leaders quaking, but for her team, she was a leader without peer, and an unforgettable force of nature with a will of steel and a heart of gold.

———————

My daily drive from Marin County to Google in Mountain View was about an hour and half. Steve Jobs lived near the campus and I sometimes stopped at his house on the way home. We often talked about "doing well and doing good," the catchphrase then in Silicon Valley.

"Larry, do you still believe in God? Do you still believe in Maharaji?" Steve asked when I answered the phone one day. Just like him; right to the point. Hardly a "hello."

"Of course I do, Steve." I had seen so many children die of smallpox, seen so many others blind or stricken by polio, and had just come back from seeing the power of nature's devastation from the tsunami, yet I had reached some personal kind of peace. "What's wrong?" I asked. "Why are you really calling?"

He had been diagnosed with pancreatic cancer and wanted to talk to me about it.

I had seen thousands of children suffering with smallpox, but I had not been gripped by the personal fear and grief that he and his family were caught in. I thought seeing all the death in India, losing my dad and grandpa, sitting in front of enlightened beings like Maharaji and Karmapa, had immunized me in some way against the pain of death. I would soon realize my faith was superficial; it would falter not long after I started at Google. Girija developed breast cancer and was operated on. Our middle child, Jon, who was on a Fulbright in China, came home to comfort his mom.

Jon became ill in Beijing a few months later and he came back to the United States for diagnosis and treatment. After scans and biopsies and months of uncertainty, he was diagnosed with lung cancer. There are no words to describe the shock our family felt. Steve jumped in, interviewing doctors, helping us find the best doctors for Girija's and Jon's cancers. Steve was a real mensch to those who really knew him. He and Jon became cancer friends, comparing notes on chemo.

After six months of surgery and radiation, Girija fully recovered from her cancer. Jon, at twenty-six, did not. Neither did Steve, who died less than a year later.

After Jon's death, I didn't believe in anything anymore. Girija and I removed all the pictures of Maharaji and Karmapa, angry at God for taking our boy, through a disease I could do nothing about. It was worse than when I was in India, angry at God because I thought he must be a lousy manager to allow little babies to die from smallpox. Losing Jon was the hardest moment for my entire family and I found it impossible to function afterward. Google was kind to me and gave me the title Philanthropy Evangelist, but I was no use to them or anyone else.

It has taken a long time, and I can still get lost in the dark hole of pain. But gradually, I understood that I have been given a new assignment, to be there for Girija and my daughter, Iris, and my son Joe, to help us stay whole, to find some things beautiful in life. I fail every day, but I also understand that part of my job is to transform my grief at losing my son into somehow being grateful that we had this wonderful person in our lives for twenty-six years. This is the hardest thing I have ever tried to do. Every once in a while, I escape my own grief for a second by remembering the tens of thousands of mothers and fathers who lost their son or daughter to smallpox while I was in India. Every once in a while, I recognize fully that the depth of their grief is as deep as mine. That sense of being in the same boat, of being human together, lasts just a second. I do not understand it. The Buddha taught that we grow old, get sick, and die, and that is true. Yet I do not understand why it needs to be that our lives are finite and our deaths so painful. I take some solace in what Maharaji often said: "It is better to see God in everyone than to try to figure it all out."

And I surely do not know how to think about these things in a way that might help anyone reading this. None of us is untouched by suffering or death. But let me answer again Steve's questions: Do I still believe in God? Do I still believe in Maharaji?

I have seen a great deal of death. But I have also seen a great deal of life and joy, and I still believe that there is much more good than bad in the world. What I did finally come to grudgingly accept is that there is more to this life than I can ever understand— solving the great mysteries of life is above my pay grade. Yes, I still believe in God. I didn't for a while, when I held so many children dead or dying from smallpox, and of course when Jon died. But doubt is the constant companion on the journey toward faith. And while the pain of loss does not go away, and I miss my son more than I can say, I also have found as I have tried to be honest, digging deep inside, that I love my two other children even more than I thought I ever could, and I realize how lucky I am to have such wonderful young human beings so close to me. There is so much for me to be grateful for. Smallpox was eradicated and I got to see Rahima Banu. Girija and I still love each other after nearly half a century. And we have since put the photographs of Maharaji, and all of our holy pictures, back on our walls.

I think still about Maharaji's prophecy: "Smallpox will be quickly eradicated. This is God's gift to mankind because of the hard work of dedicated health workers." He was saying that progress is possible, a better world is possible, that one kind of terrible suffering can be alleviated by a global, international community joining forces. He did not say that there would not be suffering. He did not say Buddha was wrong to tell us that all of us must face the truth of old age, suffering, and death. But he also said, "Sub ek," "All one." All religions are one, all nations are one, all men are brothers. I suppose we've all heard that before, and already know it someplace deep inside to be true. But Maharaji taught that this realization is only the beginning. The next step is understanding that there is something tangible to do, specific work to try to help those who suffer needlessly. Smallpox eradication is but one proof that something can be done, that little by little we can make this planet a place with less suffering. We are still finite beings, yet we can still create a world with infinitely more love, more joy, and less pain.

If after all the death and suffering I have seen, I can still find reason to be optimistic, if I can still love God and find love for everyone in my heart, then I would like this story to lift you—from your pain, your losses, and the relentless twenty-four-hour news reports of violence and hate, environmental disasters, rapes, muggings, terrorism, war, and vile racist rhetoric—and catapult you into another world, where the horror of a common enemy once brought together competing nations to prove that global efforts can accomplish great things.

Yes, I do still believe in God. Of course I do.

I want this story to steal your heart and plant a vision of what is possible. If smallpox, one of the worst diseases in history, the cause of hundreds of millions of deaths and tormenter of countless little children, can be conquered, then other miracles are surely possible. If a kid from Detroit, the first in his family to go to college, can pass through the stages of anger, self-righteousness, hedonism, and risky adventures through the minefield of drugs, prophets, and ideologies to find a harmony in an attempt to serve and honor God, so can you. Your path will be different, your obstacles different, your faith may be different, but that harmony and that pathway are always open to anyone who is ready for it.

I think back to that day I sat in front of Maharaji at Kainchi ashram, the day that began with me wanting to flee a strange cult in a foreign place and ended with me discovering I was already home. Not long after, Maharaji allowed me to use an empty room in the ashram as a makeshift medical office to treat minor medical illnesses of the local Kumaon families. He started calling me Doctor America publicly all the time after that and would playfully ask me to treat him with various Western medicines, which he would balance on his head instead of taking. The first time Maharaji balanced a tin of Tiger Balm on his head after telling me he wasn't well, he giggled and said to me, "Doctor America! Doctor America! Will you write a book? Will you write a book?"

At the time, I didn't answer. For many years, after I finished my academic book about smallpox, I tried to write a book with stories from the ashram and smallpox years, the book I was sure he was referring to, this book that you have in your hands. For forty years I have told these stories to my children and friends, but I could not write them. Looking back now I wish I could teleport myself to that day four decades ago and answer him, "Yes, Maharaji. I will write a book. It may take a long time, but at the very least, I will try."

Guru Purnima
July 19, 2016
Mill Valley

Acknowledgments

started writing this book in 1977 after Girija and I returned home to Michigan. Following the death of our teacher, Neem Karoli Baba, and the last case of *Variola major,* I wanted to tell this story. My friend Dan Goleman, then a writer at *Psychology Today* and, later, the *New York Times*, encouraged me to write about my experiences living in the ashram and working on the smallpox campaign. I was a professor at the University of Michigan by then and only had time to write with Girija a magazine article. "Death for a Killer Disease" was published in 1978 in *Quest/78*, a spiritual magazine. A few years later, I wrote an academic book detailing how we ran the eradication program, called *The Management of Smallpox Eradication in India.*

After those early efforts, I did not write much about smallpox until 2010, when Google colleague Corrie Conrad and I co-authored a chapter, "The Eradication of Smallpox from India," in *The Global Eradication of Smallpox,* which Sanjoy Bhattacharya and Sharon Messenger edited. Though I rarely wrote about my time in India again, I spoke about my experience in India in speeches over the years and even lent a few of these stories for use in other people's books, including Ram Dass's *Miracle of Love* and Wavy Gravy's *Something Good for a Change*. Other writers also wrote about my experiences in their books, writers like Richard Preston *(The Demon in the Freezer)*, Jonathan Tucker *(Scourge)*, D. A. Henderson *(Smallpox: The Death of a Disease)*, Bill Foege *(House on Fire)*, and Joel Shurkin *(The Invisible Fire)*. I want to thank all of them for preserving these stories so that I can now borrow them back again.

My colleague and friend at Google Sheryl Sandberg playfully suggested I write the entire history of my experience in India and smallpox, if only so she didn't have to hear about it again and again. Instead of mentioning smallpox in every speech, she teased, I could simply refer people to my book.

My agents, John Brockman and Katinka Matson, were patient with me, as I saddled them with unsellable proposals like "Zeropox Battle Chronicles," "The Education of Doctor America," "Talking Notes for Meeting God," and "The Business of Doing Good," which HarperCollins eventually acquired when I became an executive at Google in 2006. Mark Tauber, the publisher of HarperOne, and Gideon Weil, my editor, together inherited an unloved and unlovable contract for a book about how to do good while doing well in business, but they somehow saw the potential for a more personal work and kept the contract alive.

When my world collapsed beginning in 2008 with my wife's illness and then the death of my son Jon, I was sure I would never be able to write anything again, especially not a "business book." I told Mark Tauber that I was going to quit the book and return the advance. Instead, Mark waited patiently as I gradually came a little way out of my deep black hole and one day told me he had an idea, an offer I could not refuse. I could write a book about anything I wanted, he said. And he would increase the advance on the condition that I use the extra funds to hire someone to "work closely with you as editor and helper." He had a few people in mind for me to interview, but the first person on his list could not have been more perfect. This book would never have been written without that person, Amy Hertz, a remarkably talented woman, a celebrated publisher and editor, who had previously worked on books of people I respected immensely. She helped me with every part of this book and quickly became its principal architect, going above and beyond the call of duty and, in the process, becoming so much more than an editor or collaborator. *Sometimes Brilliant* is at least as often *Sometimes Amy*. Thank you, Amy.

I want to thank, too, the team at HarperOne. Particularly Gideon Weil, my patient and wise editor, who pushed me when I needed pushing and let me be when I needed patience. I hope he has enjoyed the ride as much as I have. And thanks to a remarkable HarperOne editor, Miles Doyle, with his lyrical edits, and for finding the spiritual core of the book. My sincerest gratitude goes to Sydney Rogers, Terri Leonard, and Lisa Zuniga, who somehow kept us all on course despite so many centrifugal forces.

But most of all, as with every element of my life, it was my loving and wonderful wife, Girija, who made it possible for this book to exist. She has suffered through the many incarnations of the book, and has lived through the many incarnations of me. I never would have worked for WHO nor would I have met our teacher Maharaji if she had not ignored my arrogance and dragged me to India in the first place. For nearly half a century, she has honored me as my wife and the amazing mother of Joe, Jon, and Iris. Speaking of our wonderful children, I have worked on iterations of this book on and off throughout their entire lives, and both Joe and Iris have remained great sports about the amount of time it has taken me. We all so much wish Jon were here to share the final product with them.

Years ago, Isao Arita and D. A. Henderson, then chiefs of the WHO global smallpox program, suggested I write *The Management of Smallpox Eradication in India.* So many people helped me with that book, and as the epidemiological building block of this book, I want to thank them again here: in addition to D.A. and Isao, Bill Foege, Nicole Grasset, M. I. D. Sharma, Zafar Hussein, R. N. Basu, Mahendra Dutta, C. K. Rao, Stan Foster, and Steve Jones all read the manuscript prepared by University of Michigan research assistants Tonya Kennedy and Mariane Zebrowski and typed by our friend Judy Gallagher. Only two people have ever told me that the book was of any use to them: President Jimmy Carter once phoned me in Ann Arbor to ask permission to photocopy twenty copies of the book for a class he was teaching at the Carter Center. (Years later, he wrote a letter nominating me for *Time* magazine's 100 list.) The second person was Dr. Jim Kim. Now the head of the World Bank, Dr. Kim visited my office at Google in 2008 as a professor at Harvard. He showed me a copy of *The Management of Smallpox Eradication in India,* teasing me about the ridiculous amount of money he had to pay for it on Amazon because it was out of print. Since then, following much-renewed interest in the campaign to eradicate smallpox, a long list of much better books about smallpox have been published. I have included some of these books in the "Further Reading" section.

The story of Rahima Banu and my visit to her is emotionally central to me, and knowing that she was the last case of killer smallpox is central to others who worked on smallpox in India and Bangladesh as well. This book is a memoir. It is not intended to be a comprehensive treatise on smallpox, its epidemiology, or its history, but because there are several other cases of smallpox that have the same importance to other epidemiologists as Rahima Banu to me, I wanted to honor some of them as well.

Rahima Banu was the last little girl with killer smallpox, the last case of smallpox in Asia, the last naturally occurring case of *Variola major,* and, for me, an emotional end to the deadly chain of transmission that scientists say began thousands or tens of thousands of years ago. But there were and still are viruses frozen in nitrogen in a few labs around the world. In 1978, at the University of Birmingham Medical School, a British medical photographer named Janet Parker contracted smallpox when the virus escaped from its container, wafted through a ventilation system, and infected her. Her family was placed under quarantine; her father died of cardiac arrest after seeing her in the emergency room. No autopsy was performed on him because of fear of smallpox contamination. Her mother, Hilda Witcomb, contracted smallpox as well but survived and, chronologically, is the last person infected with smallpox. Janet Parker died on September 11, 1978, the last person in history to die from smallpox. The doctor who had retained the sample of *Variola major* in his lab—against the directive of the World Health Organization—committed suicide while under quarantine. He left behind a note, which read, "I am sorry to have misplaced the trust which so many of my friends and colleagues have placed in me and my work."

There is another type of smallpox. *Variola minor,* also called alastrim, is a much milder and less often fatal form of smallpox. Although the two viruses look the same under an electron microscope, *Variola minor* kills one in a hundred cases, compared to *Variola major,* which kills one in three. No one could be sure that if *Variola minor* had not been eradicated, that a mutation to killer smallpox would not have taken place. Hence *Variola minor* was fought, with D. A. Henderson leading the charge, as aggressively as *Variola major* was. For many people, a Somalian cook named Ali Maow Maalin, the last person sick with *Variola minor* (October 1977), is for them the emotional center of the smallpox battle, the last case of the Variola family of viruses in nature.

I do not want to take anything away from any of these stories or diminish their importance. Each step was one of many toward a world free of smallpox. But I myself return to Rahima Banu every time I think of the long chain of transmission. Rahima Banu was the last child with *Variola major,* the end of a chain of transmission of agony and death, the end of this particular burden of suffering off the shoulders of humankind.

There would be no book if we had not conquered smallpox, and the long list of smallpox workers is still incomplete. Please forgive me for any name I have inadvertently omitted. But I want to name as many as I can remember because just seeing all these names brings me pleasure and reminds me what a multinational, multiracial, multireligious community it took to conquer smallpox: D. A. Henderson; Bill Foege; Isao Arita; M. I. D. Sharma; the remarkable Nicole Grasset, whose moniker Hurricane on High Heels does not do service to her incredible intelligence and huge heart, protecting her team and her values; the first person who took the time to teach me epidemiology was my beloved friend Zdeno Jezek; a man I wish all Indians could know better because they would be so proud is Mahendra Dutta, one of the key members of the Central Team; David Heymann; Stan Foster; Dr. Viswakarma; Don Francis; P. Diesh; Jay Friedman; H. M. Gelfand; J. S. Koopman; Mike McGinnis; G. Meiklejohn; D. Preston; the remarkable Alan Schnur; M. Strassburg; Dick Keenlyside; Roy Mason; D. M. Parkin; David Coxhead; W. M. Hamilton; J. Hatfield, P. Rotmil; B. Karwacka; T. Olakowski; K. K. Shah, who I still think should have been elected regional director of WHO; P. N. Shresta; M. Castet; J. Ryst; D. Tarantino; B. Bagar; V. Jaout; K. Markvart; V. Zikmund; Henry Smith; the heroic Afghan Abdul M. Darmangar; M. K. Al Aghbari; G. P. Marchenko; N. Maltseva; I. Selivanov; F. S. Kingma; J. M. Lane; dear Don Millar; our friends Bev Spring and Alan Morinis, who joined us as travelers in India, worked with us at WHO, and founded Seva in Canada; W. Orenstein; M. I. Rosenberg; David Sencer; Steve Solter; Joel Bremen; Mary Lou Clements, who died much too young in the explosion of a Swiss airliner; Connie Davis; S. N. Ray; my dearest friend Steve Jones, or as our children, his godchildren, call him, "Uncle Steve"; Nick Ward; Tony Scardacci; Roy Mason; my working and writing partner Lev Khodakevich—I wish his untimely death had not prevented our plan to meet in Moscow with so many years of history to reflect upon—and his wife, Lydia Khodakevich; J. P. Rikushin, who so loved mangos; Albert Monnier; V. A. Moukhopad; D. G. Olsen; Vladamir Zikmund; and that most remarkable, competent, and kind "Tata man," Sujit Gupta, and the pater familias, J. R. D. Tata; my constant companion for more than five years and my "paramedical assistant" but really my teacher, Zafar Hussein; E. M. A. Sheluchina;

A. N. Slepushkin; I. D. Ladnyi; A. I. Gromyko; J. W. Doss; Karan Singh; R. N. Basu; Edna Boyer; Jan de Vries; David Sencer; Don Hopkins, who will surely soon preside over the last case of Guinea worm; Mahendra Singh; C. K. Rao; Mohan Singh, who taught me a most important situational moral lesson and one I would wish I could translate into a general rule of life; and Justin Bhakla, who tragically lost the genetic lottery, but still led an important and meaningful life. I also want to thank those with whom I served as an administrative assistant when Nicole Grasset had to "cook up" a job description that could get me hired through the labyrinth of WHO and international rules: P. K. Anand; R. Satyanarayana, who learned English and speedwriting by listening to BBC broadcasts; M. S. Victor; K. K. Talwar; Prem Gambhiri; Mahesh Gupta; the leader of the administrators gang, R. K. Malhotra; V. B. Malik; S. Balasubramaniam; and K. K. Bajaj. I was a strange addition to your team and you were so kind to me.

How many people are lucky enough to say that their best friend is a clown, and not only that, but the clown prince of the counterculture? Thank you to Wavy Gravy and his wife and our friend Jahanara for helping me talk through these stories for forty years. After all these years, Wavy and Jahanara, and Girija and I are still married and remain friends for life. You can hardly find two couples who have been through so much and keep on truckin' together. And to all my wonderful and crazy brothers and sisters, from the Hog Farm commune to splendid Camp Winnarainbow and through the Seva Foundation, and to all the co-founders and staff of Seva, especially those who helped on this book: our beloved Suzanne and Tim Gilbert, who we dragged from Ann Arbor to northern California (it was not so difficult), Bev Spring, Aaron Simon, and Tamara Klamner.

The center of the book is Neem Karoli Baba, who we called Maharaji, and the wonderful people around him in his ashrams, especially Siddhi Ma and the other mas, Kainchi's own Vinodh Joshi and dear K. K. Shah. I also cherish the memory of Dada Mukerjee and several Indian families: the Barman, Soni, and Vaish families, who welcomed us to their India. And a then-young Ravi Khanna, who translated these wondrous words of wisdom and love. Maharaji's children, A. S. Sharma, Dharm Narayan Sharma, and Girija Bhatele, and his grandchildren, Dhananjay, Sashi, and Bobby. Some of the Westerners who lived with us in the ashrams during smallpox days have also helped with this book, especially: Ram Das, Dan Goleman, Sunanda, Mirabai, Krishna Das, Ravi Das (Michael Jeffery), Parvata, Mira, and Balaram (Peter Goetsch). I think I recounted nearly every story in this book at one time or another to Steve Jobs, who I first met when he was nineteen. I was twenty-nine. We were both in India trying in our own ways to understand Maharaji's lessons. Over four decades of friendship, Steve asked me more about the "meaning" of smallpox and the "meaning" of Maharaji than anyone else. He told me my article "Death for a Killer Disease" inspired him to join Seva. It would have meant so much for me if he could have been here to read this book. Girija and I consider ourselves very fortunate to have his extraordinary wife, Laurene Powell Jobs, as a dear friend, and his children and family as part of our extended family.

Besides Maharaji, or rather because of him, Girija and I spent much of our time in India seeking out wise teachers from a wide variety of faiths. It is too superficial to simply name these great masters, gurus, and spiritual leaders, but I write about most of them in the book and do not want to fail to thank them whether they are alive or have passed on: our friends Lama Govinda and Li Gotami; His Holiness the Sixteenth Karmapa and Jamgon Kongtrul Rinpoche, and His Holiness the Dalai Lama; our first meditation teacher, Goenka; other teachers we deeply respect like Jack Kornfield, Sharon Salzberg, the Sufi of Bhola Island, Rabbis Morris Adler and Sherwin Wine, Martin Luther King Jr., the Jesuit father who gave me communion in Bihar, and many other teachers, Christian and Jewish and Muslim and Zoroastrian and Jain and Buddhist and Hindu alike.

Financial support for this book over the years has come from the Rockefeller Foundation and from Jeff Skoll and his organizations, the Skoll Foundation, Skoll Global Threats Fund, and Jeff Skoll Group. A fellowship from the Rockefeller Foundation allowed me to live and work in Bellagio, where I was inspired by the ghosts of so many great writers.

At the height of my optimism about Google, I met Jeff Skoll, the former president of eBay. After leaving eBay, Jeff started the Skoll Foundation, a globally respected organization that focuses on social entrepreneurship. When I met him, I teased him about the fact that he wasn't all that familiar with India. "Anyone who's never spent much time in India," I used to joke, "is missing a big chunk of his life." Jeff and I agreed to meet in India, and we traveled together to small villages and big cities for a couple of weeks. I showed him villages with working polio eradication programs. Jeff even accompanied me to the Kainchi ashram, where we talked at length about Maharaji's prediction about smallpox. He is Canadian and would be embarrassed if I say too many nice things about him, so I want to bury one story about him here. When we visited Kainchi, Maharaji was gone but Siddhi Ma was there. When I introduced Jeff to her, she said to me, "He is a saint in training." I think it is true. Like me, Jeff was also concerned with pandemics, as well as climate change and global wars. He invited me to join the board of his Skoll Foundation, an invitation I happily accepted. To tackle a host of "global threats," Jeff created another foundation called the Skoll Global Threats Fund—of which I am now chairman—focused on such issues as pandemics, climate change, water, nuclear weapons, and the crisis in the Middle East.

I want to specifically thank my colleagues from the Skoll Global Threats Fund who have supported me and allowed me time away from various projects to complete this book: in particular Jeff Skoll; Jim DeMartini; Sally Osberg, who introduced me to the foundation world and to our beloved Skoll world; Annie Maxwell and Mark Smolinski; Lindsey Spindle; Lauren Diaz, who has helped with this book and all the craziness it added to my already crazy life; Bruce Lowry; and especially Veronica Garcia, who, in addition to being one of this book's loudest cheerleaders, created an archive of every speech, every photo, and every PowerPoint that I ever made, organizing my personal history into a loving, living database for this book. Because she cared more for preserving these memories than even I have, I owe her so much I can never repay her.

Grants from the World Health Organization and the University of Michigan, as well as a fellowship from the American Institute of Indian Studies, paid for the research and publication of my first book on smallpox. Part of the proceeds from the TED Prize allowed me to buy a library of reference books that I have referred to constantly in the process of writing this book.

People sometimes assume that because I wrote one of the first books on the smallpox eradication campaign in India that I was one of the leaders or visionaries of the smallpox eradication program, but that is not true at all. I was just a young kid in my first job out of medical school, the team mascot, hired as a secretary, who outstayed mostly everyone and wound up closing down the shop. Big accomplishments like the eradication of a disease are always a team sport and I was just one among the almost 150,000 smallpox warriors in India alone. And so was my smallpox partner Zafar Hussein, who was born in poverty, raised in poverty, and became my paramedical assistant and my guide. He risked his life many times for smallpox eradication and there were no big shiny awards for him. He was one of my great heroes.

Floating out to sea after leaving Rahima Banu on Bhola Island and often since, I thought about my great smallpox mentors and their tremendous dedication over such a long, sustained effort to conquer this terrible disease. I thought about D.A. and his decades-long struggle with countless bureaucracies to keep the program going and how he worked. This is the first publication I have written that D.A. did not proofread word for word, editing, suggesting, cajoling even, at every page. That is because D.A. passed away while I was still writing this book. I offer this book as a tribute to his leadership. I often had the wise counsel and help of the noble Isao Arita, who often came to India to bail me out of whatever trouble I had gotten myself into. And David Sencer, as head of CDC, and Alex Langmuir, who helped launch the Epidemic Intelligence Service program at CDC. I thought of Nicole Grasset and her fire and grace, her fierce determination to bring about the day when the world would be free of killer smallpox, and our decades-long partnership after smallpox, in Seva, and lifelong family friendship. Nicole epitomized the best in a global public servant. I think about Bill

Foege's wisdom and compassion from the day he showed me my first case of smallpox, and his ingenuity in creating the early-detection/early-response surveillance-and-containment strategy. And how he served with such dignity through his time as head of CDC and his influence on Jimmy Carter's and Bill Gates's global health breakthroughs. I am not telling any secrets to those who know him that we speak of him in almost reverential tones and all of us would like to be like Bill. It is not only in height that he stands out among everyone everywhere he goes.

And I thought about Justin Bhakla, Lev and the other Russians, the Americans, the Brits, the Swedes, the Czechs like my friend Zdeno Jezek, and the hundreds of thousands of health workers who had joined hands to defeat a common enemy. And even today I think of those who should have had a much bigger part in the book: Steve Jones, who embarrassed a UN agency into feeding and caring for homeless smallpox victims so they did not become beggars spreading the disease, went on to stop addicts from dying because of dirty needles, and served as one of the co-founders of the Seva Foundation; David Heymann, who ran the smallpox program for an Indian state, then as assistant director general of WHO led the fierce battle against SARS, and ran the WHO global polio program and innovated game-changing ideas like the Global Outbreak Response Network and CORDS, a global NGO consisting of a group of twenty-seven countries and three UN agencies. And Stan Foster, from a family of missionaries who led the Bangladesh smallpox program through tumultuous days and who had a wonderful career at CDC; Don Francis—one of my oldest friends from our civil rights and antiwar days in medical school, through running the state smallpox program in Uttar Pradesh and the Bihar state polio program, to becoming the brave hero of the early days of HIV/AIDs and the hero of the bestseller *And the Band Played On;* and Don Hopkins, who I met only briefly in India, but whose work at the Carter Center on Guinea worm disease is a treasure and part of the legacy of the smallpox experience. There were so many more young Americans who fought smallpox and went on to become warriors in the fight against AIDS and pandemic flu, and to help run the CDC and rise through the ranks of WHO.

And the Indians, oh my lord, the Indians, who seemed to never take a day off, never waiver, like "Papa" M. I. D. Sharma, who not only saved me from being kicked out of India but led the country through the massive epidemics, harsh press coverage, and frightened bureaucrats, and, in the process, made possible the WHO-India teamwork when skeptics were cropping up everywhere. My friend Mahendra Dutta later took his place at the NICD and eventually become one of the leaders of the polio eradication program in India.

Because space was limited in the book I often just refer to the Indian members of the Central Team (or Central Appraisal Team) but I would be remiss in not naming each of them: R. N. Basu, Mahendra Dutta, Mahendra Singh, C. K. Rao, R. R. Arora, and M. I. D. Sharma. In addition, Purushottem Diesh, in the early days, A. G. Acharia, head of the Bihar program, and Health Minister Karan Singh. I vividly remember him chanting Sanskrit verses from the Vedas at the funeral ceremony of the mother from Aurobindo's ashram in Pondicherry, as well as at the NICD on the occasion of the celebration of the end of smallpox. The extraordinary mapmaker professor and my friends from Tata—and they became lifelong friends—Sujit Gupta and his family, Russi Mody, and, of course, J. R. D. Tata, whose handwritten monthly letters in turquoise-colored ink I will always cherish in some ways even more than the millions he gave to redeem the honor of the Tata name and help eradicate smallpox from its last hiding places in India.

Thank you also to those who have allowed me to interview them or who have read parts of the book, or listened to my stories and offered suggestions or inspiration. Special thanks to Dan Goleman, who has always believed in this book; Elliot Schrage, who, despite a job that would take all the energy out of most people, never ceases to energize me with his wit and wisdom and warm support for this project; my guru-brother, Ram Dass, and his willingness to pour over the photos and epigraphs and nuances of this book, helping me remember and put stories in their proper context; Bill Foege, who has opened doors to so many of the firsts in my life and will always be my mentor in things both technical and moral along with his dear wife, Paula.

And to other dear friends who have helped me give birth to this book: Sheryl Sandberg; Rameshwar Das; Steve Jones; Sunanda Markus; Judge Michael Jeffery (Ravi Das); Tamam Kahn; Rep. Bob Inglis; Roger Martin; Kirk Hansen; Susan Ewens; Rev. Earl Smith; Marc Benioff; Mark Smolinski; my brother, Barry Brilliant; my batch mate at CDC EIS program and constant thought leader, Roger Glass; Barbara Cromarty; Jack Kornfield; Roger Martin; Krishna Das; Ravi Khanna; Mahendra Dutta; my mom, Sylvia Bloom; cousin Sherry Sherman; Suzanne Gilbert; Rev. Jim Wallis; Jeff Skoll, my friend and someone whose movies have inspired a generation but whose life will inspire even more; Janet Cardinell; Irene Taylor Brodsky; Salman Ahmed; Lauren Diaz; Bev Spring; and Nauren Shaikh.

I remember coming back from India and spending hours telling my mentor Ben Spock most of the stories in this book and how happy he was with the tales of smallpox because it showed that I had "returned to medicine from all that hippie stuff."

Thank you to each one of you for your help in making this book a reality. And a special thanks to our guru-brother, fellow student, teacher, and dear friend, Baba Ram Dass (Richard Alpert), who inspired us with his book *Be Here Now* to go to India, inspired us to become students of Maharaji, inspired us when we were working on smallpox and worked his butt off helping to raise money and start up the Seva Foundation, and continues to teach us and inspire thousands every day. I wrote the last chapters of this book staying at his ashramlike home in Maui with his wonderful assistant Dassima (Kathleen Murphy), looking out the window at the mango tree my daughter, Iris, planted in memory of Jon, a frequent visitor there.

Jon's mango tree is bearing fruits that are quite large and sweet these days.

Further Reading

THE ERADICATION OF SMALLPOX

Arita, Isao. *The Smallpox Eradication Saga: An Insider's View*. Telangana, India: Orient Blackswan, 2010.

Basu, R. N., Z. Jezek, and N. A. Ward. *The Eradication of Smallpox from India*. Geneva: World Health Organization, 1979.

Bhattacharya, Sanjoy, and Sharon Messenger. *The Global Eradication of Smallpox*. Telangana, India: Orient Blackswan, 2010.

Brilliant, Lawrence B. *The Management of Smallpox Eradication in India*. Ann Arbor: University of Michigan Press, 1985.

Davis, Cornelia. *Searching for Sitala Mata*. Laredo, TX: KonjitPublications, 2015.

Fenner, F., D. A. Henderson, I. Arita, Z. Jezek, and I. D. Ladnyi. *Smallpox and Its Eradication*. Geneva: World Health Organization, 1988.

Foege, William H. *House on Fire: The Fight to Eradicate Smallpox*. Berkeley: University of California Press, 2012.

Guinan, Mary. *Adventures of a Female Medical Detective*. Baltimore, MD: Johns Hopkins University Press, 2015.

Henderson, D. A. *Smallpox: The Death of a Disease: The Inside Story of Eradicating a Worldwide Killer*. Amherst, NY: Prometheus Books, 2009.

Hopkins, Donald R. *The Greatest Killer: Smallpox in History*. Chicago: University of Chicago Press, 2002.

Marennikova, S. S., ed. *How It Was: The Global Smallpox Eradication Programme in Reminiscences of Its Participants*. In Russian. Novosibirsk: TSERIS, 2011.

413

Preston, Richard. *The Demon in the Freezer: A True Story*. New York: Ballantine, 2003.

Shurkin, Joel N. *The Invisible Fire: The Story of Mankind's Triumph Over the Ancient Scourge of Smallpox*. New York: Putnam, 1979.

Skelton, James W., Jr. *Volunteering in Ethiopia: A Peace Corps Odyssey*. Denver, CO: Beaumont Books, 1991.

Tucker, Johnathan. *Scourge: The Once and Future Threat of Smallpox*. New York: Grove Press, 2002.

NEEM KAROLI BABA (MAHARAJI)

Das, Krishna. *Chants of a Lifetime: Searching for a Heart of Gold*. Carlsbad, CA: Hay House, 2010.

Dass, Ram. *Be Here Now*. Questa, NM: Lama Foundation, 1971.

———. *Be Love Now: The Path of the Heart*. San Francisco: HarperOne, 2010.

———. *Miracle of Love: Stories About Neem Karoli Baba*. New York: Plume, 1979.

———. *Polishing the Mirror: How to Live from Your Spiritual Heart*. Louisville, CO: Sounds True, 2013.

Markus, Parvati. *Love Everyone: The Transcendent Wisdom of Neem Karoli Baba Told Through the Stories of the Westerners Whose Lives He Transformed*. San Francisco: HarperOne, 2015.

Mukerjee, Dada. *By His Grace: A Devotee's Story*. Santa Fe, NM: Hanuman Foundation, 1990.

———. *The Near and the Dear: Stories of Neem Karoli Baba and His Devotees*. Santa Fe, NM: Hanuman Foundation, 2000.

Credits

Cover image: Gale Jesi.

Within Text

Frontispiece: India. Washington, DC: Central Intelligence Agency, 1979. Courtesy of the University of Texas Libraries, University of Texas at Austin.

Page 115, epigraph: From "Gotta Serve Somebody" by Bob Dylan. Copyright © 1979 by Special Rider Music. Reprinted with permission.

Page 157: "Smallpox in the World, 1972: Eradication from Indonesia" from *Smallpox and Its Eradication* by F. Fenner, D. A. Henderson, I. Arita, Z. Jezek, and I. D. Ladnyi. Geneva: World Health Organization, 1988, p. 529. Courtesy of the World Health Organization.

Page 243: "Key Leadership for the Final Phase" from *Smallpox: The Death of a Disease* by D. A. Henderson. Amherst: Prometheus Books, 2009, p. 173.

Page 286: Modified from "Figure 13.2. The World's Greatest Exporter of Smallpox" from *The Eradication of Smallpox from India* by R. N. Basu, Z. Jezek, and N. A. Ward. Geneva: World Health Organization, 1979, p. 299. Courtesy of the World Health Organization.

Page 294: From "Figure 4.14. Smallpox Incidence by Region" from *The Eradication of Smallpox from India* by R. N. Basu, Z. Jezek, and N. A. Ward. Geneva: World Health Organization, 1979, p. 53. Courtesy of the World Health Organization.

Page 305: Chart re-created from "Figure 5. The Shock" from *The Management of Smallpox Eradication in India* by Lawrence B. Brilliant. Ann Arbor: The University of Michigan Press, 1985, p. 44.

Page 337, epigraph: From *In the First Circle* by Alexsandr I. Solzhenitsyn, New York: Harper Perennial, an imprint of HarperCollins, 2009.

First Photo Insert

Page 2, bottom photo: "Dr. Martin Luther King Jr., University of Michigan, 1962." "Martin Luther King, Hill Auditorium, November 11, 1962," Media Resource Center. Bentley Historical Library, University of Michigan.

Page 3, top photo: "Larry arriving on Alcatraz to help deliver the baby Wovoka, 1970." A still taken from the movie *Taking Alcatraz* by award-winning filmmaker John Ferry.

Page 3, bottom photo: "Poster for *Medicine Ball Caravan*, the Warner Bros. movie the Hog Farm appeared in." Licensed by: Warner Bros. Entertainment Inc. All rights reserved.

Page 4, top photo: "Larry performing surgery on a local Tibetan, Nepal, 1971." Photo taken by Ruffin Cooper.

Page 5, top right photo: "Ram Dass and Maharaji, Kainchi, 1971." Photo taken by Rameshwar Das.

Page 7, bottom photo: "Front of postcard with Maharaji's prediction." Photo taken by Balaram Das.

Page 8, top photo: "Hanuman statue at Maharaji's temple." Photo taken by the author.

Page 8, middle left photo: "Sixteenth Karmapa, tickling Jamgon Kongtrul Rinpoche, Rumtek, 1974." Photo taken by the author.

Second Photo Insert

Page 1, top photo: "Nicole Grasset and Larry at WHO meeting, New Delhi, 1974." Courtesy of the World Health Organization.

Page 1, middle photo: "Dr. Halfdan Mahler, WHO director general, honoring smallpox workers, New Delhi, 1976." Courtesy of the World Health Organization.

Page 2, top photo: "Doctors R. N. Basu and M. I. D. Sharma with Saiban Bibi, last case of smallpox in India." Courtesy of the World Health Organization.

Page 2, middle right photo: "Larry receiving award from SEARO regional director Dr. Gunaratne, New Delhi, 1976." Courtesy of the World Health Organization.

Page 3, bottom left photo: "Tata Hospital doctor with smallpox patient, Tatanagar, 1974." Courtesy of the World Health Organization.

Page 3, bottom right photo: "Another view of patient in recognition card—he survived." Courtesy of the World Health Organization.

Page 4, top right photo: "Larry with smallpox-infected child near Tatanagar, 1974." Photo taken by Nedd Willard.

Page 4, middle left photo: "Smallpox-blinded beggar, Kainchi, 2005." Photo taken by the author.

Page 4, bottom photo: "Girija with Maharaji and other devotees, including R. P. Vaish, at the home of the Barman family, New Delhi, 1973." Photo taken by Balaram Das.

Page 5, top left photo: "Smallpox workers enforcing ban on travel outside the city without vaccination, Tatanagar, 1974." Courtesy of the World Health Organization.

Page 5, bottom photo: "Rahima Banu, last case of killer smallpox, Bhola Island, Bangladesh, 1975." Photo taken by the author.

Page 6, top photo: "First days at Google as executive director of Google.org, 2006." Bloomberg/Getty Images.

Page 6, bottom right photo: "Larry using an Apple II computer donated to Seva by Steve Jobs, Kathmandu, 1979 or 1980." Photo taken by Rameshwar Das, 1979.

Page 7, middle photo: "With President Barack Obama, at meeting about Ebola, Roosevelt Room, White House, 2015." Photo taken by a White House photographer.

Page 8, top left photo: "Iris Brilliant, age three, in California." Photo taken by the author.

Page 8, top right photo: "Maharaji in one of the last photos taken of him, probably in late August 1973, a few weeks before he died, taken by a Western devotee on Larry's Rollei camera." Photo was taken using the author's camera but could have been taken by any member of the satsang.

Page 8, middle left photo: "Joe Brilliant, age one, in India." Photo taken by the author.

All other photographs courtesy of the author.

Thanks to the Image Flow gallery in Mill Valley, CA, for providing photographic scanning, prints, and archival services.